Crisis and Reform
in Socialist Economies

About the Book and Editors

Providing an important overview of the growing diversity in modern socialist economies, this collection contrasts economic developments in the Soviet Union, Hungary, Poland, Yugoslavia, China, and Cuba. On the basis of empirical country studies, the authors analyze the institutional setting, economic policies, and performance of each country for the first half of the 1980s and assess the prospects for the years ahead. They examine the factors behind the success or failure of each economy and discuss the main conflicts facing today's socialist economies. This thorough evaluation provides a useful comparative view of the pressures and constraints of systemic changes in different types of socialist economies.

Dr. Peter Gey is an assistant professor and a research fellow at the Institute for Market and Planning at the University of Frankfurt, where **Dr. Jiří Kosta** is professor of economics and **Dr. Wolfgang Quaisser** is a research fellow.

Crisis and Reform in Socialist Economies

edited by Peter Gey, Jiří Kosta,
and Wolfgang Quaisser

Westview Press / Boulder and London

HC
704
.C75
1987

Westview Special Studies in International Economics

Published in 1987 in the United States of America by Westview Press, Inc.; Frederick A. Praeger, Publisher; 5500 Central Avenue, Boulder, Colorado 80301

Library of Congress Cataloging-in-Publication Data
Crisis and reform in socialist economies.
   (Westview special studies in international economics)
   Bibliography: p.
   1. Communist countries—Economic policy. 2. Economic
forecasting—Communist countries. 3. Communist
countries—Economic conditions. I. Gey, Peter.
II. Kosta, H. G. Jiří, 1921– . III. Quaisser,
Wolfgang, 1955– . IV. Series.
HC704.C75 1987   338.9′00971′7   86-32602
ISBN 0-8133-7332-8

Composition for this book originated with conversion of the editors' word-processor disks. This book was produced without formal editing by the publisher.

Printed and bound in the United States of America

∞   The paper used in this publication meets the requirements of the American National Standard for Permanence of Paper for Printed Library Materials Z39.48-1984.

6   5   4   3   2   1

Contents

Contributors

Hartmut Bechtold

Dr., University of Frankfurt, Federal Republic of Germany (FRG)

Peter Gey

Dr., Dr., University of Frankfurt, FRG

Andreas Helfer

Dipl.-Volkswirt, University of Frankfurt, FRG

Hans-Hermann Höhmann

Dr., Bundesinstitut für ostwissenschaftliche und internationale Studien, Köln, FRG

Jiří Kosta

Csc., Dr., Professor, University of Frankfurt, FRG

Jože Mencinger

Dr., Professor, University of Ljubljana, Yugoslavia

Piotr Pysz

Dr., Gesamteuropäisches Studienwerk e. V., Vlotho, FRG

Wolfgang Quaisser

Dr., University of Frankfurt, FRG

Andreas Wass von Czege

Dr., University of Hamburg, FRG

Acknowledgments

"Crisis and Reform in Socialist Economies" is the title of a research project realized at the Johann Wolfgang Goethe–Universität in Frankfurt/Main (Federal Republic of Germany) in 1985 and 1986. An international conference was held in Freudenberg on October 3–5, 1986, under the same title and was dedicated to professor Jiří Kosta on the occasion of his sixty-fifth birthday. At the conference, preliminary versions of the contributions to this volume were discussed by more than fifty scholars, from countries such as Poland, Hungary, and Yugoslavia.

We would like to express our gratitude to the Volkswagen Foundation which, through its generous sponsorship of the project, made our research possible. We are also grateful to the Bank für Gemeinwirtschaft in Frankfurt/Main for providing financial assistance to the conference and to the Gustav-Heinemann-Akademie in Freudenberg for its kind hospitality. And, last but not least, we want to thank all staff members of the University Chair for Socialist Economic Systems for their abundant support in preparing the conference and completing the final manuscript of this book.

Peter Gey
Jiří Kosta
Wolfgang Quaisser

1

Diversity and Transitions in Socialist Economic Systems: A Comparative Introduction

Peter Gey and Jiří Kosta

In contrasting the economic developments in the Soviet Union, in Poland, Cuba, Yugoslavia, Hungary, and China, this collection evaluates the pressures and constraints of systemic changes in different types of socialist economies. On the basis of empirical country studies, the authors analyze the institutional setting, economic policies, and performance of each economy during the first half of the 1980s and assess the prospects for the years ahead.

This introduction begins with an overview of the growing diversity in contemporary socialist economies, showing that today it is more difficult than ever to describe the economic structures and policies characterized as "socialist." Since the facts of, and the internal and external reasons for, the economic crisis in the countries concerned are extensively presented in the individual studies, our introductory remarks then concentrate on a comparative view of the basic issues and problems of economic reforms in the socialist countries under consideration. A comparative analysis of the economic problems, which have emerged in the past during the course of market-oriented reforms such as introduced in Yugoslavia and Hungary, is also presented in the second contribution to this book.

Growing Diversity in Socialist Economic Systems

After World War II, when the Soviet Union expanded its control over a number of Eastern European countries, there was only one model of political and economic organization ideologically considered by communist parties world-wide as authentically "socialist:" the main institutions and major policy instruments which emerged during the great industrialization drive in the Soviet Union in the 1930s. Even communist leaders such as Josip Broz Tito in Yugoslavia and Mao Zedong in China, who rejected the Soviet claim to ideological and political hegemony in world socialism, did not question the so-called Soviet model of central planning and economic guidance.

The introduction of the basic elements of the Soviet economic model showed substantial time-lags due to the fact that the specific conditions varied from country to country. But from the very beginning, the means of production in key branches of the economy were rapidly nationalized and central state agencies under communist control were established, followed by the collectivization of private farmers and small owners in the areas of industry, retail trade, and services. Even the Yugoslav government, which became politically dissident in 1948, was extremely keen to present itself as truly communist in economic terms and started full-scale collectivization in the very same year. However, both the effects of the economic blockade imposed by the cominform member states and the immanent deficiencies of a rigidly centralized planning system, including a Soviet pattern of industrialization, induced the Yugoslav leadership to move away from the Soviet-type economic system, giving up collectivization and gradually introducing workers' self-management and market relations (see below).

In the 1960s, economic reforms in discussion since the mid- 1950s, were finally introduced in several Eastern European countries. But at the beginning, the reform measures adopted were not conceptually well-founded and were not basically directed against the principles of Soviet-type planning and management. Thus, with the exception of the Yugoslav challenge to the Soviet leading power within world communism, the Soviet economic model remained essentially undisputed during the 1950s and 1960s. Although some of its elements could not be established throughout the socialist countries (i.e., in Poland, the agricultural production has persisted as family farming) and despite serious political insurrections against the communist regimes (in the German Democratic Republic in 1953, in Hungary and Poland in 1956) and ultimately the attempt at developing "socialism with a human face" in Czechoslovakia (1968), economic theory and practice in the socialist countries (except Hungary, see below) were still dominated by the Soviet model up to the late 1960s. Leftist, radical approaches, such as the Cultural Revolution induced by Mao Zedong in China and the Guevarist utopia of creating a "New Man" in Cuba existing since the mid-1960s, were not considered suitable to tackle the urgent need to intensify production and, hence, were not accepted as manageable alternatives for the more industrialized socialist economies. Finally, both the Chinese and the Cuban economic models turned out to be a type of "War Communism," causing huge damage not only in terms of economic efficiency but also in human life.

The 1970s and the first half of the 1980s witnessed an overall emphasis on pragmatism in economic policy-making. At the same time, however, the diversity in institutional settings and major policy instruments in the socialist economic systems reviewed in this collection increased considerably:

Both China and Cuba adopted more realistic approaches with regards to their economic activities but the conclusions drawn from the failure of their leftist mobilization regimes were obviously not the same. The Cuban government turned back to the Soviet model of central planning and allocation. However, compared with the orthodox model of the 1961–1965 period in post-revolutionary Cuba, this renewed attempt deals, at least conceptually, with a more decentralized version of planning and management. In contrast to this, China increasingly reduced state and collective ownership and central planning, reestablishing private property rights (mostly in agriculture, small industry and services), market relations, and real monetary terms such as prices, interest, and taxes. In addition, while Cuba started to merge the remaining family farms into producers' cooperatives, the Chinese government dissolved the people's commune and redistributed land and assets to independent family units (see the essays by Peter Gey, Jiří Kosta, and Wolfgang Quaisser in this volume).

In Poland, the severe economic problems existing since the mid-1970s and the political events of 1981 paved the way for the conceptual foundation of a far reaching economic reform, gradually introduced since 1982. Unlike the period 1958–1980 when the Polish authorities showed substantial lack of consequence and patience in the realization of reform projects aimed at the transformation of the traditional Soviet model into a decentralized economic system, the institutional and instrumental changes in the 1980s have been more stable. However, the complexity of the reform and the numerous interdependencies between the basic economic mechanisms on the one hand, and the shortages and bottlenecks resulting from the economic crisis itself on the other, proved to be the main obstacles for the realization of reform laws oriented towards recovering market equilibrium, strengthening the enterprises' position against central agencies, and evoking managers' interest in the growth of exports. In the mid-1980s, direct and indirect centralization in key industrial sectors coexists with market regulation trends in the consumer-related sectors, leading to an increasing separation of economic control forms. Thus, in contrast to the reform legislation which suggested a uniform "regulated market mechanism," the present economic system in Poland can be described as a peculiar "mixed economy" (see the essay by Piotr Pysz).

In Hungary, despite some centralization tendencies in the early 1970s, the economic reforms which began in the mid-1960s have continued over the past one and a half decades, resulting in a specific Hungarian-type socialist economy. On the basis of the leading role of the party, common property of capital goods, indirect planning and market relations, the Hungarian policy-makers developed the "New Economic Mechanism" (introduced in 1968), to a comprehensive conception of a market-oriented reform, reaching beyond the traditional limits of similar reform attempts in other socialist countries. This model not only utilizes the information, incentive and coordination functions of market relations but also redefines the role of the organs of central planning and the banking system. Moreover, the existence of different social groups is ideologically acknowledged, leading to the political consequence that organs for the representation of their interests are increasingly granted (see the contribution by Andreas Wass von Czege).

During the entire post-war period, the Yugoslav economy proved to be the most flexible and changing socialist economic system. When Yugoslavia started to follow its own economic course, the institutional setting and economic rules emerging in the early 1950s, were simply called the "New Economic System." With the abandonment of the Soviet-type centrally planned system it turned out, however, that Yugoslavia, on the basis of social ownership of the means of production and workers' self-management, planned to develop a fundamentally new economic mechanism, usually described as market-socialism. For almost twenty years, the Yugoslav economy relied upon the market mechanism for the allocation of goods and services, applying decentralized planning, financial instruments and functional budgeting. Hence, it seems to be reasonable to term the Yugoslav experience as the prototype of market-oriented reforms in Soviet-type economies, the achievements and shortcomings of which are of general interest to successor countries such as Hungary and China.

On the one hand, the Yugoslav experience of market-socialism in a developing country clearly indicates that even at the beginning of the industrialization process, high rates of economic growth are compatible with considerable improvements in the population's standard of living. In this country, from 1952 to 1971, the gross domestic product (at constant prices) annually increased by 6.3%, and the real income (excluding private agriculture) by no less than 5.8%. In addition, the Yugoslav political system, although not democratic in Western terms, was not characterized by despotism and coercion. Thus, the conclusion drawn by some Western scholars that rapid industrialization requires a high degree of centralization and political coercion as provided by the Soviet-type economic model, was obviously proved incorrect by the post-war development in Yugoslavia.

On the other hand, the Yugoslav political and economic leadership failed to implement efficient macro-economic stabilization policies since it was not willing or able to develop the legal framework and the entire range of economic institutions and policy instruments usually required by market economic systems. Namely the macro-economic control of income distribution, investment allocation and financial discipline of enterprises and governmental agencies remained inefficient. Since the end of the 1960s, the shortcomings of the macro-economic arrangements and policy instruments created strong inflationary pressures, low investment efficiency, employment problems and significant dependence on external capital sources.

In the early 1970s, far reaching institutional changes indicated that the Yugoslav economic system switched from the socialist market model of the 1950s and 1960s to a basically different model, although the main principles of social ownership and self-management were not abolished. The most characteristic feature of the new economic system, usually described as "contractual," is that the market mechanism was replaced by self-management agreements between enterprises and social interest groups. As Jože Mencinger points out in his essay on the Yugoslav economy in the 1980s, the actual economic system of "social planning" has gradually acquired many characteristics of the administrative or Soviet-type system due to the fact that the abandonment of both the market and a number of "rules of the game" of the "contractual" system made more and more government interventions necessary.

In order to stop the deterioration of the Yugoslav economy indicated by nearly every macro-economic figure, a new systemic reform was introduced in 1982. Despite highly inconsistent approaches to tackling a wide range of economic problems, its main goal is clear: it is aimed at the reintroduction of the market and the reduction of several institutional arrangements of the "contractual" system introduced in the 1970s (see the chapter by Jože Mencinger).

Last but not least, in the Soviet Union itself, changes in the economic organization are under way. It remains to be seen, however, what the real consequences of General Secretary Gorbachev's "radical reform" will be. Recently, in official state and party documents, the envisaged reform measures are summed up in five elements: (1) the effectiveness of centralized economic management is to be improved by a reorganization of the planning and administrative apparatus, (2) the economic administration is to be reduced and made more efficient in order to improve the coordination between the economic management organs at different levels, (3) the autonomy of the production units is to be widened, (4) the utilization of "economic instruments" or "levers" such as financial guide parameters (normatives) and prices is to be expanded, and (5) the collective organization and stimulation of labor is to be improved via the "brigade" working groups.

These measures obviously remain in the scope of administrative reforms introduced in other centrally planned economies in the past, which aimed at "perfecting" and "improving" the traditional administrative planning system as well. However, the pressure for efficient economic reform steps will be enormous if the Soviet Union wants to meet the economic requirements a 20th century super power is confronted with. But it is pure speculation to assume that this might provoke wider margins for reforms which could go beyond the scope of the administrative system (see the essay presented by Hans-Hermann Höhmann).

Finally, let us turn our attention to more general problems concerning the transition from the traditional Soviet-type system to a market-oriented model.

Problems of Systemic Transition

In their essay on "Stagflation Problems in Socialist Economic Systems," Hartmut Bechtold and Andreas Helfer rightly refer to Kornai, showing that he was the one to convincingly expose the Soviet-type planning system as being faced with a soft budget constraint: by striving for plan fulfillment, the decision makers at all levels of the hierarchy will always allot the financial means which are necessary to meet the targets (may it be by subsidies, price increases, tax allowances, etc.).

This practice is not only a phenomenon under the system of central-directive planning. It can become even more serious when a market-oriented reform is envisaged. We know from the Yugoslav and the Hungarian example that in such a situation some elements of the centralized Soviet-type system will come into the foreground because of ideological, political and/or social determinants (see the contributions of Mencinger, Wass von Czege and Kosta). It then turns out that the budget constraint becomes softer since the administrative forms of management were loosened while neither adequate market forces in the microeconomic sphere nor appropriate fiscal and monetary policies had been developed. Let us look at this crux in more detail.

As far as prices are concerned, two points should be considered: the price level and relative prices. The level of prices is to be seen in connection with its economic impact on growth and inflation, both of which will have social implications. One can agree with the concurring opinion of economists that in order to avoid both stagnation and overheating, an inflation rate below 2% is considered to be ideal, and one between 3–7% acceptable for handling both, reform and growth. If relative prices are to correspond to the respective scarcities of different goods, then the level of prices will, no doubt, increase. And this, in turn, again brings about inflationary pressure threatening the social consensus in the country. There is no other solution, however, but to adjust relative prices, if an economical use of resources and their rational allocation is to be achieved.

In the area of work income, the reformers have to cope with a similar conflict between economic rationality and social aspects. To raise productivity, a differentiation of wages is urgently needed. Pleading for wage differences implies, no doubt, grappling with deep-rooted egalitarianism. And yet an increase of wages might bring about inflationary pressures. Again, economic criteria and social aspects come into conflict.

Two other cases of conflicting economic and social goals might appear at the enterprise level: one consists in the contradiction between the need of a rational labor input (which implies the threat of, perhaps temporary, unemployment) and the call for job security (sometimes confused with lifelong tenure in a certain job position); the other case concerns a possible conflict between the requirement of efficient management and the demand for worker's participation in decision making. Both problems are well-known in Poland, Yugoslavia, Hungary and China. Solutions can be found, in our opinion, only in reaching a compromise between economic efficiency and social aspects.

The problem of conflicting economic and social goals, however, does not only appear at the microeconomic level, it emerges in connection with policies at the macro-level as well. Under mandatory planning, the enterprises have become accustomed to bargaining for low output targets and high input assignments. Now, with the coexistence of both command planning and market-oriented policies, the former elements causing inefficiencies did not vanish, and the implementation of indirect regulation by fiscal and monetary levers was not simultaneously developed. No wonder that in Yugoslavia a galloping price inflation took place (Mencinger), in Hungary (true, for other reasons shown by Bechtold/Helfer) a type of "stagflation" occurred, and in China the state budget fell into the red. The transition to a market-oriented system must be accompanied by tight financial and monetary policies as Chinese and foreign economists emphasized during the debates in this country.

A special problem of economic equilibrium, similar in nature to the budget deficit, is that of the deterioration of the balance of payments. Hunger for investments, for consumption, and for imports—all phenomena typical for supply constrained economies—endanger macroeconomic balances, if no effective counteracting power exists. In loosening

the monopoly of foreign trade, deficits in the balance of payments occur
with the consequence of a decrease in the foreign exchange reserves.
True, in the Hungarian case the deterioration of the terms of trade in
the 1970s was a non-systemic factor, which in addition aggravated this
situation. If an improvement in the external equilibrium is to be achieved,
an export-oriented strategy must be initiated instead of a strategy of
import substitution. This applies not only to China where the orientation
is explicit; in this context, an open-door policy means that under the
given conditions of overall shortages, imports of technology and the
acceptance of foreign loans must be directed at promising export industries
and not at domestic consumption. Here again, a conflict between long-
term requirements of economic development on the one hand and short-
term consumer interests, i.e. social aspects emerges.

In tackling the difficult task of hardening the budget constraint, the
interdependence of different policies is to be stressed. To name one
example: In neglecting rational pricing, the production and export
enterprises, using their extended discretionary power, are more inclined
to sell their products to domestic buyers than to foreign importers since
the prices at home would be higher than the prices on world markets.
To put the problem in more general terms: Only a coordinated reform
approach, comprising the various areas and processes, can bring about
the desired results. Solving the conflict between economic requirements
and social aspects, however, will always be a balancing act.

Three Basic Issues of Systemic Transition

There are three more questions which are crucial for a transition of
an economic system:

- Is a dual system bedded in a coexistence of contrary elements
  (plan/market, public/private ownership, etc.) at all viable, and if
  so, to what extent?
- Is a reform feasible, or to what degree could it be feasible, if extra-
  systemic factors such as inherited structures, shortages, growth
  patterns, etc. are unfavorable?
- Is a market-oriented reform promising if the change-over is realized
  gradually, or should the transition be carried out in one step
  ("package deal")?

Within the scope of this introduction, we can only give brief answers
to these three questions.

In answer to the first question. Systems which are of a singular, non-
mixed nature do not exist in the real world today. Certainly, this does

not mean that any mixture of system elements such as different ownerships, different mechanisms of operation, different principles of work motivations and development strategies can be chosen arbitrarily.

In the case of economic reforms under "real socialism," one issue seems to be, in this regard, of particular importance: the compatibility of market forces being used at the enterprise level and the central allocation of primary goods and investments. If the enterprise has to react to market signals, then it should be provided with discretionary competence on the combination of all factors of production. This implies a replacement of mandatory planning by market-conform, indirect regulation of resource allocation. Speaking of investments, the introduction of a capital market would then be appropriate to cope with different problems such as rational allocation of capital and balancing of macroeconomic aggregates. And finally, further reaching decentralization of property rights should be envisaged to bring motivations and initiatives better into play than up to now (see the contribution of Bechtold and Helfer).

To the second question. We could argue in two directions: (1) one cannot start before inherited structures, imbalances and shortages have been overcome, (2) one cannot wait with the reform because within the old system the extra-systemic burden will never be removed.

Argument (2) is, in our view, more convincing. Yet, one must concede that in the Chinese case the strategy of readjustment, consisting in the shift of macroeconomic structures, essentially began under the conditions of central-directive planning, and still enjoyed some success. It was not long, however, before tendencies, well known in China from earlier times, appeared anew: a propensity to accumulate ("investment hunger") and, since the quantity drive in Chinese enterprises in connection with the extended rise strengthened, an extreme acceleration of economic growth took place (the annual growth rate of national income produced rocketed from 4.9% in 1981 to 8.3% in 1982, 9.8% in 1983, 13.9% in 1984, and finally reached its peak with 16.2% in 1985). Looking at the country studies for Yugoslavia and Hungary, the investment hunger could never be stopped. It seems to us, therefore, that a desirable growth pattern ("intensification") can only be achieved in the long run if a reform of the economic mechanism has occurred.

To the third question. Reform-minded economists in Eastern Europe argue that a gradual transformation of the old system to the new one will bring about all difficulties connected with the dual system (as pointed out under question one). And, moreover, the orthodox members of the political leadership would then try to push the reform drive back. Thus a "package deal" is recommended. This argument can be backed by the negative experiences made in Yugoslavia, Hungary, and last but not least, in Poland.

The mainstream of Chinese economists plead, however, for "restructuring" the economic system "step by step," while care must be taken, it is said, to coordinate the interrelated aspects of economic life at each stage. They substantiate this view by the basic realities in China: a vast territory, a huge population, relative backwardness in economy and culture and an extremely uneven development in various aspects.

A possible counter-argument, based on East European experiences, would be that a step-by-step pace can easily lead to a general failure of the reform. But the Chinese leadership might be determined and strong enough to persist in the reform course, notwithstanding temporary difficulties. At any rate, one should take into account that hurdles, stemming from the dual system, will be a necessary concomitant of a step-by-step change-over.

We have drawn our attention mainly to Hungary, Yugoslavia and China because only in these countries has a more or less market-oriented reform been launched. We should not neglect, however, the individual reform discussions, approaches and results which can be pursued in such countries as the Soviet Union, Poland and Cuba as well. The following country studies will discuss in more detail how the economic reforms proceeded during the first half of the 1980s.

2

Stagflation Problems in Socialist Economies

Hartmut Bechtold and Andreas Helfer

Introduction

Stagflation is a controversial term among Western economists. Some economists consider it to be more political than economical and they question whether it is appropriate to apply it to socialist economies.

This scepticism may have controversial reasons. In the old Soviet-type system, overwhelming economic stagnation is obvious. At least since the mid 1970s, this has been widely discussed by numerous economists (e.g. Kosta/Levčik, 1985). But don't these economies at least guarantee stable prices?

Looking at the reformed socialist systems in Hungary and Yugoslavia, there is of course inflation, but didn't these economies at least overcome the typically inefficiency of a centrally planned system?

In fact, Hungary and Yugoslavia are now confronted by both a persistent stagnation of economic and technological development and inflation. During the first years of economic reform both countries achieved satisfactory growth rates. Since 1980, however, the reform started to lag behind expectations. The Hungarian economists Nyers and Tardos still characterize Hungary's reformed system as a special kind of sellers market: "sellers keep their superiority on the market even during recession" (Nyers/Tardos, 1984; 12). This does not seem to be consistent with the concept of stagnation as overcome by reform but is quite similar to the situation for which the term "stagflation" was created in Western economic theory.

Two explanations for this phenomenon (as shown in Table 2.1) seem to be reasonable: the first year's successes could have been due to external resources. The international debt was growing during the 1970s, and when the countries started to pay it back, the growth rates dropped. A

Table 2.1 Stagflation in Reformed Socialist Economies

	1976	1977	1978	1979	1980	1981	1982	1983	1984	1985	1976-79 (average)	1980-85 (average)
Hungary												
National income	3.0	8.0	4.2	1.9	-0.8	1.8	1.5	0.5	2.9	-1.0	3.7	0.8
Consumer prices	5.0	3.9	4.6	8.9	9.1	4.6	6.9	7.3	8.3	7.0	5.3	7.2
Net foreign debt (billion US-$)	2.9	3.6	5.2	6.3	6.7	6.9	6.6	5.9	5.1	6.0		
Growth of foreign debt (percentages)	26	24.1	44.4	21.2	6.3	3.0	-4.3	-11.6	-13.5	17.6	117.2	-11.4
Yugoslavia												
Gross domestic product at factor costs	4(a)	8(a)	7(a)	7(a)	2.2	1.4	0.7	-1.3	1.7	n.a.	6.3	0.9
Cost of living	12	15	14	20.4	30.3	40.7	31.7	40.9	53.4	n.a.	15.1	37.3
Gross foreign debt (billion US-$)(b)	7.9	9.5	11.8	15.2	18.9	21.1	20.3	20.6	20.8			
Growth of foreign debt (percentages)	19.6	20.3	24.2	35.7	24.3	11.6	-3.8	1.5	1.0		92.4	10.1

(a) Gross national product
(b) Regarding Yugoslavia there are only data on gross foreign debt available for the period 1976-78, but the net foreign debt figures available since 1979 do not differ very much from those.
Sources: Economic Survey of Europe in 1984-1985. New York 1985; 72, 82, 89, 150;
Wass von Czege (Contribution in this book); Statistical Pocket Book of Hungary 1981; 39, 111; Statistički Godišnjak Jugoslavije 1983; 160, 212; WIIW Forschungsbericht No. 108, July 1985; 41; WIIW Mitgliederinformation March 1986; 8

second explanation refers to the fact that even if the reform failed to establish a coherent economic system, it removed at least some obstacles to economic growth typical to centralized planned economies, thus freeing productivity resources for a certain period. Of course, one cannot separate both effects empirically but nothing speaks against the suggestion that both played an important role. From a theoretical point of view, however, foreign debt appears as only a modifying factor to the fundamental reasons.

The measurement of inflation raises another methodological problem. Regarding Socialist economies, inflationary problems are not considered as significant as in Western market economies since the Soviet-type prices are not realistic. Nevertheless, there have been attempts to describe the economic situation in the Soviet Union in terms of stagflation (Adirim, 1984).

This paper first deals with the aspects of the stagflation phenomenon in Western market economies during the 1970s. It then goes on to examine similar phenomena in both reformed and Soviet-type Socialist economies. The final section summarizes our proposal to overcome stagnation in the reformed Socialist economies.

Stagnation in Western Economies

In the 1970s, the industrialized countries of the Western world were faced with the most serious economic crisis since the Great Depression of the 1930s. Old branches (ship-building, textile, steel, etc.) had reached their growth limit. Increasing competition from the newly industrialized countries changed the patterns of international trade. The price-policy of the OPEC also required an adjustment process. This was delayed by several factors, the most important being highly concentrated enterprises on the one hand and the political and economical, collusions accumulated over a thirty year period of stability, on the other.

Schumpeter offered some explanations for the phenomenon that large and well established institutions are slower in adjusting to new conditions than young firms: the environment offers the prerequisites for the repetition of routine acts, whereas in the "case of new things it sometimes lacks, sometimes refuses, them: lenders readily lend for routine purposes; labor of the right type is available for them in the right place." Furthermore, most people feel inhibited when faced with the possibility of treading a new path. For this reason, it is much easier for people and institutions to imitate and to improve given innovations, when the initial innovation has been set up successfully by new entrepreneurs (Schumpeter, 1939; 100). The initial innovators must first weaken the resistance of the old enterprises and institutions, and since this is a difficult task, they must be stimulated by high innovative profits.

In addition to the resistance of the factor markets, innovators face an even more tangible idleness of the commodity market. The demand for a new commodity does not grow uniformly, but follows a life cycle. The introduction phase of a new product is a trial and error process. Innovations cannot be planned. Few entrepreneurs, normally outsiders, introduce a product or production process. If they are successful and their product is accepted by the market, demand will rise, first by growing, then by diminishing, and finally by decreasing rate due to the increasing market saturation. The products will then be standardized for mass production, leaving little room for valuable ideas on improvements.

In the early phase of the growth-cycle, young enterprises prevail in the new industries; they are not constrained by their own hierarchical administrative apparatus and can be very innovative. In the latter stages of market development, concentration begins and the institutional order becomes rigid; the most successful young enterprises may have expanded to large and powerful firms without both the innovative capacity for changing their production and for introducing new products and production processes and a strong motivation to do so. As a rule, large corporations need to be forced to innovate by the rising competition of young, expanding firms (Mensch, 1979; 57). When the market has reached its growth limit and powerful firms are unable to shift resources to innovations, entrepreneurial activities are required in order to avoid economic stagnation.

In a stable, unchanging environment a slow reaction is tolerable. But the economic situations change constantly. Changes in consumer tastes, discoveries of new resources, the variation of scarcities on the world market, etc. change the price-relations and require adjustments of the production-functions. The variation of resource allocation depends on innovations. Data show that important innovations were generally introduced by recently established firms in times of crises (Mensch, 1979; 122). In line with Schumpeter and Olson, this fact can be explained as follows: As time passes, every existing system shows a self-generating tendency opposed to fundamental changes and adjustments. According to Schumpeter, innovations are "as a rule embodied . . . in new firms which generally do not arise out of the old ones but start producing beside them . . . in general it is not the owner of stage-coaches who builds the railways" (Schumpeter, 1951; 66).

For this reason, overcoming stagflation means stimulating flexibility and innovations in order to guide investments from low-level productivity towards dynamic growth. The less flexible the factors are, the greater the difference will be between money and credit available vis-à-vis produced goods which consumers also desire.

Stagnation Turns into Stagflation

In the course of the seventies, it became evident that old branches lacked the economic dynamics to shift resources from old to new production lines. The economic policy (subsidies and tariffs for endangered industries, job creation programs, exclusive rights and governmental regulations) slowed down the process of structural change and took away competitive pressure from structurally weak industries. Upcoming, modern industries were handicapped by these government activities. Limited capital was thrown into old industries, while young industries, much more dependent on the capital market, were crowded out and thus could not compensate economic losses due to the decline of old branches. The Keynesian fiscal policy sabotaged the functions of the capital market, hindering the economy to shift to new structures of production.

Following the ruling economic theory, the economic policymakers had to pump credit-financed public expenditures into the national economies. This Keynesian policy, however, failed to overcome the crisis because the multiplying effects proved to be much smaller than expected. Deficit-spending barely helped the old industries, increased the budget deficit and brought up interest rates, as it was temporarily higher than the returns on productive investments. The growth rate dwindled, while the consumer price index went up. Keynesianism, far from being a medicine, turned out to be yet another disease of the Western economies, at least in monetarist economic terms: "There is every reason to suspect that productivity trends, profit margins, the availability of profitable investment opportunities, and the propensity to invest are systematically related to the failures of economic policymaking in the 1970s" (Lindberg, 1985).

Monetarists maintain that borrowing, as well as increased taxes, crowded out private spending and absorbed resources that might otherwise have been used for productive private capital investment. One effect was an upward pressure on interest rates, another was, so Milton Friedman, higher monetary growth, causing inflation. The reduced incentives to invest and the crowding out of private investments by high government spending inhibited economic growth and caused stagflation (Friedman, 1983; 220).

In the framework of the Schumpeterian theory of business cycles, this outcome is hardly surprising: Stagnation appears since the consumers do not want to buy the products offered to them by the sellers, and the sellers are not quick enough to adjust their production structures.

The government (if still following Keynesian economic thinking) creates an additional effective demand through state orders. The sum of subsidies and payments add to aggregate demand without producing compensating supply. Incomes increase, but people still do not want to buy even some of the products offered to them. Inflation and stagnation become one.

According to this view, stagflation results from a government policy which supports old, highly concentrated firms and worsens growth possibilities for upcoming, young, innovative entrepreneurs. For a short time, the politicization of the economy helped endangered firms to avoid adjustment processes and to escape the discipline of the markets. But at the same time, inflation was provoked in several ways: The market position and price-policy of highly concentrated branches were stabilized; growing sectors had to pay higher capital costs, suffered from taxes on inputs, and, hence, were unable to lower their prices at the same pace as their production methods improved. When only a few established firms exist in a given economy (having great market power and little innovative initiative), which tend towards a national economy with a relatively rigid production structure, and which respond to additional demands with increased prices, then collusions and interest groups will flourish (Olson, 1982).

Apart from boosting inflation, the policy of deficit-spending also effects the chances of overcoming stagnation. The capital market soon became overburdened by the governments' excessive borrowing. Financial resources from the old industries did not find their way into the new ones but were wasted on government activities. However, further real economic growth involves structural change. Scarce resources must be shifted from one sector of the economy to a more productive one. The speed and efficiency of this adjustment process depends on the flexibility of the input factors: capital, labor and management (entrepreneurial) skills. Thus, a policy which lessens the flexibility of capital aggravates the problem of stagflation.

Stagnation in Socialist Economies

While according to socialist theory crises appear as an aspect of capitalism, it turned out that changing scarcities, new world market patterns, and the changing demand on Western markets contributed to serious economic crises in Socialist countries as well. Whereas in the West, the development of new technologies already forms part of the problem's solution, it worsens the problems of the socialist countries. Socialist countries have hardly played a role in innovative contributions (Kornai, 1975; 276). The decline of growth rates, the increase of debts, and the worsening of the foreign trade situation, in both quantitative and qualitative terms, draw a clear picture of stagnation.

This is true not only of the old Soviet-type economies, but also, at least in principle, of the reformed Socialist systems in Hungary and Yugoslavia. The reasons for stagnation in Western economies, i.e. the behavior of bureaucracies and large enterprises, are obviously true in socialist countries as well. And since both bureaucracy and economic concentration are more developed here than in most of the capitalist countries, their impact on the economic situation is greater.

Even in post-reform Hungary, entrepreneurship is limited to small firms and agricultural cooperatives. Medium and large-scale projects are normally initiated centrally (Kornai, 1985; 17). In terms of supply and demand, the effects of these restrictions are obvious: despite all reform attempts, statistical analyses prove Hungary to be a seller's market. The input stocks of Hungarian firms are nearly eight times as high as their output stocks, whereas in Western countries, where a buyer's market prevails, the output stock is usually higher than the input stock (Kornai, 1985; 7).

The situation in Yugoslavia is quite similar with the exception that besides market coordination, self-management is also a basic pillar of the economic system. Basic decisions are delegated to the workers' councils which elect the managers and determine the distribution of the firm's surplus. But the experience with this market-type socialism in Yugoslavia substantiates the troubles of a Socialist market economy already discussed in the case of Hungary. This leads to the suggestion that these troubles can be traced back to the lack of a working capital market.

In Yugoslavia, workers are granted the right of disposition but not the right of ownership, which consists of two basic elements: the exclusivity of rights and voluntary transferability of rights (Pejovich, 1983). Consequently, the employees, although formal "owners" of their firm, are actually not allowed to sell their shares. Hence, they try to take as much as possible from the enterprise, and they certainly are not motivated to increase employment since every new employee is considered as an additional claimant of future distribution. The system tends to extract capital from the firms and to keep out growing parts of the labor force.

Inflation in Socialist Economies

Actually, it is not an easy task to measure price increases in Socialist economies. Enterprises carefully hide them behind "quality improvements" which usually do not exist, and the statistics deal with official prices only disregarding the fact that many commodities are not available at these prices in the official shops. One can only buy them for a

substantially higher price in the notorious "exquisit" shops (as they are
called in the GDR) or on gray and black markets. Furthermore, inflation
is frequently accompanied by long waiting lines, increasing shortages
and booming black markets.

This does not mean, however, that there is no inflation in traditional
Socialist economies. For example, there are wide-spread discussions on
the inflation in Poland, where the first cautious steps towards reform
have just been initiated. The editorial staff of the Polish newspaper
Polityka already constructed a kind of commodity basket in 1984
(Polityka, 1984) in order to get some realistic quantitative information
on inflation in Poland. A quantitative analysis of this kind is, of course,
quite weak; it turns out that open inflation appears and can be measured
when commodity markets are more or less free, as it is the case the in
reformed Socialist systems.

Today, three Socialist countries have substantially reformed economies:
Yugoslavia, Hungary and China. In these countries, serious attempts
were made to reintroduce market and monetary relations.

As the reform is generally accompanied by inflation, it is argued that
in freeing prices, the previously hidden inflation is revealed. From this
point of view, the solution to the inflation problem appears to be a
matter of time: sooner or later, the cumulative effects of formerly
postponed price increases, inherited from the centralized system, along
with inflation, will disappear (Zafir, 1979). Contrary to this, we suggest
that open inflation is a typical element of reformed socialist systems
and will not disappear due to the introduction of the commodity market.

The following considerations focus mainly on the Hungarian, but
also on the Yugoslav experiences, since in China there is no theoretical
literature on inflation problems despite a kind of anti-inflation propaganda.
This, of course, is due to the relatively short reform experience in this
country and might also have something to do with the more liberal
scientific atmosphere in Yugoslavia and Hungary.

Excursus: What Rules the Behavior
of the Hungarian Firm

In his Oxford lecture, Kornai asked whether "a semi-monetized
economy, in which prices and money do not genuinely influence the
macrovariables of production, investment and employment," can be
described in Malinvaud's terms as "repressed inflation." He came to the
conclusion that "the main characteristic features of such a system—
chronic shortage, strong expansion drive, quantity drive, unrestrainable
investment spirit—can be observed when the price level is stable. But

they would also persist if the price level began to change and a slow or accelerating inflation evolved" (Kornai, 1982).

According to this theory, the reform could be interpreted as a loosening of the brakes formerly put on inflation, thus switching from suppressed inflation as a typical element of Soviet-type economies, to open inflation as a typical element of reformed socialist systems. The fundamental cause of inflation persists due to the fact that the economic entities do not really change their patterns of behavior since they are not integrated in a comprehensive structure of prices and incentives. Instead, they simply use their newly-acquired freedom for boosting prices.

> The sector functioning under a soft budget constraint does not react to price increase by reducing demand. As I emphasized earlier, the firm is able to pass on any increase in prices of inputs sooner or later to the buyer or to the state budget. . . . As a consequence of the chain of cause and effect . . . there is no trade-off between inflation and shortage. Shortage is reproduced, at a stable as well as at a falling or rising price level, as long as the institutional conditions for its chronic reproduction exist (Kornai, 1983; 28).

The idleness of Hungarian firms with regard to innovations and their readiness to increase prices seem to have their roots in the framework which determines the firm's behavior. In 1968, Hungary abolished the centralized command economy. Step by step, the state-owned firms became free in their production decisions. But did Hungary become a market economy thereby? In our opinion it did not. As of today, 93% of the industrial output is produced in state-owned firms, subordinated to governmental authorities. These institutions select the managers and determine the real behavior of the firm through various formal and informal channels.

In addition, Hungary has a very centralized economy. The Hungarian market shows a great number of monopolies, and free choice for buyers exists only in theory. Only 715 state-owned firms control 93% of the industry; 37% of the firms have more than 500 employees (Kornai, 1985; 8). Furthermore, there is a great gap between intention and reality of the Hungarian New Economic Mechanism:

> The internal division of the organization of government management of the economy has remained unchanged: The branch ministries and the internal division of such organs as Gosplan, the Ministry of Finance and the State Bank have also been retained. In other words: The old organizational structure of a planned economy has remained essentially unchanged (Bauer, 1976; 69).

The state authorities play an important role in everyday entrepreneurial decision-making. The system of central allocation of resources was abolished but nevertheless, central impairments prevail (Bauer, 1983; 305).

In practice, managers are able to influence the economic position of the enterprise and its profitability only to a minimum extent. For them, it is an easy task to show that low profitability or even losses were caused by external factors (Bauer, 1976; 71). The agencies which control management are not profit-minded, they simply want to stay in power and maintain their functions. Their main interest is oriented to maximizing their budgets for reasons of public reputation, influence, salary, etc.

Consequently, the abolition of the Soviet-type system did not subordinate the Hungarian enterprises to the control of the market; the direct dependence of the firms on the government apparatus has been kept in tact. The enterprises are still a part of the comprehensive branch-territorial hierarchy. These hierarchies have many means with which to influence a firm's policy and to undermine market functions.

Obviously, these shortcomings in the Hungarian reform can explain why there is still economic stagnation despite all the attempts to improve the economic system. Monopolies are no more innovative than state bureaucracies and the Hungarian economy still appears to be a mixture of both. But even if a firm were willing to introduce a new product, a production method or simply a significant improvement, it would face serious obstacles.

The Lack of Factor Flexibility

In Socialist economies, the innovator's situation is even worse than in capitalist ones. Kornai describes a tendency in the behavior of the socialist enterprises called "investment hunger":

> In a socialist economy there is no firm or nonprofit institution which does not want to invest. There is no saturation. Investment hunger is permanent. . . . The leader's power, social prestige, and consequently his own importance grow together with the growth of the firm or nonprofit institution. Many feel that it is greater to be the director of 10,000 than of 5,000 (Kornai, 1980a; 191–193).

Needless to say, the chances to obtain the necessary investment resources actually grow with the importance of the manager and his firm. The result is a permanent tautness of the investment plan, further aggravated by the notorious underestimation of investment costs. Thus, new enterprises not only have fewer incentives than in a capitalist market economy, but also suffer from the fact that there is no way to shift resources from old branches to innovative ones, even in an economic crisis.

Enterprises do not try to acquire extra profits by innovations; instead, they try to achieve a favorable initial position for their bargaining with higher authorities. To put it in Olson's terms, many collusions exist, both between different firms, and between firms and trade unions or parts of the agencies (Olson, 1982). Mutual information is available, as well as cooperation, before decisions are made on investments, foreign trade, etc. Enterprises have only small autonomy in making investment decisions. While in a market economy, under the conditions of a "hard budget constraint," the capital market ensures that investment decisions are oriented towards economic calculations and expectations, the politization of investment decisions automatically foresees that (formally or informally) organized groups and factions (including the state and its various agencies) struggle for the distribution of capital. Here, power plays the crucial role, not economic rationality based on market relations.

The Bypass of the Capital Market

In our view, it is this politization of the investment-savings decision that is responsible not only for the stagnation of the economy, but also for the inflationary pressure. We would like to call it the bypass of the capital market. Only at the first glance does it appear that enterprises in reformed socialist economies are as interested in profit maximation as those in capitalist economies. Profit is intended to be the basic indicator of economic success. In order to ensure that the motivation of workers and management is guided by profit motivation, their income is directly connected to the firm's profit (Bauer, 1976; 67).

But as Kornai has shown, the "budget constraint" of the Hungarian firm is weak. This means it is possible to increase the profitability of a firm not only by lowering its costs, producing more sophisticated products and improving marketing strategies but also—and in Kornai's view mainly—through bargaining with higher authorities. Centrally allocated subsidies, investment funds and soft bank loans determine the cashflow and through it the performance and expansion chances of an enterprise.

Under the Hungarian New Economic Mechanism, the redistribution of a firm's financial income is especially important (Kornai, 1980b; 314). For this purpose, generous subsidies are most often used. Subsidies for exports, for wages, on prices, etc. soften the links between both the material incentives of enterprise management and the economic performance. A very differentiated, impenetrable tax system exists in Hungary. There are dozens, if not hundreds, of different income flow channels, and the various taxes and subsidies are controlled by different agencies. These two factors make it impossible to create a rational price system that would reflect marginal costs.

To some extent, even the fiscal redistribution is a subject of bargaining. Kornai came to astonishing results, contrasting pre-redistribution profit with post-redistribution profit: The amount of money which had been moved from and to firms by financial authorities was twice as high as the original profits; the subsidies were nearly 10% higher than the profits. Differences between the profitability of firms were nearly totally leveled (Kornai, 1985; 9).

Due to redistribution, neither internal investment funds nor credits granted by the Central Bank are very strongly related to profitability. Once more, access to the decision-making authorities and political bargaining power are required to receive external resources. "As a result, the investment activity actually accomplished in the firm will not really depend on either pre or post-redistribution profitability" (Kornai, 1985; 16). Both the political determination of bank loans and the widespread use of subsidies and differentiated taxes not only paralyze the effects of profit orientation with regard to incentives, but also provide a way to cover a deficit-ridden budget.

As two Soviet authors (V. Belkin and V. Ivanter) have pointed out in the case of the Soviet Union, enterprises often borrowed the money they paid into the budget, thus exaggerating their revenues: "Conditions are created for financing the national economy . . . in excess of the material resources available" (Nove, 1985; 152). It is obvious that the almost unlimited right of the government to put its hand into the enterprises' pocket still invites a kind of inflationary budget in Hungary as well.

Meanwhile the shortcomings of direct interventions and administrative control are reflected in Hungary. An important attempt to diminish the power of intervening central authorities by strengthening a firm's autonomy was made with the introduction of the so-called "New Forms of Management." In the future, the large firms will be run by enterprise-councils, which have the right to elect their manager (see the essay by A. Wass von Czege in this book). But considering the background of the Yugoslav performance, the question should be raised as to whether the allocation problems can be changed by such a reform.

In Yugoslavia, investment-saving decisions were further biased by the capital extracting logic of self-management. Enterprises able to meet their investment requirements through their own means, are the exception (Mencinger, 1986). This means that there was a very low self-investment financing rate (under 50%) (Sirc, 1983; 130) which had to be supplemented by bank loans. The wage-price spiral and the inflationary financing of investments by soft bank loans led to the highest inflation rate in Europe.

Capital was scarce in Yugoslavia as well, but noone paid attention to this; in fact, capital was nearly a free good. Under such conditions, enterprises tended to use all available capital, disregarding the profitability of investments. The waste of capital on one hand, and the increased freedom of enterprises with regard to pricing and income distribution on the other, led to an inflationary gap between demand and supply. The situation deteriorated dramatically in the 1970s when the interest rate on short-term loans was usually lower than the inflation rate (Cicin-Sain/Mates, 1985; 184). The inflationary gap brought the established firms into a monopolistic position. The permanent disequilibrium of the capital market led to a permanent disequilibrium of the commodity market.

While Yugoslavia now has the highest inflation in Europe, the Hungarian inflation is still well below the rate of some Western countries. Nevertheless, this is a serious problem for both the economic and political equilibrium of the Hungarian society. As a result of the reform, inflation rose after 1968 when it proved impossible to maintain the strict wage control (Wiles, 1974; 122) of the former years without harm to the economic reform.

Possible Consequences

In Yugoslavia, the poor market performance caused economists and political leaders to again trust in planning (Mencinger, 1985; 200). Price controls were introduced, and government interventions sabotaged the function of the market mechanism. Sustained government interventions and frequently changing rules fed inflationary expectations (Mencinger, 1986). Slowly but surely, the Yugoslav economy began to slip into an administrative system, while in Hungary there was a slow-down of the reform process which never reached the radicalism of the Yugoslav version as far as political and ideological questions were concerned.

In Hungary, after many attempts to improve the centralized system, even leading economists came to the conclusion that there is no alternative to the market, nor can the market be simulated (Csikos-Nagy, in: Frankfurter Allgemeine Zeitung, 11 November 1984; 12). Presently, economists in Socialist countries themselves widely agree that in more advanced economic stages, directives largely need to be replaced by incentives and disincentives. At the same time, enterprises must be granted a considerable degree of independence and they should be encouraged to exercise initiative. A combination of social or state ownership of the production means and a limited implementation of market mechanisms in the planning system, are believed to be more efficient than pure systems could be. Market-socialists propose that very important decisions, such as long-range investment projects, should be made by state authorities, while the market should be responsible for everyday tasks. Management should act within a framework of limited rights, granted and supervised by the state.

Overcoming Stagflation Requires Working Capital Markets

With regard to technical progress, experience shows that a mixed economy, with markets for some commodities and limited enterprise-autonomy, might be a bit more successful than a full-fledged Soviet-type economy. Obviously, enterprises in Hungary and Yugoslavia are somewhat more flexible in introducing new methods or products and have even been more successful in their attempts to enter foreign markets.

But technical progress is only one aspect of innovation and certainly not the most important. The decisive innovative element is the creation of a new market. In other words, the appeasement of human needs which have not yet been appeased by the production of commodities (Kornai, 1975; 261–267). For example, the creation of a new product, the "personal computer," for accounting purposes in small business and the production of scientific papers, is innovative and not merely the technical addition of chips, screen, floppy disks, and a keyboard. Thus, neither the chip-producing enterprises nor the assemblers of personal computers expand with the market, but rather those firms which successfully persuade consumers that a computer is a useful tool, even if their products are not the most advanced in technical terms. The entrepreneur restrains stagflation, not the engineer.

Innovation, however, assumes the right to acquire resources. Successful entrepreneurs, who wish to carry out "new combinations" (as Schumpeter puts it) cannot finance themselves by returns on investments but depend on the capital market (Schumpeter, 1939; 50). The capital market (free banking activities, equity financing, stock exchange) mediates between innovators and capital owners.

Schumpeter particularly stressed the necessity of a well-functioning banking system which reshuffles scarce resources to innovative entrepreneurs. This is not an easy task. The Schumpeterian banker has to know, and should be able to judge, what his credit is used for. He must be independent from the government as well as from the entrepreneurs he is lending money to; he must be able to evaluate the situation based exclusively on the expected profitability. Subservience to the government or to public opinion would paralyze a banking system (Schumpeter, 1939; 166).

Even in capitalism, large banks are sometimes overstrained by fulfilling these difficult tasks. Therefore, in the USA, specialized capital firms with a very high technical competence arose, which finance uncommon innovations like the personal computer. They are faced with high risks but also with very high profit prospects (e.g., the venture capital firms which financed the Tandem computer firm. For each invested dollar they received one hundred dollars (Financial Times, 1983; 19; Kröber et al.; 36). This quite unusual profit obviously reflects the idleness of Western banks.

The banking system in Hungary and Yugoslavia is even worse. In the case of Hungary, banks are more or less subservient to the government, whereas in Yugoslavia, they are under the control of the credit-seeking firms themselves. During the last years, however, various attempts have been made to increase the role of commercial banks in both countries. In Hungary, the monetary functions of the National Bank were separated from their commercial functions. In Yugoslavia, investors were made to compete for loans and variable interest rates, thereby ensuring that capital was distributed according to economic efficiency. But these mechanisms missed their goals. As no effective sanctions existed for those who did not fulfill their credit contract obligations, investors were not overly concerned with interest rates and risks. It was not to be expected that a factory would be closed due to its inability to service its debt (Cicin-Sain/Mates, 1985; 180).

Kornai described the chances for innovation within a given economy in terms of *pull* and *push* situations. According to this concept (Kornai, 1975; 276), in a permanent *pull* situation (which means a permanent excess demand), the development of a new product is nearly impossible since nothing forces the enterprises to innovate. Of course, a *pull* situation prevails in a booming market economy; this is the situation Schumpeter had in mind when he wrote about the cyclical upswing of the market economy. In this case, the lack of innovation does not do any harm because of sustained demand for the established products. But a *pull* situation can also be created artificially by the government if it pumps money into the economy during an economic recession. In this case, innovation remains impossible even during the recession. This is exactly the situation in Hungary and Yugoslavia, where permanently available soft loans worsen the conditions for innovations and thus produce economic stagnation.

At the same time, this financial policy is automatically coupled with an inflationary monetary policy. If a firm is not in the position to meet its debt service, then additional money will be made available to provide support. It is basically of no concern whether the banks give additional unsound credits, as is the case in Yugoslavia (they can do so because they are not efficiently restricted by the monetary policy), or whether the government directly intervenes with subsidies, as is true for Hungary. Both policies not only sabotage any incentive for innovation, they also increase inflationary pressure: "As in all communist countries, the main technical source of infltion is short loans to enterprises by the central bank which are unwisely granted and not paid back" (Wiles, 1974; 129).

Corresponding to this, inflationary pressures proceed from the demand side of the economy: if there is no capital market, the households are not able to use their superfluous purchasing power for investments in innovative branches. "People do not save to form capital. The institutional, and legal framework for this does not exist. . . . Savings in general can be defined as delayed demand for consumer goods" (Birman/Clarke, 1985). The more true this is, the less possibilities there are for long-term savings as provided by the financial system. There are neither bonds nor pension funds, and there is little life insurance in Soviet-type economies (Nove, 1985; 153). Thus, additional inflationary pressure results from the high amounts of money hoarded either in cash or in short-term saving accounts which turns into suppressed or open inflation as the case may be.

Stagflation in Hungary and Yugoslavia seems to have the same roots. Since the reform of the economic system stopped, either at the consumer or at the investment goods market, it was not possible to guarantee the free flow of capital, both from large, old enterprises to dynamic, new ones, and from households to the enterprises as a whole. Investment decisions are made at the political level, determining the firms' behavior even in the reformed systems on all recently established markets. Although it is easier for a firm in Yugoslavia to obtain a loan than it is for a firm in Hungary, this is of no significance in principle, however the latter country has a lower rate of inflation. In both countries the capital flows to the strongest firms and not to those with better prospects. Under the conditions of a "soft budget constraint," this leads both to inflation and to stagnation.

Capital Markets and Socialist Ideology

In a working market economy, profit results from marketing, innovation and productivity. Besides profit, there is no other effective indication of performance, and it is a bonus for the risk of uncertainty. Since the future is unknown (least of all by state bureaucracies), the risk progressively increases the farther a decision reaches into the future. The profit incentive is a means to direct capital into its most efficient utilization (Drucker, 1978; 9).

A well-functioning market economy requires certain conditions: First of all, the prices must transmit correct signals to firms and consumers alike. Relative prices should reflect relative scarcities. Secondly, firms need incentives to act according to the variation of relative prices. Therefore, clear-cut rights of disposition and property are of vital importance.

An essential prerequisite for a working market system is contractual freedom. Buyers and sellers must have the same legal rank; hierarchies or subordinations are incompatible with market relations. While government actions are always based on authority relations, market systems are based on exchange relations and the activities of economic entities are personally motivated. Personal income and private wealth is the main incentive. The owners are motivated to seek the best use for their assets. Therefore, property rights must be guaranteed. Furthermore, a market system demands that market participants are fully responsible for their decisions because otherwise they could enjoy the benefits without being confronted with the risks. In addition, the market must provide free access for new competitors. Successful small firms should have both the right and the real chance to expand. Incentives for entrepreneurs and capital available for recently established and growing firms, are the main features of a dynamic market.

For Marx, profit was a symbol of exploitation since it was created by labor. For Schumpeter, profit was a reward for successful innovations: an entrepreneur who introduces a new product initially has no competitors; he is a monopolist, receiving a monopolistic profit. An entrepreneur, who lowers his production or marketing costs also gains profits. In either case, a profit will be a made only until competitive firms enter the market. Thus, an entrepreneurial profit in an open market economy is only of a temporary nature and must be earned by improving economic efficiency. "It is the expression of the value of what the entrepreneur contributes to production in exactly the same sense that wages are the value expression of what the worker *produces*" (Schumpeter, 1951; 153).

Accordingly, the non-innovative firm earns no profit. What is normally called profit could be interpreted as costs: as a cost of a major resource, namely capital, and as a necessary insurance premium for the real and largely quantifiable risks and uncertainties of economic activities. The only exception are real monopolistic profits which are mostly gained due to a lack of government competition policy (or due to an open anti-competition policy, respectively). In a stationary economy, both the entrepreneurial profit and the entrepreneurial function would be absent. Of course, the firms would calculate opportunity costs like interest on capital funds, and in some cases there would be monopolistic profits, windfalls and perhaps speculative profits too, but no entrepreneurial profit (Schumpeter, 1939; 105).

Assuming this is true of Socialist economies as well, we face the principal problem of evaluating goods in a Socialist economy. Socialist theory does not help much in this respect. Marx had no concept for the economic process in the future Socialist society. He hoped market relations and private ownership of production means would be overcome by concentration. According to this economic model, the sphere of production determines the sphere of distribution. In the final analysis, prices are determined by values and, thus, by costs. In such an economy, the decisions of the economic entities and the process of competition have already taken place before the relative prices are formed. Of course, this model can neither reflect consumer preferences nor the usefulness of goods, and it does not really intend to.

Nearly fifty years ago, Ludwig von Mises raised the problem of economic calculation under socialism. In a planned economy, he argued, prices reflecting the relative scarcity of commodities were at best formatted for consumer goods. Even under the conditions of rationing, the consumers could exchange goods and, thus, find a price in real terms. This possibility could not exist for investment goods, not only because it would be forbidden to barter them, but also because there would simply be no buyer or seller without property rights being legally established. But without rational evaluation of investment-goods, no rational economic accounting would exist. He resumed: "Where there is no free market, there is no pricing mechanism; without a pricing mechanism, there is no economic calculation" (Mises, 1972; 81). Mises forecasted that for this reason, socialism would only work as long as it is still surrounded by capitalism (Mises, 1920; 100). The practice of trade among CMEA countries has proved that he was right: The intra-bloc trading is realized on the basis of world market prices; the so-called transferable rouble is adjusted monthly to a basket of principal Western currencies, and the dollar is increasingly used as an account unit within the CMEA.

We would like to take Mises' argument one significant step further. In simple terms, he denies the possibility of coming to a rational economic choice without a market for investment goods since the value of the machines depends on the value of the commodities being produced with these machines, but not on the production costs of the machine (this is in line with the modern decision-oriented theory of the firm which does not care about sunk-costs). Thus, an optimum allocation of the resources requires a link from the consumer goods market to the investment goods market in the way that the former determines the latter. If there is no link, there will actually be market clearing prices and a market equilibrium on the consumer goods market, but the economy remains beyond its optimum.

If this is correct, the same is true for the allocation of capital itself. Presently, the majority of the Socialist economists and even politicians accept a market for consumer goods. From their point of view, this is due to the complexity and variability of the consumers' demand. But in evaluating investment goods according to their usefulness for the production of consumer-goods, we face the same problems. Hence, the most radical reform-proposals in Socialist countries even attempt at establishing market-type relations between enterprises (usually called "horizontal" relations as opposed to the "vertical" relations between the enterprise and the state authorities) in order to allow them the exchange of capital goods without the formal abolition of the social property of the means of production.

But what about capital itself? It is not the homogeneous good it is often considered to be. The evaluation of capital in its actual form, i.e. shares and different credit risks, within a developed capitalist economy, takes place in the most sensitive markets of all, due to the fact that it reflects both the permanently changing consumers' preferences and the altering production functions. In fact, the evaluation of stocks and loans on the capital market is identical with the social evaluation of information. There is no reason why this task is easier done by a state authority than the evaluation of goods and services. It can be drawn from experience that the shortcomings of a planned economy cannot be abolished without the creation of capital-markets.

Although acknowledging the industrial capitalist as a creator of technological progress, Marx considered the financial capitalist to be a totally useless and miserable figure, who earns most from new developments without any contribution (Marx, 1972; 113). Contrary to this, Schumpeter idealized the function of the banker already in his earliest writings (Schumpeter, 1951). The banker evaluates innovative proposals and strips the chaff from the wheat. He gives the innovators the financial means they need to carry out their proposals and has, therefore, a decisive function in the innovation process (in practice, however, Schumpeter was not very successful in this respect).

Conclusions

It seems that the only way to solve the stagflation problem of reformed Socialist economies is the introduction of capital markets: The central allocation of investment resources proved to be insufficient to bring capital to the innovative sector of the economy. Rezsö Nyers, the father of the Hungarian economic reform, refers to this point when he writes:

"concentration of forces from the largely diminished resources would cause serious losses . . . new channels of capital reallocation have to be opened . . . to cede the unused assets to other enterprises or small ventures" (Nyers/Tardos, 1984; 8–9).

It appears that one basic argument against capitalism must be reversed: Capitalism looks to the future, socialism to the past and not vice versa. The reason for this is that economic chances are evaluated on a capital market which is impossible in a Socialist economy. If Schumpeter was correct in asserting that the main aspect of capitalism is the innovative entrepreneur who tries new combinations and obtains the required resources from the capital market, the existence or non-existence of capital markets is the distinctive aspect of a market economy.

References

Adirim, A., 1984: Besonderheiten der Stagflation in der UdSSR, in: Osteuropa, Vol. 34, No. 11; 921–935

Bauer, T., 1976: The Contradictory Position of the Enterprise under the New Hungarian Economic Mechanism, in: Co-existence, Vol. 13

———, 1983: The Hungarian Alternative to Soviet-Type Planning, in: Journal of Comparative Economics, No. 7

Birman, I./Clarke, R. A., 1985: Inflation and Money Supply in the Soviet Economy, in: Soviet Studies, Vol. XXXVII, No. 4, October 1985; 494–504

Čičin-Šain, A./Mates, N., 1985: The Development and Role of the Major Economic Policy Instruments in Yugoslavia 1951–1972, in: Gey, P./Kosta, J./Quaisser, W., ed., 1985; 175–196

Drucker, P., 1978: People and Performance: The Best of Peter Drucker on Management. London

Friedman, Milton, 1983: Bright Promises, Dismal Performance. San Diego/ New York/London

Kornai, J., 1975: Anti-Äquilibrium. Über die Theorien der Wirtschaftssysteme und die damit verbundenen Forschungsaufgaben. Berlin/Heidelberg/New York

———, 1980a: Economics of Shortage, Vol.A. Amsterdam

———, 1980b: Economics of Shortage, Vol. B. Amsterdam

———, 1982: Growth, Shortage and Efficiency. A Macrodynamic Model of the Socialist Economy. Oxford

———, 1983: The Reproduction of Shortage, in: J. Kornai: Contradictions and Dilemmas. Budapest 1983; 6–32

———, 1985: The Dual Dependence of the State-owned Firm: Hungarian Experience (unpublished manuscript)

Kosta, J./Levčik. F., 1985: Economic Crisis in the East European CMEA Countries, Study No. 8., Research Project Crisis in Soviet-Type Systems

Kröber, G. et al., Innovation und Wissenschaft. Berlin

Lindberg, L. N., 1985: Models of the Inflation-Disinflation Process, in: L. N. Lindberg, and C. S. Maier, ed., 1985: The Politics of Inflation and Economic Stagnation. Washington; 25–50

Marx, K., 1972: Das Kapital, Dritter Band, in: Karl Marx, Friedrich Engels, Werke, Vol. 25

Mencinger, J., 1985: Yugoslav Economic System and Performance of the Economy in the Seventies and Early Eighties, in: Gey, P./Kosta, J./Quaisser, W., 1985; 197–210

——, 1986: The Crisis and the Reform of the Yugoslav Economic System in the Eighties (in this Volume)

Mensch, G., 1979, Stalemate in Technology. Cambridge

Mises, L. v., 1920: Die Wirtschaftsrechnung im Sozialismus, in: Archiv für Sozialwissenschaft und Sozialpolitik

——, 1972: Economic Calculation in the Socialist Commonwealth, in: A. Nove/D. M. Nuti: Socialist Economics. Harmondsworth

Nove, A., 1985: Money Supply and Inflation in the Soviet Union, in: G. Fink, ed., 1985: Socialist Economy and Economic Policy. Wien/New York; 149–156

Nyers, R./ Tardos, M., 1984: The Necessity for Consolidation of the Economy and the Possibility of Development in Hungary, in: Acta Oeconomica, Vol.32; 8–12

Olson, M., 1982: The Rise and Decline of Nations. London/New Haven

Pejovich, S., 1983: Innovation and Alternative Property Rights, in: Schüller, A./ Leipold, H./Hamel, H., ed.: Innovationsprobleme in Ost und West. Stuttgart/ New York; 41–49

Polityka, 1984: Koszyk Polityki, in: Polityka, 29. 12. 1984; 3, German Translation in: Osteuropa, Vol. 35, No. 9; A504–A508

Schumpeter, J. A., 1939: Business Cycles, Vol. I. London/New York

——, 1951: The Theory of Economic Development. Cambridge

Sirc, L., 1983: Workers' Self-Management and Innovative Behaviour, in: Schüller, A./Leipold, H./Hamel, H., ed., 1983; 123–134

Wiles, P., 1974: The Control of Inflation in Hungary. January 1968–June 1973, in Economie Appliquec, Vol. 25; 119–147

Zafir, M., 1979: A fogyasztói árakról—július 23, a utan, in Figyelö, No. 47 (1979); 1 and 4. German Translation in: Osteuropa, Vol. 32, No. 5; A274–A275d

3

Soviet Economic Policies Under Gorbachev: Problems and Prospects

Hans-Hermann Höhmann

The economy enjoys high priority within contemporary Soviet politics. The goals were both the acceleration of economic growth and a fundamental change and improvement in the conditions for growth, to be brought about by the transition from a primarily *resources*-based, extensive economic pattern to a predominantly *productivity*-based course of development with the aid of the frequently called-for "intensification" of the economic processes. Even before coming to power, General Secretary Gorbachev urged that this intensification should be afforded the same political resonance as the industrialization in the early phases of Soviet history (Pravda, 10 December 1984).

Acceleration and intensification have remained the declared "leitmotivs" of the re-orientation of economic policy envisaged by Gorbachev, indeed they are cardinal elements in his policies as a whole. In his concluding address to the 27th Party Congress, the General Secretary summarized by saying: "The idea of acceleration permeated our entire activity before the Party Congress. It stood in the focal point of attention at the Party Congress and was reflected in the revision of the Party Programme and in the changes to the Statutes, and also in the major directions of the economic and social development of our country for the 12th Five-Year Plan and up to the year 2000" (Meyer, 1986; 496–497).

And indeed, the policy declarations of the revised Party Program for the most part equate ideological objectives, such as the "perfection of socialism" and the "move forward to communism," with the process of "acceleration of the socio-economic development" of the Soviet Union. The ultimate utopian goal of history has taken second place to the road leading to that goal, defined in terms of economic and social-policy criteria. To use the terminology of A. Wallace (Wallace, 1961; 148): elements of "transfer culture" have once again—and conspicuously— gained in significance compared to the "goal culture" that prevailed up to now.

The Need for a Policy of Acceleration

Prominent Soviet politicians and also economists, sociologists and scientists have been clearly expressing the need for more rapid economic growth and the progressive intensification of the production processes for quite some time. The speeches and discussion rounds at the 27th Party Congress again yielded both a vivid picture with regards to the required economic performance and a multi-faceted confirmation of the complex functional deficiencies which are presently confronting Soviet economic reality. More economic growth, better product quality and more rapid technological innovation are desirable, indeed essential for a number of reasons, of which the most important are the following:

- the high demands made of the investment process and capital formation if further growth is to be assured, the conditions essential to structural modernization created, and resources made available for expensive regional projects;
- the demands made by the defense sector, which would remain high even if—rather improbable at present—arms control agreements were to bring significant relaxation;
- the urgent need to improve satisfaction of consumer demands— the Soviet economic program intentionally speaks of social and economic development—in order to assure adequate motivation for improvements in productivity and to shore up the political loyalty of the population with economic incentives;
- the increasing costs of USSR's hegemonial foreign policy within and beyond Eastern Europe;
- and last but not least the need for real progress to consolidate the legitimation of the USSR's communist system, since the purported ability to generate superior economic performance is this system's raison d'être.

It is hardly possible to specify what level of economic growth the USSR would require in order to be able to attain its established objectives. Nevertheless, it can be assumed that in the sectors indicated there are certain critical thresholds below which it must not be allowed to fall. In the capital formation sector, these are the *growth and modernization threshold*, in the armaments sector the *threshold of military and strategic parity* in the balance of power with the USA, and in the consumer demand sector the *motivation and loyalty threshold.*

In this connection, it is reasonable to estimate that a course of development above these critical thresholds would require growth at an annual average of about 3.5% in investment, 3% in arms spending, and approximately 2.5% in terms of expenditure of national income for consumer purposes; this would allow an increase in private consumption of about 1.5% per capita. Such an increase in the main fields of spending would in turn presuppose growth of the Soviet gross national product at an annual average rate of 2.5–3.0%. If it proved possible to attain such a growth rate, there would be adequate economic reserves available to finance Soviet domestic and foreign policy and conflicts over spending could be kept to a minimum, thus benefiting economic and budgetary stability.

In fact, the annual growth rate of the Soviet economy since the end of the 1970s has been only slightly more than 2%. The reasons for this were the slowdown in the expansion of the supply of the production factors, i.e. labor, capital, and natural resources, and also the significant deterioration in the growth of productivity. Since the drop in the growth of the supply of economic factors is likely to continue in the coming planning periods—the figures quoted by Prime Minister Ryzhkov in his address to the Party Congress corroborate this (Meyer, 1986; 321)—, it will only be possible to realize the objective of accelerating economic growth if it proves practicable to reverse the unsatisfactory productivity trend of past years.

The inadequate development of productivity in the Soviet Union can be attributed to a variety of reasons (elaborated in detail by Höhmann, 1984). Even though, in the long term, these causes are al intimately linked with the Soviet system, it is nevertheless possible to draw some distinctions from a short-term perspective. Such a differentiation is absolutely essential, especially since it is only on this basis that the chances of success for the re-orientation of economic policy so vehemently advocated by Gorbachev at the Party Congress can be assessed.

The productivity problems in the Soviet economy can be traced back to the interaction of four groups of factors: exogenous factors, structures and process policy factors, system-inherent factors, and secondary factors which intensify the effects of these primary factors.

The main *exogenous factors* are weather conditions, seasonal fluctuations in working hours, and the international trade situation. While better weather conditions appear possible for the future (several of the past years have been plagued by abnormally bad weather), the terms of reference in foreign trading have deteriorated significantly, e.g. the drop in the oil price and the fall of the dollar. For seasonal reasons, the available working time will be somewhat better in the initial phase of the 12th Five-Year Plan.

The *structures and process policy factors* include first and foremost the consequences of Soviet investment policy. The cutback in the rate of investment, the fragmentary allocation of available funds, and the pronounced increase in costs have had the same adverse effect on productivity as have some of the shifts made within the structures of sectoral and regional investment. Corrections to these phenomena are planned, and, within limits, possible. Foremost along the deficiencies in process policy to date—some of them likewise amenable to correction—are dysfunctional planning pressure, lack of balance in economic planning, and finally the general deterioration in the style of centralized economic management in the latter phase of the Brezhnev era. This was also frequently emphasized in the discussions at the Party Congress.

Worthy of mention among the *system-inherent* factors is the declining ability of Soviet economic planning to cope with its major duties: it failed to steer the economy properly towards the objectives established by the political leadership, coordination of the economic process was inadequate and allowed many forms of "second economy" to emerge, efficiency dropped (indicators: high costs on the input side, inadequate quality on the output side, little inclination to innovate in the production process). These in-system obstacles to increased productivity are to be combated by new reforms. The approaches embodied in, and the prospects for, the success of those reforms will be discussed later.

The *secondary factors* finally served to intensify the outlined shortcomings through their cumulative ratcheting effects on the existing bottlenecks and have contributed considerably to the much lamented loss of motivation among the working Soviet population. Conversely, if it should prove possible to achieve improvements due to corrections in structures and process and system policies, positive ratcheting phenomena could also be expected to take effect. In this context, however, it should be pointed out that the nuclear accident at Chernobyl has given rise to new adverse trends, to be precise, in the field of motivation, which will be difficult to offset.

Gorbachev's Economic Policy Concept

What instruments does Soviet economic policy have at its disposal for solving the outlined growth and productivity problems and for attaining the goal of the "acceleration of socio-economic development"? In his address to the Party Congress, Gorbachev again spoke of "restructuring" (perestroika) and of a "decisive turn-about," indeed of "radical reform." Ryzhkov followed up on this, and by now the concept of reform has, after a long absence, once more found a place in the Soviet discussion arena.

All this is indicative of a willingness to finally take resolute action, to radically overhaul the Soviet economic policy and modernize it in terms of substance and methods. Nevertheless, a radical change of the socialist system of planned Economy in the USSR is not intended for the time being. Instead, all that can be expected in the foreseeable future is a repetition of the familiar combination of corrections to economic policy with isolated, partial elements of restructuring in systems policy, i.e. reforms "within the system." But of course, this gives no indication of the potential future success of such a policy, nor of its span; for far-reaching partial-reforms would appear possible even within the framework of the traditional planning system, as well. One possible approach is the "sectoralization" of reform measures of a staggered range, which Gorbachev propagated at the 27th Party Congress and which is now going into tentative implementation with special arrangements for agriculture and light industry. This approach will be discussed in more detail below.

Generally speaking. Gorbachev's economic strategy, expertly backed up by the Soviet Prime Minister, provides for two stages of "restructuring." In the first stage, the "activation of the human factor," much invoked in the speeches and documents of the Party Congress, is to be attempted with the aim of tapping existing reserves which have been inadequately exploited thus far. Improvements in organization, more discipline in labor relations, planning and plan implementation, and the intensification of "material incentives" are envisaged here. Then the improved performance effects achieved in economic policy and in the economic system in the short-term are to be perpetuated such that it eventually proves possible to attain even the high rate of acceleration in economic growth planned for the 1990s. This also includes the greater flexibility in system policy already mentioned. On the other hand, Soviet economic policy is not likely to allow itself to be put under to much pressure by the "goals up to the year 2000." If it proves possible to attain the acceleration in growth planned for 1990, and if, in particular, this can be combined with a perceptible rise in the Soviet standard of living, the tentative planning targets for the 1990s could well be adjusted downwards without any loss of authority for the leadership. But once again, the crucial factor is rapid success; success that can make itself felt to the Soviet man on the street. Especially in the wake of Chernobyl, the public will need to be shown that it is not just a production factor (and frequently a poorly protected one at that) but is also taken seriously as a recipient of benefits achieved by improved economic performance.

Gorbachev's economic policy, as endorsed by the 27th Party Congress, can only be seen as a package of diverse measures with regards to its conception and probable functionability. Precisely the decision not to attempt a reform involving changes to the system itself, a reform that could aspire to a new "strong"economic mechanism with considerable weight in its own right (though this in itself gives no indication of its functionability), makes it essential to search for exploitable potentials for growth and productivity in many fields of economic policy.

The implementation of such wide-ranging measures, however, will depend on the quality of the acting central economic management. Soviet leadership is concerned primarily with how it can strengthen the authority of the central economic organs and how it can significantly improve the style of economic policy. The poor "muddling through" image in the latter years of the Brezhnev era was rooted precisely in this aspect. Reference was made on this on several occasions at the Party Congress. The goals to be achieved now are fewer contradictions, greater stringency and more discipline in the implementation of economic directives. And indeed there are many ways in which better economic management at the central level could contribute to the desired improvement of the economic situation. Following are a few of the possibilities:

- improvements in motivation as a result of a clear political line which helps to establish authority and takes effect via the "charisma of action men" (again, much will depend on how the leadership deals with the Chernobyl situation);
- establishments of better balance by avoiding excessively high planning targets that would only over-strain the economy;
- enforcement of the priorities established for modernization by curbing the familiar inflation of pretensions on the part of the regional and sectoral bureaucracies and the resulting harmful consequences in the form of capital fragmentation that is an obstacle to increased productivity;
- creation of a highly capable management, especially at the upper echelons of the management hierarchy, by dismissing incompetent managers and recruiting new ones.

By and large, a correction in the style of centralized economic management as practiced up to now can be expected to release significant performance reserves. The extent of which cannot be predicted at present as the period of observation is still too short, quite apart from the fact that "centralized economic management" in socialist planned economies is a category in economic policy that has not been sufficiently investigated to date even by Western experts in East European studies.

With regards to the substance of future Soviet economic policy, the 27th Party Congress has endorsed the aspects bearing Gorbachev's mark from the very beginning. His package of economic policy measures includes, firstly, measures in the field of *manpower policy*. Emphasis in this field continues to be placed on all-round discipline. Breaches of discipline are to be combated, whatever their nature, as are other vices such as theft, bribery, drunkenness, greed, toadyism and cajolery. Incompetent officials and those lacking initiative are to be replaced, the level of professionalism of economic managers is to be improved. The wage distribution system is to be modified to bring remuneration more into line with performance. A further goal is to expand the system of material and "moral" incentives with the aid of improving motivation and increasing productivity. Steps are to be taken against all forms of illegal income from the "shadow economy" and corruption. Therefore it is likely that Soviet penal law in economic matters will be tightened up. On the other hand, broader leeway is to be established for legal economic activity on the part of the individual, particularly in the provision of services.

Secondly, major emphasis is placed on *corrections to structures policy* which is largely intended to benefit scientific-technological progress. Large-scale promotion of basic and applied research aims at bringing about a technological break-through which is to go so far as to enable the production facilities to be equipped with robots and computers and the application of biotechnologies. As plausible as this package may appear, its implementation is likely to be difficult. The traditional institutions and procedures of the socialist planned economy are familiar obstacles to innovation (Berliner, 1976). And wherever modernization has been achieved, it has always involved major capital expenditure. In the light of the worsening shortage of capital, however, this entails a serious weakening of one of the cornerstones of modernization policy as practiced to date.

In order to introduce technological innovations into the production practice, to establish the basis in terms of machinery and equipment that is essential to the success of investment policy, and to perceptibly raise the scrapping coefficient in the interests of modernizing the capital stock, machine building is given high priority within the framework of the envisaged re-structuring of the economy. "New generations" of machinery and equipment are intended to bring about a transition from "evolutionary to revolutionary" changes in technology and to make significant increases in labor and capital productivity and considerable savings in material, energy and input products possible. In turn within the machine building sector the construction of machine tools and instruments, computer technology, electrical and electronic engineering, in short the "catalysts of scientific-technological progress," are to be given special backing, for instance by preferential treatment in the allocation of investment funds.

Foreign trade, too is to be put to work in the service of the further development of the economy and in particular of the modernization drive (Meier, 1986). In the first instance, the intention is to mobilize the USSR's East European partners in the CMEA to deliver more goods and to raise their quality standards. A "complex program for the scientific-technological progress of the CMEA countries up to the year 2000" covering five key sectors—electronics, automation technology, nuclear power, new materials, and biotechnology—has been designated as the "nucleus" of comprehensive specialization and cooperation. Nevertheless, reciprocal trade will remain in the foreground of economic relations within the CMEA. The future of this trade, however, stands under the uncertain auspices of the changing oil price situation which makes it necessary to renegotiate the existing agreements on prices and quantities. The USSR will attempt to offload some of the burden of the deterioration in its terms of trade onto its partners. Cut-backs in the USSR's oil exports to CMEA would be one way of achieving this, as would increasing the share of machinery and industrial equipment in Soviet exports and demanding higher quality products as imports from the CMEA countries.

But the intention is also to expand economic relations with the Western industrialized nations. This involves improving the institutional background conditions and eliminating obstacles to free trade. Key commodities on the import side, besides the old favorite grain, are machinery, industrial equipment and technology. Here too, however, falling oil prices, the drop in the value of the dollar and the slowdown in oil production have had a drastic effect on the Soviet terms of trade. For this reason, the USSR can be expected to pursue a cautious and selective import policy. At any rate, Ryzhkov gave a clear signal to that effect with his call to "strictly regulate the expenditure of foreign reserves on imports." In the coming years the Soviet Union must endeavor to increase its sales of industrial semi-finished and finished products on Western markets. However, this would require a higher capacity for export-oriented production, something that can hardly be achieved without reforms to foreign trade. Steps to this end are apparently already in preparation and include the reorganization of the foreign trade apparatus, the transfer of foreign trade functions to major Soviet production enterprises, and the founding of joint ventures with Western companies. But all these measures are likely to fall short of the changes in the smaller CMEA countries.

Changes in Systems Policy

Gorbachev's statements on economic policy since his coming to power in March 1985, document his view that economic revival and the intensification of the economic processes cannot be attained without a thorough "perfecting," "improvement" or "restructuring" of planning, management and the economic mechanism. For instance, the General Secretary declared as early as at April 1985 Plenum of the CC of the CPSU: "Whatever questions we discuss, from whatever side we approach the economy—everything boils down to the need to seriously improve management and the economic mechanism as a whole" (CPSU, 1985; 14).

In later speeches Gorbachev underlined the need for corrections to systems policy. At the same time, an economic experiment already introduced under Andropov, to try out new forms of planning and incentive mechanism for Soviet industry was extended, and the discussion within the Soviet Union on reform—which had already picked up perceptibly in the Andropov era—was further intensified.

Measured in terms of the pressures for reform and of the discussion on economic policy, the revised Program of the CPSU, published in draft form in late October 1985 (Pravda, 26 October 1985), at first appeared to place little emphasis on changes in systems policy. The call for a "restructuring of planning" or the "creation of an overall system of economic management and planning" had given way to the vaguer and more familiar slogan of "perfecting" and is also not included in the final version eventually passed by the Party Congress. However, the Program does contain an adequately assorted selection of building bricks which provides material for numerous and even a few more far-reaching changes "within the system" of the planned economy and furthermore, which matches up precisely with the catalogue of changes and initiatives familiar from Gorbachev's speeches. Indeed, it contains everything which would be needed for the modernization of an administrative planned economy and that could consequently be "called up"—provided there were a logical and consistent model of institutions and functions, a strategy for implementation that holds promises of success, a capable personal basis, and expedient flanking measures in terms of structures policy. This is where the crucial present-day shortcomings and the future tasks lie, but also the reserves which can be drawn upon for improvements in Soviet systems policy.

At the 27th Party Congress, Gorbachev established new points of emphasis. As already mentioned, the concept of reform found its way back into Soviet economic language, and the attribute "radical" was introduced as a sign of determination. At the same time, however, it also became apparent that the future Soviet systems policy is to remain within the bounds of the attempts, familiar from the past, to rationalize the planned economy system by introducing organizational improvements and more modern planning methods, to make it more efficient by introducing new planning indicators and bonus systems, to relax it by selective decentralization—especially in sectors that do not enjoy any major political priority—and to use indirect steering instruments ("normatives") on a larger scale for the purpose of controlling the economy. The centralized planning functions are to be relieved of unnecessary details in order to recover the ground lost in terms of controllability of the economy. As in the past, the main areas of reform are the organizational structure of planning, management and the production units, planning methods, and the system of economic levers, economic mechanism intended to convert planning targets into activities at the production unit level, which are in keeping with planning considerations and with actual demand.

The principle of the envisaged restructuring in systems policy, as advanced by Gorbachev and endorsed by Ryzhkov, bears the mark of such moderate reformers as Academician N. P. Fedorenko (Fedorenko, 1984) and A. G. Aganbegjan (Aganbegjan, 1985). The latter, in particular, has frequently confirmed that he numbers among the General Secretary's advisors—but that, of course, says nothing about the intensity, form or importance of such advisory activities. Another aspect repeatedly emphasized at the Party Congress was the need for better scientific substantiation of policies, but politicians and economists alike lament the lack of any practicable "Political Economy of Socialism." What is particularly lacking are investigations into the totality of those relations of interaction that emerge in a more strongly de-centralized administrative planned economy and which have to be controlled by expedient economic policy. Thus, models for reform are not developed on the basis of new and self-supporting theoretical foundations but rather derived from, and in response to, the major contemporary shortcomings in the Soviet planning system of today: excessive bureaucratization and simultaneous inadequate steering of the economy, unsatisfactory coordination and poor efficiency.

The strategy of progressively more relaxed directive planning in the non-priority sectors of the economy, with extended market functions and more emphasis on parametric steering, is an attempt to mitigate one of the fundamental contradictions of present-day economic planning which Fedorenko so vividly described (Fedorenko, 1984; 3):

The root of all evil lies in the fact that, in the present mechanism, there is no agreement between the planning directives which give expression to the overall state interests and the system of economic levers. Because these levers are not coordinated with the planning objectives, they work against them at every step. For this reason, the major emphasis within the management mechanism is placed on administrative methods, and as many economic decisions as possible are concentrated at the center. This, in turn, makes management sluggish and leads to a lack of responsibility.

Now, what is Gorbachev's plan for combining the two types of steering instruments possible within an administrative planned economy—direct dictates stipulated by the planning authorities and indirect "economic levers" couched in terms of value parameters—as harmoniously as possible, thus helping to alleviate the present dysfunctions in the system? In his address to the Party Congress he summed up the principles of the envisaged changes in systems policy in five elements which are also to be found—in a different form but essentially the same in nature— in Ryzhkov's planning Report:

Firstly: The effectiveness of centralized economic management is to be improved by extensive and far reaching changes to the organizational structure of the planning and administration of the economy and by refraining from attempting to regulate unnecessary details. The main task of the central economic management is to implement expedient economic policy strategies. These include ensuring the attainment of the most important economic objectives, the establishment of favorable structural proportions in the economy to facilitate growth and modernization, and ensuring a "balanced" development.

Secondly: With a view to improving the organizational structure, the economic administration apparatus is to be reduced by eliminating superfluous administrative organs, Gosplan is to be made into the scientific center and general headquarters of economic planning at the central level, better allowance is to be made in the structure of the administration for the interministerial interests of related branches, the link-ups between economic management organs at the branch and territorial levels are to be improved in the interests of a "complex economic and social development of the Republics and regions," and at the production unit level both high-efficiency large-scale enterprises and also small and intermediate-size businesses are to be promoted.

Thirdly: The autonomy of the production units is to be backed up by restrictions on directive indicators dictated from above, by extended capacity for contractual relations, and by greater financial self-sufficiency for the associations and enterprises. The enterprises are to be put into a position to earn their funds largely by their own efforts on the basis of "full economic accountability." Also, more credit funds are to be made available. The material/technological logistics system is to take on more and more the nature of state-run trading in means of production.

Fourthly: The more widespread use of "economic instruments" is envisaged as a means of steering the economy and at the same time as a lever for improving efficiency. In this context, the "normative method," in which the economic activity of the associations and enterprises is influenced via financial guide parameters (normatives)—comparable to taxes at different rates—is to play a particularly important role. Performance-based normatives are to be applied, for example, in the formation of the various financing funds for the enterprises, and these funds in turn determine the development of the wages and social security benefits payable by the enterprises. An extension of the function of prices—in particular their use as levers for more technological progress and better product quality—is also included in the "economic instruments" strategy.

Fifthly: And finally, the envisaged tightening up of planning, improvements in the organizational structure, and extended decision-making freedom on the part of the production units are to be accompanied by an extension of elements of worker participation in an attempt to improve motivation and to legitimate the system. The more integral application of the "Act Governing the Worker's Collectives" is called for, but reference is made above all, and despite many shortcomings in practice to date, to the favorably assessed example of the brigades within the enterprises. The relatively closed-shop working groups of the brigades are regarded not only as an effective form of collective organization and stimulation of labor but also as the expression of self-administration and democracy—concepts that were prominent in the speeches and documents of the Party Congress.

These basic principles of Soviet systems policy still take their bearings in many respects from the reform course followed in the past. However, they do embody some new elements and revive some earlier approaches that have been discussed but never implemented in the past, such as elements of the Kosygin-Liberman reform of 1965. The aspects distinguishing the new strategy from the policies of the latter phase of the Brezhnev area are, apart from an unmistakable determination to take action, the greater emphasis on the need to decentralize and economize, but also the idea of more selective changes in systems policy in specific sectors ("sectoralization"). Thus, Gorbachev at the 27th Party Congress announced extensive decentralization measures to be applied in the agriculture, in the production of consumer goods, and in the services sector. In the meantime, the Central Committee and the Council of Ministers have also passed a number of joint ordinances to this effect for the agricultural sector (On the further perfecting of the economic mechanism in the agro-industrial complex, Pravda, 29 March 1986) and for light industry (On the improvement of planning and economic stimulation and the perfecting of production management for mass demand commodities in the light industry, Pravda, 6 May 1986). The intention has also been announced of introducing similar provisions for other sectors. Of particular importance is the envisaged development of systems policy within the framework of Soviet industry which, in the course of the coming year, is to be completely re-geared towards new planning, steering, and bonus allocation procedures that have been developed and tried out within the terms of reference of a "large-scale experiment" (Höhmann, 1985; 153). The basic idea shared by the provisions introduced for the agro-industrial complex and light industry is to link-up extended decision-making freedom on the part of the production units with a cutback in the numbers and greater stability in the use of directive planning indicators, closer orientation of economic activities to market conditions, and a significant uprating of economic "normatives" as instruments of indirect control.

However, the General Secretary himself has attempted to suppress any exaggerated hopes of what his reform policy might achieve: "We are only at the start of our path. Under the conditions prevailing in our country with its immense and complicated economy, the restructuring of the economic mechanism is going to take time and energetic efforts. There may be difficulties, and we are not immune to miscalculation . . . " (Meyer, 1986; 70). The reasons for possible difficulties were made only too apparent at the 27th Party Congress. On the one hand, bureaucratic inflexibility and arbitrariness were criticized, on the other, attention was drawn to ideological reservations which had still not been reconciled, for instance against the more widespread use of "commodity/money relations" or the intensified application of forms of parametric control. In response to such attitudes, Gorbachev and Ryzhkov stressed the immutable validity of the "principles of socialism," the yardsticks of which Gorbachev immediately went on to define in pragmatic terms as follows: "The supreme criterion for perfecting management, indeed for the entire system of the socialist conditions of production, must be socio-economic acceleration, the actual strengthening of socialism" (Meyer, 1986; 77).

Prospects and Perspectives

The prospects for the success of Gorbachev's systems-policy course as re-affirmed and re-accentuated at the 27th Party Congress of the CPSU can be regarded as open. Of course, the USSR's future systems policy retains the familiar mixture of direct steering instruments and economic levers, which embodies its insoluble contradictions with regards to functionability. In particular, it permits, it even opens the door to a return to more direct administrative interventions, whether in a gradual or in an abrupt process. This could be dangerous, especially if price-induced misallocations were to lead to discrepancies between the performance of the production units and the politically established central-level priorities.

For these and other reasons, Western observers as a rule hold a sceptical view of the prospects of future "reforms within the system" and—like many a voice from the currently reviving Soviet reform scene—consider more far reaching reforms along market socialism lines to be essential. The question is, however, whether such a perception does not under-estimate the potential for intra-system improvement while at the same time over-rating the feasibility and the chances of success of more radical reforms—not only in general but especially under the conditions pre-vailing in the Soviet Union at the present time.

As far as the chances of future limited reforms are concerned, the link-up with oft-tried principles is not to be equated per se with the certainty of renewed failure. To be sure, fundamental functional defi-ciencies will remain. Every economic system has them. But what is just as certain is that there are a number of fields of action that can be tilled better than they have been in the past with the aim of improving the functioning of the economy. For instance the organizational and pro-cedural set-ups could be made consistent, the implementation of changes in systems policy could be expedited, reforms could be better backed up by accompanying measures in the field of process and structures policy, their personnel and motivational basis could be improved. More first-hand experience, intensive observation of economic reforms else-where, and more research with a closer bearing on practical economic policy could likewise make a contribution to progress in systems policy. After all, we should bear in mind that the Soviet leadership cannot realistically intend to jump straight into the best of all economic worlds, but must be content with achieving some selective improvements in the level of performance of the economy.

With regards to the problems of, and the limitations on, radical reforms involving changes to the system, attention is commonly drawn—and rightly so—to the retarding effects of certain political and social factors. But almost as serious as these are the reform-impeding elements of the Soviet economic and social structures. Of particular significance are the following:

- the size of the country and its unbalanced economic structure, which adds its own specific risks to those of any extensive reform;
- the multinational composition of the USSR, which harbors the danger of centrifugal tendencies to the detriment of the central state in the event of far-reaching reforms along the lines of market socialism;
- the traditional lack of market economy thinking and entrepreneurial potential in Russia and the USSR, coupled with the likewise traditionally strong tendency towards intervention on the part of the state authorities;
- the USSR's role as a world power, with the consequence that economic forces have to be kept available at short-term disposal and that, for this purpose, the traditional deployment instruments of central steering has to be preserved—if not in practice then at least in principle;
- the special weight of the military industrial complex, but also of other state tasks and expenditures—for instance in connection with regional policy—which would be difficult to finance from a market-economy budget, and last but not least
- the long time spent under the centralized administrative planned economy system, with all its behavior-forming and structure shaping effects.

Under these conditions, an absolute prerequisite for any far-reaching reform would be that new, quasi-"pre-market-economy" economic and social structures compatible with the reform are created or at least allowed to emerge before-hand. Implementation of the present strategy of technocratic/conservative modernization need not by any means necessarily give way to radical reforms, but it could help to establish economic and social structures which would facilitate more far-reaching reforms. Better management practices, a higher standard of technology, increasing manager responsibility, intensified foreign trade relations, a higher level of education, and an improved standards of economic and organizational science could, in the more distant future, create conditions beneficial to reform that cannot be envisaged in the short to medium term. So the 27th Party Congress may yet, in retrospect, take on greater significance than some of the more disappointed commentators in the West are prepared to credit to it today.

How, then, are the chances of the Soviet economic program, the prospects for the "acceleration of the socio-economic development" of the USSR to be assessed? Even if it can be taken for granted that it will not prove possible to attain all the planning targets established, the revised, streamlined and re-profiled economic policy aspired to by Gorbachev nevertheless holds promise of some effects in terms of improved performance and more stable growth—at sufficient to prevent a protracted and thus politically dangerous drop below the critical thresholds defined earlier. The decisive factor will be, however, whether Gorbachev succeeds in developing charisma and building up his own personal authority. Both will be required if sustained improvement in the quality of centralized economic management is to be achieved, which in turn is a prerequisite for the success of the economic policy package outlined. One early and difficult test of Gorbachev's abilities will be whether he manages to come to grips with the adverse repercussions of the Chernobyl nuclear accident. In light of the latest drop in motivation, caused by the human suffering involved, the persistent population's fears, and due to the shortages in power supply and agricultural products—at least on a short-term and regional basis—this is likely to be no easy task.

References

Aganbegjan, A. G., 1985: Na novom etape ekonomicheskogo stroitelstva, in: EKO 8; 3–24

Berliner, J. S., 1976: The Innovation Decision in Soviet Industry. Cambridge (Mass.)/London

Fedorenko, N. P., 1984: Planirovanie i upravlenie: kakimi im byt? in EKO 12; 3–20

Höhmann, H. H., 1984: Bilanz der Ära Breschnew, in: Dietz, B., ed.: Zukunftsperspektiven der Sowjetunion; 24ff. München

———, 1985: Wirtschaftsreformen in der UdSSR, in: DIW quarterly 2; 153ff.

Meier, C., 1986: Dynamik oder Stagnation? Perspektiven sowjetischer Auaenwirtschaft nach dem 27. Parteitag der KPdSU, in: aktuelle Analysen des Bundesinstituts für ostwissenschaftliche und internationale Studien, No. 14

Meyer, G., ed., 1986: Sowjetunion zu neuen Ufern? Dokumente und Materialien. Düsseldorf

Wallace, A., 1961: Culture and Personality. New York

Towards the 27th Party Congress of the CPSU. Materials of the Plenum of the CC of the CPSU, 23 April 1985. Moscow 1985

4

The Polish Economic Reform: Central Planning or Socialist Markets?

Piotr Pysz

The development in Poland after 1945 is characterized by continual socio-economic crises. Approximately ten years passed from the time the Communist Party took control in 1944–45 until the first crises in 1954–56. The next social and economical upheaval took place twelve years later, i.e. in 1968, and lasted until 1970. The third crises, which had been the most serious, occurred from 1979–82. The Polish political leaders reacted to this with a program of crises-management measures. Economic reforms have always been included as a part of these measures. The reform plan was to deal with the 1979–82 crisis exceeded the traditional threshold, below which most of the economic reforms in Poland and other socialist countries had failed. The reform attempted to combine the "regulated market mechanism" with the necessary changes to the social and political spheres of the system, particularly in the method of government. For this reason, we can talk about the reform of the economic system as a whole. The purpose of this essay is to help find answers to the following questions: To what extent, if at all, were reform concepts successfully implemented from 1982–85? To what extent has the government returned to the traditional planning system, so familiar from previous reform attempts?

Characterization of the Reform Concept

The characterization of the Polish reform concept includes two basic elements: (1) the desired model of the reformed economic system, and (2) description of the "transition path" from the existing command management system to the reformed system. The implementation of the reform was planned to take about three years, covering the period 1982–

84. After this time, it was expected that the Polish economic system
would resemble the final model, with regard to both the political and
institutional mechanisms, as well as the economical operation.

Desired Model of the Reformed System

The official outline of the economic reform was based on three pillars,
the so-called "3 S's": autonomy (samodzielnosc), self-management (sa-
morzadnosc), and self-financing (samofinansowanie). The previous structure of enterprise subordination to superior organs was to be replaced
by an equal partnership, within the framework of mutually binding
regulations. The superior authorities would have the right to intervene
in an enterprise's activities only on the basis of well-defined legal criteria,
and only in certain cases. Self-management was seen as the institutional
guarantee of the stability of an enterprise's independence. The workers'
councils, elected by the workforce, were to obtain significant decision-
making power in the strategic management of this economic unit; the
enterprise's director would retain control of operation. The workers'
councils would have the right to appoint the director through a voting
procedure, as well as the right to dismiss him. By enforcing the rule
of enterprise self-financing, profit was to be made the cornerstone of
the financial system. After paying taxes and repaying credits, the workers'
councils would have the right to divide the remaining profit between
the development fund and consumption.

Other elements of the economy's organizational structure, primarily
the organization of the State economic apparatus, were to be adopted
to the above mentioned changes in the enterprise status. The number
of branch ministries was to be reduced to two, or even one, and their
functions were to be changed. Instead of aggregating and breaking down
plan targets to and from subordinated organizational units, their duty
was to manage industrial policy/technical progress, foreign trade, ini-
tiation of structural changes, etc. The logical supplement to these changes
at the branch ministry level was to be the liquidation of the intermediate
level between the ministries and the enterprises, i.e. the liquidation of
the enterprises' obligatory associations (zjednoczenia). This was planned
to coincide with the reorganization of the Planning Commission, which
was to be transformed from an operative planning and economic control
organ into an advisory agency, focussing its attention on analysis, pre-
planning studies, and on preparing appropriate variants of the national
plans for the Cabinet and Parliament (Sejm). This would require some
changes in the organizational structure of the Planning Commission
itself, previously characterized by the domination of branch divisions
over functional ones.

Along with radical changes of branch structures within the economic system, its functional organs, i.e. the Ministry of Finance, the Ministry of Labor, Wages and Social Affairs, the Ministry of Prices etc., were to be strengthened. The latter, not being in direct control of the enterprises, were to influence their behavior through universal and relatively stable indirect instruments (rates of taxation, wage rates, credit policy, etc.). Some changes were also to be carried out in the banking system. First of all, the importance of credit contracts and enterprise credit-worthiness as criteria for granting credits was to be increased. All of these changes in the organizational structures of the State economic apparatus were regarded as the institutional guarantee of an enterprise's independence, according to the principles of autonomy, self-management, and self-financing, spelled out in the reform's outline.

The changes envisaged in the central planning of the economy referred both to its socio-political and its systemic aspects. Highly exclusive decision-making processes, typical in the command management system, were to be replaced by participation on the part of institutions representing various social groups in the planning process (for example trade unions, consumers' organizations, academic and professional associations).

The pluralization of participation in central planning demanded a diversity in the interests articulated therein. This in turn implied an increase in the role of Parliament (Sejm) as a mediator in the social planning process. The socialization of central planning also required a more precise separation of the functions of the respective institutions participating in the management of the economy, thus enabling a more precise definition of their responsibilities. The reform design includes in this point, among other things, a number of postulates referring to the party authorities (Kierunki, 1981; 12).

Regarding the systemic aspect of central planning, the proposed transition from daily management to long-term strategic management on the part of the central authorities, is of crucial significance in terms of economic development. A five-year socioeconomic plan was to play a dominant role in the planning process, as opposed to yearly plans, as had formerly been the case. This plan, being of an indicative nature, would concentrate on determining the most important socio-economic proportions, conditions for external and internal equilibrium, the structural and spatial conditions for economical growth, etc. This indicative character is linked—in the reform outline—to the discontinuation of the break-down of plan targets for plan executors.

The reform's outline envisaged the self-regulating market mechanism as having a crucial impact on allocation and distribution decisions within the economy as a whole. Consistency between central planning decisions and market decisions was to be achieved mainly through legal regulations and by universal indirect instruments of economic control (budget and monetary policy including credit policy, price policy, taxation, etc.). These instruments were to meet two requirements. On the one hand, they should conform to the logic of the market mechanism, i.e. not disturb the self-regulating adaption processes between demand, supply and prices. On the other hand, they should guarantee the realization of the macro-proportions outlined in the central plan. The reform concept considers the possibility of divergences between the plan's decisions and the operation of the self-regulating market mechanism. In emergency situations (national security, natural calamity) or in the case of meeting international obligations, the State economic apparatus would have the right to include a specific assignment to an enterprise's production plan, or to stipulate production beyond target. Considering the foreseeable wide usage of indirect, and in some cases even direct instruments of control, one can say that the reform outline proposed the creation of a "regulated market mechanism."

Reform Implementation

Two different points of view were the subject of a lively discussion in 1980–81 on the method of reform implementation. One of these may be summarized as "market equilibrium first, then the reform." The second point of view was based on the assumption that market equilibrium could be achieved only if a comprehensive and highly concentrated reform was introduced. This can be summarized as: "The reform first, then market equilibrium." The official view of reform implementation combined these two ideas. This is reflected in the following quotation from the reform outline:

> The reform will be realized in a comprehensive way and as quickly as possible. The new economic mechanism, and the organizational structures adapted to them, will create the conditions necessary to restore economic equilibrium, and in that way contribute to creating conditions favorable for the success of the reform itself. . . . The condition necessary for a successful economic reform is an economic policy which would enable the practical function of the new systemic arrangements. The reform of the planning and management system cannot in itself fulfill the expectations it created, and, in particular, it cannot eliminate the various sources of disequilibrium in the economy (Kierunki, 1981; 52, 63).

As a result of this compromise, the method of reform implementation included two basic elements. One of these was the "crucial reform package," which was to be introduced at the very beginning of the implementation process. This was a set of basic legal regulations and indirect economic instruments which were to create the systemic conditions for changing the behavior of economic entities and thus of the economy as a whole, in accordance with the desired model of the reformed economic system. Furthermore, this plan included a set of so-called transitional measures which deviated from this model. These were primarily direct instruments of economic control necessary for the continued rationing of the means of production and the organizational structures which would control the rationing system. The necessity of transitionally maintaining this mechanism was justified by the serious market disequilibrium and by the disequilibrium in foreign trade. At the same time, it was emphasized that these transitional mechanisms should not conflict with the logic of the new system, and if so, then these conflicts should not be of a severe nature nor be long-lasting (Kierunki, 1981; 58).

The task of integrating these two semi-contradictory elements of reform implementation was turned over to the economic policy makers. The reform implementation was to start with a reduction of final demands for consumer and investment goods. It was expected that this would favorably affect microeconomic efficiency and the allocation of production factors. By adjusting the final demands to the existing supply of final goods, producers were to be confronted with the barrier of elastic demand. This demand would flexibly react to price and quality changes and would force producers to improve efficiently since inefficiency could not any longer be easily shifted to the consumers and/or investors via price rises and quality reduction. This would gradually reduce the overall demand for intermediate goods and place the producers in front of a barrier of limited demand as well. This gradual loosening of the demand constraint within the economy would eventually affect the markets for production factors by limiting the demand for labor and capital, and would contribute indirectly to a further stabilization of the markets for consumer and investment goods. As a result, the market mechanism could take over the allocation and distribution functions within the economy. Production factors and final goods would then be directed first to the producers and consumers who were able to make the best use of them. Thus, overall allocative efficiency would be improved.

The gradual marketization of the economy would also lead to the elimination of shortages which justified the transitional retention of direct economic control instruments and the maintenance of organizational structures deviating from the model of the reformed system. The self-regulating market mechanism and indirect instruments of economic control would replace various forms of production targets and resource allocation limits for the enterprises. These changes in instruments would diminish the need for the intermediate State organs. As a result of their gradual loss of functions, they would be liquidated, or given new tasks. In summary, it can be said that in the process of reform implementation, the economy was to be gradually freed from mechanisms of a transitional character and to approach as nearly as possible the final model of the reformed system.

The Course of the Reform Implementation

The reform of the traditional planning system began almost one year before its announcement in July 1981. In the second half of 1980, the formation of the union "Solidarnosc" started a democratization of the society. The economic crisis and political conflicts radicalized a large part of the society, which in turn caused "Solidarnosc" to change their existing strategy. Instead of the typical union demands (wage increases and a reduction of working hours), emphasis was placed on furthering the democratization process (Rapport, 1986; 169). The political leadership reacted to this development in September 1981 by imposing martial law. This significantly affected the reform, which formally began on 1 January 1982. On the one hand, the socio-political changes were reduced to a minimum: The reform lost its institutional guarantees (independent unions, self-administration of labor, pressure from public opinion, etc.). On the other hand, the chances of successfully implementing the reform through a reduction of final consumption increased.

This reform, which was now basically of an economical nature, was implemented relatively true to the guidelines set down in the reform concept. Already in December 1981, the Polish parliament passed two fundamental reform laws on state-owned enterprises and on the self-administration of the employees of such enterprises. During 1982, and thereafter, further economic laws were passed which originated from the reform concept. The laws were intended to create an economic mechanism which would adapt the national economy to market regulation and indirect economical control. In addition, it was hoped that this would prevent a return to a centralized planning system. The development of the reform since 1982 is described below.

Economic Policy

At the beginning of 1982, the political leadership introduced some radical measures aimed at reducing the final demand within the economy. The prices of basic food-stuffs were increased by 140–150%, while the prices of industrial consumer goods increased by approximately 95%. The rise in food prices was partially supplemented by financial compensations. Despite this, during 1982 real income of the population dropped by 25%. This went hand in hand with a decrease in the volume of net gross capital expenditure by approximately 12% (Maly Rocznik Statystyczny 1986; 107, 119). This reduction in final demand, however, did not occur without error. First, the compensation turned out to be too high in relation to the price increases, i.e., the price increases could have been higher. In other words, the decrease in real income of the population by 25% in 1982 still was not large enough to stabilize the consumer goods market.

However, this error could have been quite easily corrected, if a second error had not been made at the same time. According to the system reform concept, three types of prices were introduced at the beginning of 1982: official prices, regulated prices and free prices. The latter were to be made freely on the market as a result of bargaining between buyers and sellers. Fearing spiraling prices and hyperinflation, the political leadership started to put strong informal pressure on sellers immediately after the reform began. The name of the game was to show moderation in setting prices and to link them mainly with production costs (Jaruzelski, 1985; 77). This pressure was not without its effects. Empirical research has shown, that as a rule sellers did not fully exploit the possibilities of achieving a profit rate which would correspond to the existing supply-demand relations on the market, and instead set this rate approximately twice as high as the regulated prices (KRG, 1984) This was, however, not enough to stabilize the market.

Despite the above mentioned errors, the reduction in final demands contributed to a relaxing of external and internal constraints on economic growth. It helped, for example, to change the structure of hard currency imports. The share of investment and consumer goods in total imports could be decreased and that of intermediate goods necessary for the functioning of the economy correspondingly increased. In addition, there was a structural change in the import of means of production. Most significant were the reductions in feed and grain imports from 8.7 million tons in 1981 to 5.2 million tons in 1982.

The hard currency saving achieved as a result of these structural changes could be used to increase the current supplies to industry. An increase in the money value, as a result of a reduction in final demand, in turn created favorable conditions for increases in labor supply, mainly through overtime. Combined with the administrative pressure it enabled the lengthening of the work week and, thus, increases in coal production. In the first quarter of 1982, the latter had already increased by 15%, as compared to the first quarter of 1981. This in turn contributed to breaking the coal and electric energy supply barriers, which had made a strong impact in 1981. This factor also appeared to have been helpful in lowering the foreign trade barrier. Following the drastic reduction in hard currency imports during the first quarter of 1982 (this corresponds to a drop to 59 in the first quarter of 1982, in comparison to an index of 100 in the forth quarter of 1981), hard currency imports grew throughout the remainder of 1982, and achieved a 98% level by the end of the year.

By the middle of 1982, the complex of economic policy measures presented above had created a situation which was compatible (at least generally) to the reform design. Equilibrium had not been achieved on the investment and consumer-goods markets, but some progress had been made in terms of reducing inflationary pressure (Pysz, 1984; 35). With regards to supply, it succeeded in slowing-down the decreases rate of sold industrial production. In the first quarter of 1982, this drop equalled 11% (compared to the first quarter of the previous year), and in the second quarter it was limited to 4.5%. The continuation of this economic policy would have eventually led to equilibrium on the final goods market and to the furtherance of the equilibrium on the remaining markets. From the political leadership's point of view, however, the time factor was here the most important.

By introducing martial law in Poland, the political leadership recovered their position of power, but this could not be considered as stable enough in 1982. The resistance of the underground "Solidarity" movement continued, the strikes, banned by martial law, were still organized, and in large cities mass demonstrations of "Solidarity" supporters took place. "In such circumstances, the main lines of economic policy were dominated by non-economic considerations and decisions, aimed at basic social stabilization" (Kuzinski, 1986). The priorities of stabilizing political leadership as a rule lead to a shortening of the time span of an economic policy. Thus, the more the necessity of instituting martial law was emphasized by the political leadership (in part to prevent the total destruction of the economy), the greater was the need for the rapid and widely spread success of this policy in 1982. The political leadership attempted to establish some sort of economic legitimacy for their highly unpopular decision of introducing martial law, and were thus forced to make a decision of far-reaching consequences. The leaders had to choose between two possible methods of rejuvenating economic growth.

The first relied on the continuation of the economic policy provided by the systemic reform concept. Thus, it would have been necessary to await the results of the attempt to reduce final demand and for their impact on the entire range of interrelated factors, finally including the start of intensive economic growth. Indirectly, this plan had, in addition to numerous advantages (i.e. growth would then actually be a result of systemic reform), some disadvantages as well. These included: a relatively longer wait for the renewal of economic growth and the high uncertainty accompanying this. This uncertainty concerned both the length of expectation time and the amount and structure of a possible increase in social production. Therefore, this variant of the economic policy demanded strength from the political leadership, a long-term planning, and the ability to act in situations of high uncertainty.

The second method of inducing economic growth was basically taking advantage of the opportunities which appeared as a result of the loosening of some of the external and internal constraints. It could be described as the "impatient growth" method. To increase production in the shortest possible time, it was necessary to activate the workforce. This could not have been achieved by increasing the number of employees, as is typical in the command management system (Pysz, 1984; 40). In the short-run the supply of labor could be increased only by lengthening the work week (mainly more overtime) and by increasing labor intensity (increase in work output per time unit). Given the lack of other incentives, this type of workforce utilization would be possible only by making the wage fund dependent on production at an enterprise level. "At the beginning of the reform in 1982, methods of linking wages with production growth and labor productivity were desperately sought for" (Dryll, 1984).

In the second part of 1982, the political leadership opted for the method of "impatient growth." The fundamental change in the priority of economic policy goals presented above, had consequences similar to those of the introduction of martial law. Martial law had kept the socio-political aspects of the reform to a minimum and in the second half of 1982, the continuation of the economic policy measures, which could have assisted the reform implementation, was virtually abandoned. As a result of these concessions, out of three sections of the reform outline, interrelated to some extend, only one section was left, which deals only with the economy mechanisms (instruments of economic control, or-ganizational structure).

Instruments of Economic Control

In August 1982, the Cabinet's Resolution No. 182 introduced a significant change in the obligatory payments to PFAZ (labor retaining fund), from those outlined in the system reform concept. The original function of this mechanism was to reduce the growth rate of average wages. If their increase in individual enterprises exceeded a set level for a given year, the surplus would be subjected to progressive taxation. The PFAZ payments resulting from this were to be paid from the portion of the enterprise's profit remaining at its disposal after paying income tax. The changes introduced by Resolution No. 182 were aimed at partially loosening the restrictions resulting from the PFAZ payments. Exemptions from PFAZ payments were linked to the production growth. For 1% of production growth the enterprises could obtain 0.5–0.8% of the wage fund increase. Within this general rule, individual enterprises might negotiate with appropriate departments of the economic apparatus to secure changes in the coefficient adapted to their specific situations. In situations considered exceptional, the enterprises could apply for a corrective coefficient exceeding the generally binding upper level of 0.8. As a basis for computing production growth in the second half of 1982, results were not taken from the second half of 1981 but from the first half of 1982. Considering the decrease in industrial production in the first two quarters of 1982, this was the lowest possible reference point (Jozefiak, 1985; 48).

The reorientation of the function of the PFAZ wage fund tax from restraining the increase of average wages to stimulating production growth, led to the differentiation of this indirect instrument of economic control. This possibility was already given in Resolution No. 182, permitting negotiations between enterprises and organs of State economic control as to the size of the wage fund corrective coefficient, depending on the increase of production. Apart from this formal considerations, the differentiation of the PFAZ mechanism resulted from two other factors. First, in individual branches as well as in enterprises, there existed highly differentiated technical, organizational and economic conditions for achieving production growth. Second, the degree of utilization of production capacity varied greatly among branches and enterprises from 1979–82. This was mainly due to the differences in the supply of production means. The following dilemma in economic policy resulted from this situation: If the diversified conditions for production growth are not taken into account, this would lead to an economically unjustified, and more importantly, politically dangerous differentiation of wages. These would increase faster in those branches and enterprises where production growth would be relatively easy to achieve due to the reasons mentioned above. On the other hand, the varying conditions for the increase in production growth within the individual branches and enterprises, unavoidably called for a differentiation in the wage determination process.

The differentiation of obligatory PFAZ payments significantly affected enterprises' behavior. Once again it became clear that in the most important operational matters they are more dependent on their relationships to State economic control institutions than on the sales of their products and services on the market (Jezioranski, 1984). In bargaining with these institutions, the enterprises have traditionally held a strong position, resulting from their oligopolistic or even monopolistic power within the market, from the information monopoly connected with this and the supply gap. This was fully confirmed by the 1982 economic results, when average wages increased 12% more than expected. This non-planned wage growth took place mainly in the second half of 1982 (Kolodko, 1984). The surprisingly large income effect of putting the increase in social production before other economic policy targets induced the political leaders to take some deflationary measures in order to protect the consumer goods market from the highly destructive spiraling price inflation.

The application of indirect control instruments has been developing since the turn of the Year 1982/83 into two contradictory targets of economic policy: preferred economic growth and market equilibrium. One can explain this process as follows: various deflationary measures were initiated to at least partly reduce the disequilibrium on the consumer goods market and to finalize the large investments of the 1970s as quickly as possible. However, the application of indirect instruments led to difficulties in financing current production in some branches and enterprises. Under the pressure of affected economic entities and out of fear that the deflationary policy would stop the production growth, not only in individual economic units but also in the economy as a whole, concessions were almost a rule. Various exemptions from generally binding rules were permitted. This gradually extended the scope of diversification of the indirect instruments which began by introducing exemptions from the obligatory PFAZ payments.

The above mentioned process is worth illustrating with some examples. In 1983, the deflationary measures consisted mainly of lowering of the correction coefficients which linked production growth in the enterprise to the exemption form PFAZ payments, as well as in a more restrictive price policy aimed at strengthening the State control over prices and at limiting the scope of contractual prices to the benefit of official prices. The enterprises reacted to this tight money policy with demands for various reductions and exemptions, alleging that these were necessary fore keeping the achieved production levels or for further growth. In 1983, this led to a very rapid growth in the number of exceptions (Dabrowski, 1983). In 1984, the policy of tight money was still attempted, using a still more extensive set of indirect control instruments. The range of free prices was reduced. Moreover, a price freeze (with only some exceptions) was introduced. These arrangements were supplemented by the introduction of "justified costs" as a basis for free-price determination. The more elastic usage of turnover tax rates added to the picture. The corrective coefficients, accompanying the PFAZ payment exemptions, were tightened even more than in 1983. Apart from this, the depreciation allowances, which according to the reform concept were to supply the enterprises' development fund, were now divided between enterprises and the state budget.

However, in 1984, the tight money policy did not bring the expected results in the form of equilibrium on the consumer and investment goods markets. It did not succeed in significantly diminishing the inflow of money to enterprises (Interview, 1985). Instead, this policy lead to the intensification of a process of permanent correction of the financial distribution at the enterprise level. The money was rigorously taken from the economic units which were in good financial situation and given to enterprises having financial difficulties. To achieve this, various individualized subsidies, tax exemptions, changes in amortization schemes, etc. were applied. In the first case, the measures were justified by the necessity of restricting the total demand and of achieving market equilibrium, while in the second, the justification was fond in the necessity of stimulating production growth (Pysz, 1985; 24).

In 1985, the usage of indirect instruments continued to be developed under the pressure of ever-growing contradictions between the two targets of the economic policy: economic growth and market equilibrium. The main reason for this was the evident exhaustion of the existing, relatively simple reserves of economic growth, activated by the lowering of some internal and external barriers in the previous years (Bugaj, 1984). As a result the direct stimulation of production growth in the individual branches and enterprises became more important. Otherwise the deceleration of the production growth observed in 1985 (3.2% national income growth, compared to 5.6% in the previous year) would turn into stagnation. These factors restricted the range of deflationary policy measures and thus indirectly reduced the chances for achieving market equilibrium. The State economic organs exploited this situation by enforcing their position vis-à-vis the supervised enterprises. "It is considered to be desirable that as many enterprises as possible find themselves in a situation which forces them to search for help. This prompted the so-called 'high cross-bar' practice, enabling a further increase in the State organs' superiority" (Raport Konsultatywnej, part 2). The State control organs were able to keep enterprise production activities in line with central planning projections by making certain requirements a prerequisite for receiving favorable treatment.

The gradually developing individualization of indirect instruments led to the situation described as "indirect centralization" (Jozefiak, 1985; 47). Individualized instruments of indirect control did not, however, become a substitute for traditional direct instruments. On the contrary, the two instruments complemented one another or even overlapped. In the years 1982–85, the systematic expansion of the scope of various forms of rationing of production factors can be observed. A particularly flagrant example are the State orders, constantly increasing in number: from 0 in 1982 to 30 in 1983 and 111 in 1984 (Raport, 1984; 48). In addition, the scope of obligatory rationing is expanding in the area of intermediate goods, with the branch trading networks having mandatory rights in buying and selling. In 1985, an additional set of direct instruments was added to the instruments used in the rationing process, i.e., the system of supervisory branch ministries evaluating enterprises' directors. The most important evaluation criteria are: the volume and growth of sales, average wages, etc. With the help of this system, the branch ministries aim to restore the direct flow of information between themselves and the enterprises (Kowalska, 1986).

In summary, one can say that the evolution of the various indirect policy instruments took a course in direct contrast to that outlined in the reform project, mainly because the market was not activated in its allocative and distributive functions. Enterprises were not open (with the exception of some market segments) to influence objective market information (equilibrium prices, demand), which would direct and coordinate their activities. The functions not fulfilled by the market had to be, out of necessity, taken over by the remaining instruments (direct and indirect). The execution of these functions was intertwined with the continuous individualization of indirect instruments. The universal scope of these instruments' influence was in fact exactly the opposite of that described in the reform concept. Instead of adapting to the logic of the self-regulating market mechanism, they adapted themselves to conditions similar to those of the traditional command management system. The direct instruments of economic control assumed the allocation and distribution functions and expanded their range of application. This unexpected revival of direct control is an evident contradiction to the reform concept which assumed a significant restriction in this area. The processes presented above were also linked to an increase in the number of both direct and indirect instruments. This produced a highly complicated set of instruments. An economic system set up in this way can be described as "overregulated."

Organizational Structures Within the Economy

The implementation of the reform began in 1982, in a period characterized by the existence of significant elements of organizational structures inherited from the command management system. The partial reorganization of the State control apparatus in the middle of 1981, admittedly led to a decrease in the number of branch ministries from nine to six, but their basic functions did not undergo any significant changes (Mujzel, 1984; 66). This situation was also not significantly affected by the liquidation of the trusts (Zjednoczenia) in the first half of 1982. They were replaced by obligatory and voluntary associations which are almost identical to the branch structure of their predecessors (Mujzel, 1984; 68). Some inconsistencies in reforming the organizational structure of the economy can at least be partially explained by the functional tasks of branch ministries and associations. They were to operate the transitional, direct instruments, outlined in the reform concept mainly with regard to rationing factors of production.

However, the existence of this type of organizational structures meant that during the reform implementation process the "Rubicon" of systemic changes had not yet been crossed. Thus, the alternative of returning to the wide application of direct control instruments was still open. If this type of "escape-route" had not been available to the political leadership, they would have found themselves under a great deal of pressure. The political desire to force a final demand reduction to the limit, above which it would have began propagating market equilibrium and implementing a self-regulating market mechanism, should have been stronger. Apart from this indirect influence on economic policy, comparatively well-developed branch structures could influence the decisions on national planning. As these decisions are almost always produced by bargaining and a coordination of interests between the respective organs of economic control and political leadership. As a result, a kind of "institutional equilibrium" is created, its shape being dependent on the balance of forces and on the amount of information available (Jozefiak, 1981; 26). It is characteristic, that this state of affairs is nearly always connected with trying to balance production and demand, mainly through increasing the output of production means (Dobozi, 1979; 680). This is, however, in contradiction with the reform principles which seek to achieve this goal through the reduction of the economy's final demand.

It is known that the market mechanism did not take over the allocation and distribution functions of the economy in 1982. These functions had to remain in the domain of the State economic apparatus and this, in turn, required the use of instruments capable of performing them. The relationship between the functions of the State economic control apparatus and the evolution of instruments could not but influence the economy's organization. This was expressed, firstly, by the fact that, despite the provisions of system's reform concept, the re-building of the State control machinery, started in 1981, was not continued consistently. Thus, no further progress was made in decreasing the number of existing branch ministries. Second, no evident change in their functions can be seen as they continue to focus their efforts on the "directional conformaty" of enterprises' plans with the national economical plan. One indication of this is that the branch ministries did not substantially reduce their control over branch trading networks, which exercise mandatory trade rights in the buying and selling of certain inputs, contrary to the intentions of the reform concept (Jozefiak, 1985; 49). Through the possibility of making decisions on deficit input allocation, the ministries have retained a highly efficient method of putting pressure on the enterprises. Third, the intended re-building of the ministries' internal organizational structure aimed at limiting or liquidating departments dealing mainly with operative control, also not took place.

> The analysis of the employment situation and of changes in the number of departments and offices shows that this process has not proceeded according to the original plan. There is a tendency towards the recreation of traditional organizational structures of sectorial and branch ministries (Raport, 1985; 5).

Fourth, an increase in the "processing capacity" occurred within these ministries. The number of employees in the six branch ministries was 3,706 in 1982 and increased to 4,108 in 1984 (Rocznik, 1985; 500–501).

At the intermediate level between enterprises and branch ministries, the number of obligatory associations decreased from 45 to 36. This is, however, of no significance. Nine obligatory associations in the mining industry were simply turned into nine multi-plant enterprises, the so-called "gwarectwa." In addition, the evolution of functions, contradictory to the reform principles, is visible in the voluntary associations, which are organized according to the branch principle: "in their operation the relics of 'command management' (rationing, negotiating the reductions, norms, preferences) and coordinating enterprises' activity are the most noticeable" (Mujzel, 1985). Moreover, there is a dangerous tendency towards creating so-called superinstitutional economic organizations, which in fact are gigantic multiplant enterprises with monopolistic positions within the market. To name a few examples, a nation-wide agricultural equipment enterprise "Agroma" was formed in 1984, and the highly controversial "Unity of Iron and Steelworks Enterprises" was formed in 1981 (Dryll, 1986).

According to the reform outline, the functional departments were to concentrate their activities on influencing the operation of the self-regulating market mechanism, or in other words on its "fine tuning." Establishing this additional market control measure was meant to guarantee the character of the "regulated market." Furthermore, this was to enable the coexistence of the plan and market and also to ensure the possibility of achieving the most important goals of economic policy expressed in the general outline of the national plan. The functional ministries would control the overall indirect instruments. The functional department's positions, their extended tasks and the instruments used, were defined and legally protected by appropriate regulations. Despite this , the functional ministries could not perform the duties subscribed reform outline in the implementation process. This was due mainly to the method of market operation. Without the market-clearing prices and the related adjustment of production and investment, the indirect economic control instruments (monetary policy, taxation, credit policy, etc) can also not function properly (Nasilowski, 1986). In this case, the individualization of this instruments is almost unavoidable. Instead of "fine tuning," direct control of economic activity of individual branches, and in some cases even of individual enterprises, is used. The universal instruments of indirect control obtain branch character, and the process of "enbranching" takes place (Fallenbuchl, 1985).

This forces the functional departments to cooperate closely with branch ministries. Consequently, the branch ministries serve as a kind of intermediate link, subdividing parameters established at the level of the functional organs (this refers e.g. to creating means for wages, differentiating the rate of amortization paid to the budget, controlling supplies). The branch ministries do not limit their cooperation with functional departments to the role of a passive intermediary. Moreover, they represent the interest of the supervised enterprises vis-a-vis functional departments, acting as their advocates (Raport, 1985; 5). At the lower level of the economy's organizational structure, obligatory associations and voluntary ones started to play a similar double role. As a result, the numerical values of indirect instruments are broken down to the level of the enterprise.

The functions fulfilled independently by branch ministries, as well as their cooperation with functional ministries, resulted in strengthening their position within the overall economic organizational structure. Taken together, these factors enabled them to apply relatively successfully for various concessions under threat of possible decreases in the production of goods and services particularly in demand on the market (Raport Konsultatywnej, part 2). In summary the following may be stated:

> Just as in the past, the feature characteristic of a centralized control of the economy prevailed. One of those features is the real domination of the sectorial and branch structures over the functional ones. The former make the most important economic decisions, to which the latter rather passively adapt (Jozefiak, 1985; 52).

The functions performed by the branch ministries and functional departments, as well as their cooperation, were to be integrated at the

Planning Commission level. This would promote the transition from planning in quantity terms, characteristic of the command management system, to planning in monetary terms. "The actual functioning of the economy is the reason why the partial and material categories are the main premises in the planning process" (Raport Konsultatywnej, part 2). This calls for the continued existence of the current Planning Commission's structure, with well developed branch departments. Therefore, the branch structures, well-known for their economy-disintegrating impact, still exist in the institution which was designed to integrate the economy. We should consider this while assessing the Planning Commission Act of 1984. On the one hand, it maintains the principle of its responsibility for the execution of the national plan. On the other, the Act grants to the Commission the right to design systemic changes. This holds the danger of subordinating the systemic policy to the requirements of the current control of material proportions outlined in the national plan (Jozefiak, 1985; 8). The above mentioned danger intensified in 1985. With the liquidation the of Plenipotentiary State's Economic Reform Office, the Planning Commission obtained, as a Government policy adviser, a semi-monopolistic position.

The interrelated degrees of the enterprises' independence and self-financing can be said to constitute a "mirror image" of the policy instruments used and the functions performed by the State apparatus. The conclusion of the above considerations is that the reform failed to even approach the realization of its key goals. Instead, a reverse tendency occurred, i.e. the gradual reduction of enterprises' autonomy and self-financing, as compared to the situation in 1982. The report of the Consulting Economic Council states that:

> No one seemed to foresee that the functioning of the economy in the middle of 1984, and probably during the next year would be characterized by such a limitation of enterprises' choice, by such significant differences in the mode of operation individual segments, and such a wide scope of detailed State regulations (KRG, 1984).

This places a doubt on the possibility of the existence of enterprise self-management, for without the appropriate decision-making the enterprises would have nothing to decide upon, and this will sentence them to gradual decay. Thus, the "3 S's" within the enterprise structure still remain a theoretical possibility and not a practical reality.

Conclusions

During the years 1982–1985, the development of the reform remained in the legislation phase and the new economic mechanism had little influence on the behavior of economic entities. The main reason for this was that the market, it its allocative and distributive functions, failed to become efficient. But despite this, the reform is not yet over after four and one-half years, and the present economic system cannot be compared to a traditional, centrally planned economy. The legal guarantees for the preservation of the reform could at least slow-down the repression of the new economic mechanism (especially in comparison to the quick failures of earlier reform attempts). Political goodwill was also not lacking, which is demonstrated by the fact that a second reform phase has been suggested (Referat, 1986). Interventions, which do not seem to follow any given rule, are becoming more and more common. They appear to serve as a correction of undesired developments rather than as an enforcement of special economic policy goals.

The present economic system in Poland can be described as a peculiar "mixed system." On the macroeconomic level, there is neither a consistent central planning, nor a functioning market. Many of the economic processes are characterized by the type of self-operation, which is kept running by the individual economic entities, within the frame of their traditional behavior, already familiar from central planning systems. Within such a mixed system, it has not been possible to overcome the functional problems of the traditional planned economy, or the extensive development strategy of the previous decades. The planners could not fulfill one of the main goals of the Three-Year Plan (1983–1985), i.e. to increase the share of consumer goods produced (Podstawowe, 1983). In contrast to the premises of the plan, the consumer goods production increased only at about the same rate as the manufacture of capital goods. The realization of structural goals, with regards to investments, was just as unsuccessful (a stop on some large projects of the 1970s, more consumer-oriented sector, etc.).

The indirect centralization of the system took place during the years 1982 to 1985, mainly in the key economic sectors, with the help of the individualized, indirect control measures and the distribution of production means. Here, the branch sectors of the economic apparatus were maintained and non-enterprise economic organizations were formed. Important production branches such as coal, electrical energy, cement, sugar and meat, were removed from the general reform regulations, which gave the branch ministers a number of possibilities of direct intervention in the economic activities (Jozefiak, 1985). Another development could be seen in the consumer goods industry of the incorporated sector and in the private sector. The regulations of the economic reform were introduced to the incorporated sector (local small industry) already in 1981, and in principle were not removed. The small manufacturers could adapt easier to the consequences of the economic crisis than the key sectors, which was reflected in their higher economic growth rate in the 1980s. In this area, a few of the rudiments of market regulation were also developed (Raport Konsultatywnej, 1986).

The question is whether the present "mixed system" can continue to exist on a long-term basis. The experience made in the first half of the 1980s would speak against this: the system was neither able to introduce structural changes, nor was it able, with the aid of indirect economical control measures, to motivate enterprises to strive for an increase in efficiency. Moreover, the economic policy cannot serve as a substitute for the reform much longer, as was the case from 1982 to 1985 (Pysz, 1985; 32). The political freedom (increased after the imposition of martial law) to support an austerity policy, aimed at providing the economy with more imported intermediate goods, has become restricted over the years. There are strong social barriers against an abstention policy. These have emerged as a result of the prohibition of the union "Solidarnosc," as well as of new unions, and from the pressure exercised from the territorial state organs who are responsible for the political stability in their areas. Investments can also not be easily avoided as the capital assets in the Polish economy are sorely outdated. Therefore, investments for modernization and replacement purposes are badly needed. In addition, within the frame of the present system, the pressure for investments made by the economic apparatus, has not yet been stilled. But does this open up the possibility for a rejuvenation and acceleration of a market-oriented reform, which is expressly demanded by many economists?

However, there is a basic barrier set up against a market-oriented reform: politically acceptable changes are usually not economically efficient, while modifications which appear useful in economical terms must be seen as unrealistic in terms of the political philosophy (Pysz, 1983). Here it is important to mention the inner logic of the economic system. The system's basic elements and behavioral patterns have adapted to one another over the years to such an extent that it would not be easy to change or replace them. Therefore, the market-oriented form of this tightly woven system must be overcome. The necessary "reform threshold" must be placed quite high (Balcerowicz, 1985). However, in the years 1982–1985, the reform basically could not cross this threshold which explains its lack of efficiency. This experience shows that a consequent, market-stability oriented economic policy forms the necessary, although not sufficient, requirement for a transition to market regulation. But such a policy faces the socio-political and system-related barriers mentioned above.

One can assume that in the future, as in the past, the self-operation of the economic system will be increasingly supplemented by planning and market regulations. In direct contrast to the reform outline which suggested a uniform concept, this intensifies the separation of control forms. In the key sectors, the traditional planning system has actually been re-introduced through further indirect centralization using individualized economical control measures, as well as direct regulations. With regard to the consumer-related sectors, it can be assumed that market regulation trends will increasingly take hold. This leads to some important questions with regard to the future of the Polish "mixed system." Can various control forms in different economic sectors co-exist, and if so, to what extent? And how will adaption processes among these sectors be achieved? But the most important, unanswered question is, how this economic system will develop on a long-term basis, and whether it will follow the more consequent models of Hungary or the GDR.

References

Due to technical reasons Polish letters and accents were not used in the references.

Balcerowicz, L., 1985: O zrodlach trwalosci systemu nakazowo-rozdzielczego, unpublished paper. Warszawa

Bugaj, R., 1986: Dlaczego kryzys sie przedluza, in: Tygodnik Powszechny, No. 1, 1986

Dabrowski, M, 1983: W szponach mody na ulgi, in: Zycie Gospodarcze, No. 49, 1983

Dobozi, I., 1979: Surowcowe uwarunkowania polityki gospodarczej Europy Zachod niej i Wschodniej, in: Ekonomista, No. 3, 1979

Dryll, I., 1984: Place w cuglach, in: Zycie Gospodarcze, No. 33, 1984

――――, 1986: Gra we Wspolnocie i poza, in: Zycie Gospodarcze, No. 17, 1986

Fallenbuchl, Z., 1985: The Present State of Economic Reform in Poland, unpublished paper. Washington D.C.

Interview with Prof. J. Pajestka, 1985: Reforma nie jest jeszcze procesem nie odwracalnym, in Zycie Gospodarcze, No. 3, 1985

Jaruzelski, W., 1985: Rede vor dem Sejm der Volksrepublik Polen, in: Wojciech Jaruzelski: Ausgewählte Reden 1981–1984. Berlin (DDR)

Jozefiak, C., 1981: Koniecznosc i kierunki rekonstrukcji systemu ekonomicznego, in: Libura-Grzelonska, U. (ed.): Cele i zakres reformy gospodarczej. Warszawa

――――, 1985a: Wirtschaftsreform in Polen auf halbem Weg steckengeblieben, in: Europäische Rundschau, No. 1, 1985

――――, 1985b: Bilans okresu przejsciowego—ceny reglamentacja place, in: Zycie Gospodarcze, No. 4, 1985

――――, 1985c: Proba oceny przebiegu reformy gospodarczej. Warszawa

Kierunki reformy gospodarczej—Projekt, 1981. Warszawa

Kolodko, G., 1983: Psucie monety, in: Polityka, No. 4, 1983

Kowalska, M., 1986: Sila tradycji—systemy ocen przedsiebiorstw po roku, in: Zycie Gospodarcze, No. 9, 1986

KRG o systemie funkcjonowania—warunki dzialania przedsiebiorstw, 1984, in: Zycie Gospodarcze, No. 45, 1984

KRG o systemie funkcjonowania—zalozenia kierunkowe i propozycje, 1984, in: Zycie Gospodarcze, No. 47, 1984

Kuzinski, S., 1986: Polityka gospodarcza a realia spoleczne, in: Zycie Gospodarcze, No. 1, 1986

Maly Rocznik Statystyczny 1986. Warszawa

Mujzel, J., 1984: System funkcjonowania gospodarki i jego ewolucja w Polsce, in: Mujzel, J./Jakubowicz, S. (ed.): Funkcjonowanie gospodarki polskiej— Doswiadczenia, problemy, tendencje. Warszawa

———, 1985: O przyspieszenie reformy, in: Zycie Gospodarcze, No. 51/52, 1985

Nasilowski, M., 1986: Potrzeba szerszego spojrzenia, in: Zycie Gospodarcze, No. 10, 1986

Podstawowe uwarunkowania planu trzyletniego, 1983, in: Zycie Gospodarcze, No. 12, 1983

Pysz, P., 1983: Wirtschaftsreformen in Planwirtschaften? in: Orientierungen zur Wirtschafts- und Gesellschaftspolitik, No. 17, 1983

———, 1984: Die Preisreform 1982 auf dem Konsumgütermarkt in Polen, in: Berichte des Bundesinstituts für ostwissenschaftliche und internationale Studien, No. 12. Köln

———, 1985: Konzeption, Bilanz und Perspektiven der polnischen Wirtschaftsreform 1982–1985, Berichte des Bundesinstituts für ostwissenschaftliche und internationale Studien, No. 34. Köln

Raport o realizacji reformy gospodarczej w 1984 roku—ocena i wnioski kierunkowe, 1985. Warszawa

Raport—Polska 5 lat po sierpniu, 1986. London

Raport Konsultatywnej Rady Gospodarczej—Gospodarka w latach 1981–1985, part 1, in: Zycie Gospodarcze, No. 14, 1986

Raport Konsultatywnej Rady Gospodarczej—Gospodarka w latach 1981–1985, part 2, in: Zycie Gospodarcze, No. 16, 1986

Referat Komitetu Centralnego PZPR na X Zjazd PZPR, 1986, in Trybuna Ludu, 30 June 1986

Rocznik Statystyczny 1985. Warszawa

5

The Cuban Economy Under the New "System of Management and Planning": Success or Failure?

Peter Gey

Introduction

After more than a decade of drastic systemic changes, the disaster of the 1970 "big sugar harvest" (gran zafra) marked the end of the experimental stage of the Cuban revolution. Subsequently, the communist leadership started the "institutionalization" of the economy which was formally approved in December 1975 when the First Congress of the Cuban Communist Party (PCC) passed a resolution to implement the new System of Economic Management and Planning (Sistema de Dirección y Planificación de la Economía—SDPE). Thus, more than ten years later, a thorough review is in order: Has the new system reached full maturity, or is it still struggling through adolescence? And what are the results and problems of the Caribbean-style Soviet planning in Cuba?

This essay focuses on the more recent development of the Cuban economy. However, several attitudes of the state and party leadership, namely the current ambiguous policies towards the private sector and a strong preference for subjective approaches in tackling economic problems, trace back to behaviour patterns which emerged in the second half of the 1960s. Since 1965, the institutions and policies following the Soviet model, which had been adopted in 1961, were largely restrained or fully abolished. From then on, the Cuban economic model was influenced by the "search for something new," beyond traditional market relations and central planning.

In order to create the objective conditions for the "New Man," an unselfish and egalitarian human being, a "Revolutionary Offensive" was launched in 1968, eliminating the remainder of small private businesses in industry, construction, services and retail trade. Material incentives in monetary terms such as profits interests and taxes were further restricted or entirely abolished. Instead, moral incentives and labor mobilization were developed to meet ambitious production targets. Hence, the so-called Sino-Guevarist approach resulted in a mobilization regime with high emphasis on ideology and puritanism.

The economic results of the Sino-Guevarist model were disastrous. While official statistics quote a 4.4% annual growth in the Global Social Product (GSP) for 1966–1970 (1967–1970 at current prices), Western estimates suggest no real growth over the period and indicate a sustained deterioration of GSP by 15.6% in 1970 compared with 1967 (Pérez-López, 1985). The Cuban leadership acknowledged the failure of the Sino-Guevarist model and began to develop a more pragmatic approach to the economy. In the first half of the 1970s, a reintroduction of Soviet-type planning and management appeared, marking a fundamentally new era in post-revolutionary Cuba, although, as will be explained in more detail below, this was notably modified by some characteristics of the "moral economy" (S. Roca).[1]

The Actual Performance of the Economy During the Second Five-Year Plan, 1981–1985

The discrepancy between the goals and the actual performance of the 1976–1980 plan (GSP grew at a pace of 3.5% per annum, falling 42% short of the target of 6.0%)[2] made Cuban planners more cautious when setting targets for 1985. The annual average GSP growth rate was set at 5.1%, which was higher then the actually accomplished rate in 1976–1980, but lower then the 6% target for the previous five-year plan. In his comment on the 1981–1985 plan, Castro said the targets did not correspond to the revolutionaries' impatience to resolve people's problems but reflected realism and good sense with regards to Cuba's limited resources (Castro, 1980; 9).

The actual average increase in GSP from 1981–1985, however, surpassed the target by far. At constant prices, the Cuban GSP expanded at an annual average rate of 7.3%. Labor productivity in this period increased by 5.2%, 58% higher than the annual target rate of 3.3%. Total investment targets were also exceeded by 13 to 18%, though the second five-year plan had favored consolidation above expansion. Performance in the consumption sphere was mixed: Social consumption grew considerably from 1981–1984, expanding at a rate of 7.1%. The annual growth of private consumption from 1981–1984, however, was only slightly higher than the moderate rate of 2.5% of the previous frugal period (Table 5.1).

Official statistics indicated not only vigorous growth of the Cuban economy during the period 1981–1985 compared with 1976–1980, but also quote it as the highest growth rate in Latin America for the period in question.[3] There are, however, reasonable doubts about the reliability of Cuban macroeconomic data which refer to (1) the effects of inflation on GSP, (2) high degree of unfulfillment of physical targets in key branches of the economy, and (3) unfavorable and deteriorating external circumstances.

Effects of Inflation on GSP

In 1985, the State Committee of Statistics published series of macro-economic indicators for the period 1975–1984 which for the first time were reconstructed at comparable prices (AEC 1984, 1985; 88/89). This recalculation of the economic activity indicators used 1981 as the base year, when significant changes in the system of wholesale prices were made. Prices for the basic industrial, agricultural and constructional products as well as freight tariffs which were frozen in 1965, were to be fixed at a significantly higher level in order to take into account international prices for petroleum products, whose variations on the world market had thus far been ignored (ECLA, 1983; 308/309). Official data indicate that wholesale prices rose substantially. Compared with 1980, GSP in 1981 increased by 25.9% at current prices and by 16.0% at constant 1981 prices, suggesting inflation in the range of 10%. The question is, however, whether Cuban statisticians succeeded in eliminating the effects of the price reform on macroeconomic data.

It is reasonable to assume that the remarkable growth of Cuba's GSP at constant prices in 1981 is still affected by inflation. At the end of 1980, when the planners were confronted with declining international sugar prices, the overall target for 1981 was set at a relatively modest 4%, i.e. below the annual average GSP growth of the current five-year plan which was set at 5.1%. Some months later, when the wholesale price reform was brought into effect, GSP was expected to increase by 8% in 1981, and at the end of the year, the president of the Central Planning Board reported that actual growth was 12% (Pérez-González, 1982; 23). This was not all of the GSP news for 1981: The following statistical yearbooks for 1982 and 1984 indicate that the GSP in 1981 increased by 15.6 and 16.0%, respectively (AEC 1982, 1983; 98; AEC 1984, 1985; 89), and in April 1985, Vice President Carlos Rafael Rodríguez quoted 15.1% (C. R. Rodríguez, 1985).

Table 5.1 Selected Cuban Economic Indicators: Actual Performance and Planned Goals 1976-1990 (At Constant Prices of 1981)

	Actual Performance						Planned Goals 1981-1985(a)	Actual Performance 1981-1985(a)	Planned Goals	
	1976-1980(a)	1981	1982	1983	1984	1985			1986	1986-1990(a)
Global social product official	3.5	16.0	3.8	4.9	7.3	4.8	5.1	4.3	3.0-3.5	5.0
J.Pérez-López	2.2	5.2	0.8							
National income	3.0	20.8	5.0	5.5	7.4	n.a.	n.a.	n.a.	4.0-4.5	n.a.
Investment (b)	13.3	3.4	3.0	3.4	4.0	4.1	15.2-15.8	17.9	n.a.	23.1
Labor productivity	3.4	n.a.	n.a.	n.a.	n.a.	3.6	3.3	5.2	2.5-3.0	3.5
Personal consumption	2.5	3.8	2.9	1.2	3.1	n.a.	4.0	n.a.	n.a.	
Social consumption	14.6	19.3	2.4	10.0	9.4	n.a.	3.0	n.a.	n.a.	

(a) Annual average growth rate
(b) Billion pesos, at current prices
Sources: AEC, 1982; 102; AEC, 1984; 84-89; BNC/CEE, 1985; 2; Castro, 1980; 6-9; Castro, 1986a; 2-9; Mesa-Lago, 1982; 114; Pérez-López, 1985; TRAB, Dec. 30, 1985; 2

Thus, there was a great deal of dynamics in Cuban statistics which probably did not reflect those of the 1981 economic activity, but methodical problems in tackling with the effects of the 1981 wholesale price reform. A second reform of wholesale prices has been announced for 1989, beginning with a revision of fuel prices and other basic goods already in 1986 (TRAB, 8 May 1986; 1). For this reason, it is hazardous to evaluate the feasibility of the 1986–1990 growth goals (Table 5.1).

Unfulfillment of Physical Targets

The preliminary data on the physical output in key branches of the economy in 1981–1985 does not correspond with the global overfulfillment of the second five-year plan. In the sugar industry, which is still king and one of the cornerstones of Cuba's industrialization strategy, the average output from 1981–1984, as well as the estimated output in 1985, was about 7.5 million tons, but still 2.0 to 2.5 million tons short of the 1985 goal. Because of the serious drought in 1985 and hurricane "Kate" which caused serious damage throughout the island in mid-November shortly after harvesting began (GRS, 8 December 1985; 4/5), the sugar industry was even less in a position to produce "more or less 8.0 million tons," as Fidel Castro described annual sugar production for the period (Castro, 1986a; 2).

In the nickel industry, the output has been stagnant at an average of 34,000 tons since 1968, although total investment in the last decade amounted to 1.2 billion pesos (TRAB, June 9, 1986; 1). The new plant "Ernesto Che Guevara" in Punta Gorda, which was expected to start operation by 1980, was opened in November 1985 (TRAB, Oct. 10, 1985; 1) but the first stage, capable of producing 10,000 tons, was not ready until January 1986 (GRS, Jan. 27, 1986; 1). The nickel output goal for 1985, however, included the total capacity of the Punta Gorda plant at 30,000 tons which could not be realized (Table 5.2).

Actual performance in other branches of heavy industry was also badly off target. The production of electricity, steel, and cement fell 19%, 77% to 79%, and 35%, respectively, behind target. The fishing and citrus fruit industries, two success stories of the Revolution, reached historical highs in 1985 but missed their goals by 28% and 44%. This is also true of the textile industry which was below the planned targets by about 39%. Also, the production of coffee, rice, beans, milk, radios and probably refrigerators, which are important products for domestic consumption or export, lagged considerably behind the 1985 targets (Table 5.2).

Table 5.2 Physical Output of Selected Products in Cuba: 1960, 1980, 1984,
1985, and Goals 1985 (In Thousand Metric Tons Unless Specified)

	Actual Output 1960	1980	1984	1985	Goals 1985
Sugar	5943	6554	7514	7619(c)	9500-10000
Citrus fruits	73	268	600	732	1300
Coffee	42	19	23	24(c)	46
Eggs (106 units)	430	2327	2557	2500(c)	2300
Rice	323	352	555	529(c)	630-640
Beans	37	9	12	10(c)	35
Pork	38	54	88	92(c)	85
Milk(e)	767	893	915	889(c)	1000-1300
Fish	31	186	200	215	300
Nickel	13	38	33	33	69
Electricity (106 kwh)	2981	9896	12292	12199	15000
Steel	63	304	338	413	1800-2000
Cement	813	2831	3347	3182	4900
Fertilizer	438(a)	1059	1036	1160	1250
Textiles (106 m2)	116(a)	159	172	205	325
Cigars (106 units)	591(b)	167	302	366	360(d)
Refrigerators (103 units)	0	26	24	26	n.a.
Radios (103 units)	0	200	253	236	500

(a) 1963
(b) 1959
(c) Author's calculation based on official data
(d) Estimate based on official data
(e) State sector
Sources: Output 1960 and Goals 1985: Mesa-Lago, 1982; 118/119; Output
1980, 1984: AEC, 1984; 149-156, 201, 214, 276/277; Output 1985:
BNC/CEE, 1985; 9, 19-21; Castro, 1986a; 2-4; Proyecto, 1986; 10/11

Adverse External Circumstances

As in the previous quinquennium, a coincidence of unfavorable external
factors had a negative impact on Cuba's foreign trade and balance of
payments from 1981–1985. This once again highlights the structural
weakness of the Cuban economy, which a quarter of a century after the
Revolution, still relies predominantly on its revenues from sugar exports.
At the same time, Cuba's dependence upon supplies from market
economies (machinery, industrial raw materials, foodstuffs, and quality
consumer goods) has continued to be substantial, in spite of the fact
that in the early 1960s, its external trade was basically reoriented away
from the USA and towards the Soviet Union and the other socialist
countries. For trade purposes, the island needs convertible currencies
which, in turn, depend first and foremost on the international sugar
price (Gey, 1983). Hence, in order to improve Cuba's position in the
world economy, the external trade scheme in the second five-year plan

Table 5.3 Percentage Distribution of Cuban Exports by Product,
1958, 1965, 1975, 1980-1984

Years	Sugar	Tobacco	Minerals(a)	Fishing	Fuels	Others(b)
1958	80.6	6.8	3.8	0.8	-	8.0
1965	85.5	4.8	7.4	0.9	-	1.1
1975	89.8	1.8	4.7	1.8	0.1	1.8
1980	83.7	0.9	4.9	2.3	4.2	4.0
1981	79.1	1.3	7.9	2.3	4.2	5.2
1982	77.2	2.1	6.1	2.0	6.9	5.7
1983	74.0	1.9	5.4	1.9	10.6	6.2
1984	75.5	1.0	5.5	1.7	10.1	6.2

(a) Mainly nickel
(b) Mainly fruits, cement, and rum
Source: AEC 1984, 1985; 300, 302; and author's calculations

has been aimed at substituting imports from, and diversifying exports to the market economies, although raw sugar is to remain by far the most important Cuban export product, yielding even greater revenues (Castro, 1980; 9).

At a first glance, Table 5.3 indicates that Cuban external policies have been rather successful in diversifying exports. The share of sugar exports compared to total exports, which amounted to 85% of the export value from 1976–1980, declined from 83.7% in 1980 to 75.5% in 1984. This, however, was mainly the result of two opposed external circumstances: a sharp decline in international sugar prices from almost 30 cents per pound in 1980 to 5.20 cents in 1984 (IMF, various issues), reducing the share of sugar over the total value of exports, and an extremely favorable arrangement with the USSR, permitting the re-export of Cuban petroleum imports from the USSR to market economies. The latter enabled Cuba to balance Soviet petroleum products with sugar at 850 rubles per ton, while Western European trading partners paid only 80 pesos per ton. A high Cuban official alleged in 1985 that this marked a difference of ten to one (C. R. Rodríguez, 1985).

Cuba still meets its energy requirements almost entirely by means of imported oil from the USSR, but at the same time, petrol now ranks as the most important source of foreign exchange after sugar (Table 5.3). This, however, could not fully compensate for the adverse effects of the external economic situation which in the first half of the 1980s was characterized by a high interest level on the international money market, increasing prices for goods imported from the West and, primarily, by the drastic decline of the international sugar price. In 1982, when

Table 5.4 Distribution of Cuba's Exports and Imports by Socialist and
Market Economies, 1975-1985 (At Current Prices, in Million Pesos)

Years	Total Exports	Imports	Socialist Economies(a) Exports	%	Imports	%	Market Economies Exports	%	Imports	%
1975	2952	3113	2002	68	1605	52	950	32	1508	48
1976	2692	3180	2090	78	1864	59	602	22	1316	41
1977	2918	3462	2443	84	2341	68	475	16	1121	32
1978	3440	3574	2916	85	2849	80	524	15	725	20
1979	3499	3688	2884	82	3053	83	615	18	635	17
1980	3967	4627	2786	70	3613	78	1181	30	1014	22
1981	4224	5114	3179	75	4114	80	1045	25	1000	20
1982	4933	5531	4172	85	4908	89	761	15	623	11
1983	5535	6222	4765	86	5414	87	770	14	808	13
(Goals)							1197		875	
1984	5462	7207	4893	90	6058	84	569	10	1149	16
(Goals)							1272		965	
1985(b)	5983	7905	5310	89	6640	84	672	11	1265	16
(Goals)							1353		973	

(a) Comecon, China, Albania, Yugoslavia, North Korea, and Viet Nam
(b) Preliminary
Sources: AEC, 1982, 1983; 317; AEC 1984, 1985; 289; BNC, 1982; 15, 62;
BNC/AEC, 1985; 22/23

Cuba had to renegotiate approximately 1.3 billion dollars, or one third of its debt in convertible currencies, the National Bank of Cuba adopted guidelines for the future debt management based on very low sugar prices, assuming 8 and 10 cents per pound in 1984 and 1985, respectively, which were still considerably undercut by actual sugar prices of 5.20 and 4.06 cents per pound (BNC, 1982; 62; IMF, various issues).

The government reduced imports of the intermediate and capital goods required for the production of consumer goods in order to utilize hard currency for increasing export production (Gutierrez et al., 1984; 250). But despite its austerity program, exports to market economies in 1984 and 1985 fell about 50% short of target, reducing the proportion of Cuba's exports to the West from 30% in 1980 to 10 and 11% in 1984 and 1985, respectively (Table 5.4). On the other hand, it was also not possible to reduce imports from market economies in 1984 and 1985 to the extent set by the National Bank of Cuba in 1982. Imports from Western economies in 1984 exceeded the limit by 19% and in 1985 by 30%, leading to an unfavorable export/import ratio of about 50% (Table 5.4). After the sharp cut in Western imports by 38% in 1982 and the continuing low level in 1983, this additional importation was obviously necessary due to the increasing demand for modern technology and industrial raw materials not available in the CMEA. In sum, the tough restrictions on imports from market economies barely allowed the utilization of production capacities on a scale necessary to generate an annual average growth of GSP as reported for the years in question.[4]

Conclusions

As pointed out in this chapter, the effects of the wholesale price reform in 1981, the high degree of unfulfillment of physical targets in 1985, and adverse external conditions in the first half of the 1980s suggest that real economic growth in Cuba from 1981–1985 was probably not 7.3% p.a., as official data indicates, i.e., almost 50% higher than the goal set by Cuban planners who expected a relatively modest annual growth of GSP of 5.1% (at constant prices). Alternative estimates of Cuban macroeconomic indicators, however, are not easy to make. In a study prepared for the U.S. State Department, J. Pérez-López used the "bottom up" approach to construct indexes of real GSP growth for Cuba during 1965–1982.[5] Although only the first two years of the second five-year plan have been assessed, it is worthwhile to note that according to the estimated index, the GSP increased by 5.2% in 1981, biassing the average growth rate over the period considerably less than the official data which quotes a rate of growth of 16.0%. For 1982, the estimated index implies GSP growth at a rate of 0.8% compared to the 3.8% in the official statistics (Table 5.1).

It should also be considered that the performance of the Cuban economy can only be partially attributed to Cuba's actual efforts. Its links with CMEA countries have protected the island not only from otherwise catastrophic repercussions of international price trends, but also resulted in substantial financial aid and technological assistance. Although Cuban authors frankly admit that "without access to socialist markets and supplies, the Cuban Revolution would have quite possibly failed" (Gutierrez et al., 1984; 249), figures on total CMEA contributions to Cuba have not been officially reported so far. According to the author's estimates, subsidized Soviet purchases of Cuban sugar alone amounted to 40% of the value of Cuba's total exports in 1976–1980 (Gey, 1983; 50). The total cumulative Soviet economic aid, including repayable loans and nonrepayable subsidies given to Cuba in 1960–1979 was assessed at 16.7 billion dollars (Mesa-Lago, 1982; 150), and more recently, at over 32 billion dollars in military and economic assistance over the years (Duncan, 1986).

These estimates of the total aid provided by the Soviet Union must probably be revised upwards. When Fidel Castro characterized savings as the most important source of resources the country has at hand, he added: "We dispose of abundant resources since what we have received from the USSR alone in one quinquennium, including merchandise, freightage, and credits, sums up to more than 20 billion rubles" (Castro, 1984; 6). To put it in true perspective: based on an exchange rate of 1 ruble = 1.2 peso for 1981 (author's calculation based on Mesa-Lago/ Pérez-López, 1985; 63), Soviet aid in 1981–1985 amounted to 88% of the value of total Cuban exports and to 20% of GSP (at current prices).

To be fair, in terms of public health, Cuba has made better use of its foreign aid than most other Latin American countries. The ratio of doctors to inhabitants was raised from 626 in 1980 to 443 in 1985, the lowest ratio in the area, and there were 5.4 hospital beds for every 1,000 inhabitants compared to 4.9 in 1980. The infant mortality rate was reduced from 19.3 in 1979 to 16.5 for every 1,000 live births in 1985, and life expectancy for both sexes rose from almost 73 years in 1980 to 74.2 in 1985 (Castro, 1980; 8; BNC/CEE, 1985; 7; Castro, 1986a; 4).

Investment Efficiency, Capacity Utilization, and Production Costs

Considering the performance of the Cuban economy in the first half of the 1980s, macroeconomic indicators and production figures have to be complemented by empirical data measuring economic activities on the micro level. Such data are hard to obtain, but top Cuban officials and mass media recently provided illuminating information about the actual economic conditions in terms of efficiency.

Investment Efficiency

In his report to the Third Congress of the party (Castro, 1986a; 6/ 7), Fidel Castro presented a long list of problems obscuring construction and investment planning. In the construction industry, investment efficiency was poor since resources were dispersed among too many projects. New activities were introduced into the plans, although the necessary elements and constructional capacities had not been assured. As a result, many projects could not be finished at the set date. Investment efficiency was further reduced by delays in the technical documentation and poor quality of materials.

Castro acknowledged that the evaluation and execution of investments have been among the most serious problems in the country's development. He said: "There is not a lack of examples: New industries and agricultural development in uninhabited areas without accommodation facilities for the workers; . . . irrigation systems which lack water pumps or electricity to make them work; absence of electricity lines in workshops and installations; new housing areas without urban infrastructure, etc."

The most striking examples for delays of investment projects were reported at a meeting of the representatives of 900 enterprises from the city and province of Havana on 25/26 June 1986. Commenting on the oral intervention of the party secretary of the Boyeros electronic enterprise, Castro stated that in addition to the 11 years already spent on this project, one has to add nearly 11 years more until it might be finished. He called a construction period of 21 years "out of one's mind" pointing out that due to "grave problems" in the planning process, the equipment would become obsolete by the time the plant is finally completed. Castro also criticized that at Boyeros 400 pieces of equipment were stored outside, "badly warehoused and badly treated" (TRAB, 26 June 1986; 1). The next day it was reported that in the Ariguanabo textile industry investments have been delayed by 17 years, mainly due to the "custom already enthroned," i.e. that too many projects were started at the same time without one of them being finished. Castro indicated that enterprises frequently preferred to initiate new projects in order to fulfill the plans, in terms of value, in the most beneficial and easiest way since the first stages of investments generate much more income, the last stages being more difficult to realize (TRAB, 27 June 1986; 1).

Capacity Utilization

According to Fidel Castro, in 1981–1985 the economic system was not sufficiently successful in utilizing the existing industrial capacities. The "Commander-in-Chief" pointed out some general problems such as the scarcity of skilled workers and the instability of the labor force which were two of the main reasons for the slow assimilation of new installations. He noted the lack of all types of containers which "systematically" affected several production processes, causing underfulfillment of some exports and consumer goods. Castro then went on to describe industries where capacity utilization was low, including almost every branch of the economy: sugar and sugar by-products, textiles, cement, chemicals, machinery, agriculture, transportation (Castro, 1986a; 6).

The 1982 Statistical Yearbook presented a table on capacity utilization of tractors used at state farms. This table, which was not reproduced in the Yearbook for 1984, provided information on the structure of the time funds and the reasons for the non-utilization of the tractors in different years. It turns out that in 1970, at the peak of the Sino-Guevarist period, only 22% of the tractor capacity were utilized. This rose to 30% and 53% in 1975 and 1981, respectively, and was stagnant in 1982. (In other words, a Cuban state farm needs two tractors in order to have one that works.) In one of two cases, the tractors could not be used due to technical malfunctions (AEC 1982, 1984; 243).

Production Costs

To the author's knowledge, there is no information on production costs in Cuba, with the exception of agriculture and sugar production.[6] Both sectors are, however, of significant importance to the country's overall economic position. Since the mid-1960s, Cuba's development strategy has aimed at a rapid and fundamental modernization of the country's traditional crop—sugar—which was supposed to be transformed into an effective "accumulation source." Furthermore, foreign currencies generated by the sugar sector are to be used for the importation of Western technology in order to modernize non-sugar cane agriculture and other branches.

From the very beginning, Cuba's so-called "agro-industrialization" created considerable costs. The country made huge efforts to develop the mechanization of the sugar harvest (cutting and lifting), the cleaning of the cane in "conditioning centers" and the modernization and expansion of the sugar mill capacities. The data available on the distribution of state investments in the 1960s show that the share of total investments in sugar and non-sugar agriculture increased from 24% in 1963 to about 40% in 1965 and 1966 (Mesa-Lago, 1981; 45). These figures indicate that in Cuba the investment share allocated to the agricultural sector were the highest any CMEA country has ever made.

In 1978, Humberto Pérez (then head of the Central Planning Board—JUCEPLAN), reported that both sectors (which are directed by different agencies: the Ministry of Agriculture/MINAGR, and the Ministry of Sugar Industry/MINAZ, which is responsible for the growing of sugar cane as well as for its industrial processing) were running at a loss although prices of relevant imported products, i.e. fertilizers, pesticides and oil, had not changed since 1968. He stated that these might be even more unprofitable when domestic prices are adjusted to international or CMEA prices as the upcoming wholesale price reform has planned (Pérez González, 1978; 185).

About two decades after the Cuban "agro-industrialization" began, neither MINAGR nor MINAZ could yet cover their costs. In non-sugar cane agriculture, losses amounted to 473 million pesos in 1980, decreased to 46.5 million pesos in 1983, and increased once more to 114 million pesos in 1984 (TRAB, 3 October 1985; 4). Losses in the sugar sector in 1984 were not far behind those in MINAGR enterprises and amounted to 115 million pesos (TRAB, 6 September 1985; 1). Differences in production costs per ton of sugar indicate that this was only partially due to an increase in input prices: costs ranged from 115 pesos per ton of raw sugar to an astronomic 418 pesos, produced in an enterprise which had recently started operations. In total, from 144 "Agro-Industrial Complexes," only 66 were profitable (TRAB, 12 September 1985; 1). Thus, only the subsidies pumped by the Soviet Union into Cuba's sugar production keep this industry alive.[7]

The Current Stage in the Implementation of the SDPE

When Fidel Castro presented the outline of the SDPE at the First Congress of the PCC in 1975, it became evident that Cuba would not revert to the pre-reform Soviet model which had been already tested from 1961–1965 but planned to implement the economic reform model adopted by the Soviet Union in the mid-1960s. Compared with the Stalinist model, the new System of Management and Planning is considerably more sophisticated, and the Cuban leadership soon became aware of the complications linked to self-financing, labor norms, development and incentive funds, economic calculation and other elements of the SDPE. At the final session of the first national survey on the SDPE in February 1979, where the current phase of the new system was investigated, the president of JUCEPLAN stated that the system would not be in full operation by the end of 1980 as scheduled by the first party Congress. Even the forthcoming quinquennium 1981–1985 was still not viewed as a period of "harvesting" the fruits of the system, but one of "cultivating" the basic mechanisms to make the system function as prescribed by the outline (Pérez González, 1979; 47/48).

The daily newspaper of the Cuban Labor Confederation "Trabajadores" has released extensive information about the serious difficulties the new system is still faced with in the mid-1980s, and at several meetings, Cuban officials presented a thorough analysis of the shortcomings in the SDPE. As can be deducted from this information, one decade after implementing the Soviet reform model, the Cuban economy is actually struggling with the results of highly centralized and cumbersome economic mechanisms similar to those of the traditional Stalinist model. Systemic elements such as self-financing, price flexibility, and incentive and development funds, which conceptually determine the difference between the centralized and the decentralized model, obviously do not play a fundamental role in Cuba's economic activities.

In May 1985, summarizing the results of the fourth survey on the problems facing the SDPE, Humberto Pérez stated that economic calculation, i.e. self-financing, appeared only in conceptual terms but not in practice. "We have operated formally, covering the monetary-mercantile and financial veil over preceding styles which are still prevailing." The head of JUCEPLAN portrayed actual planning procedures in Cuba as basically physical gross-output oriented planning: "We attempt to fix centrally how many kilograms of steel are required to construct a piece of equipment but we do not attach sufficient importance to the costs of raw materials this equipment might require; on the other hand, we do not deal energetically enough with those indicators which emphasize that production increases more than material consumption." As in other socialist countries, the high degree of centralization in decision-making does not produce a corresponding degree of integration of economic activities, but leads to an "anarchic execution of the elaborated plan" (Pérez González, in: TRAB, 27 May 1985; 1). Furthermore, it was reported that less efficient enterprises with idle capacities are favored above efficient ones, which have fewer possibilities of increasing output—a typical phenomenon in centrally planned economies (TRAB, 25 May 1985; 1).

The national survey also found that there was little progress in the field of "internal economic calculation" (cálculo económico interno), which was to be applied in recently established "brigades." The brigade system had been considered as an important potential for increasing productivity since it was hoped to increase the workers' interest in the economic results of their enterprises by establishing smaller production units or "brigades of the new type" (brigadas de nuevo tipo). These brigades are supplied with machinery and equipment, energy and raw materials, labor force and wage funds. They have their own production plans to fulfill, their own accounting and incentive funds. Brigades which are successful in saving resources or increasing profits are allowed to pay bonuses up to 40% of the respective salaries, excluding those workers which are to be penalized.

In 1981, the Ministry of Agriculture was the first state agency to organize in 9 enterprises with a total of 3,020 workers 19 "permanent brigades" (brigadas permanentes). It took another two years until two enterprises in the textile industry established 37 "integral brigades" (brigadas integrales), covering 1,470 workers. The number of permanent (agriculture) and integral (industry and construction) brigades totalled 2,061 in September 1985 and was expected to increase to 2,141 by the end of the year. Instead, it decreased slightly to 2,055 in May 1986 (1,242 brigades, or more than 50% existed in the agricultural sector). In September 1985, the total number of workers integrated into brigades was 121,634, or a modest 5% to 6% of the labor force in the productive sphere (GRS, 9 February 1986; 4; TRAB, 25 November 1985; 4).[8]

In principle, the brigade members are to be paid according to the team's contribution to the total enterprise profit. Since the "cálculo económico interno" is only applied in a very limited number of brigades (due to the non-profitability of many enterprises, organizational problems and other reasons), salaries are in general still to be linked to labor norms. Although the wage and bonus system has been considerably improved, it is, however, still far from its full operation.

While in 1978 the number of workers paid by norms was about 672,000, it rose to 1.2 million at the end of 1984. In the same period, payment of bonuses increased from 209,700 to almost 1 million (TRAB, 8 April 1985; 4). Hence, less then one half of the total workers in the productive sectors of the economy are covered by the SDPE wage and bonus system. From almost 3 million labor norms, only 23% are technically substantiated, which results in unjustified bonus payments; the premium system is too complicated and inefficient (in the Guantánamo province, bonuses for the 1981 coffee harvest were paid in 1985 when half of the former pickers had already moved away); and massive adjustments of actual plans often caused "debacles" (TRAB, 8 April 1985; 4; TRAB, 3 December 1985; 5). The Cuban Labor Confederation pointed out that the internal labor organization was only partially responsible for this: "The basic deficiencies detected in the development of the brigade organization of the labor force refer to planning and control, incentives and organization. An important part of these problems . . . can be attributed to the deficiencies still inherent in the original SDPE. It should be noted that many of these were not caused by the brigades but became manifest when the latter were introduced. This is the truth" (TRAB, 16 May 1986; 4).

Ambiguous Attitudes Towards the Private Sector

Gradually, the shift to the Soviet reform model in the 1970s introduced new policies towards the private sector of the Cuban economy: on the one hand, the collectivization of the small peasants and the transformation of the private plots of state farm workers and cooperative members into collective plots for self-consumption; and on the other, the opening of free artisan and peasant markets. Although there is no public discussion on the island, it can be drawn from official statements and articles that the existence of a private sector in Cuba's socialist economy is extremely controversial. More than that, while the transformation of private farms into production cooperatives have been consequently carried out, recent policies towards the private sector have shown that private activities, as included in the Soviet-type economic model, are likely to be totally eliminated in Cuba.

The Collectivization of Small Land Owners

After the two agrarian reforms in 1959 and 1963, raising the share of state farms in the country's total land to 70%, private farms had been more or less tolerated, although it was planned to transform or integrate those into state farms in the long run. In the early 1960s, to control the peasants, the government established a state purchasing organization for agricultural products ("Acopio") and initiated various types of cooperatives, such as the peasant associations (asociaciones campesinas) similar to the peasants' mutual-aid associations in Eastern Europe, the credit-and-service cooperatives and the agrarian societies (sociedades agropecuarias). The members of the latter, comprising only a tiny fraction of the Cuban peasants, owned the land, livestock and equipment collectively. For this reason, the agrarian societies are now officially considered the predecessors of the new production cooperatives (cooperativas de producción agropecuaria—CPA) which were initiated by the V. Congress of the National Association of Small Farmers (Asociación Nacional de Agricultores Pequeños—ANAP) in 1977 (Domínguez, 1978; 447–463). In the beginning of the collectivization process, it was argued that CPAs were "historically" necessary, substituting the unproductive private minifundium with large-scale and technically advanced production units (Gey, 1984a; 211).[9] The subsequent result was that the state and party leadership concentrated primarily on the institutional preconditions of integrating formerly private producers into centralized planning (Pérez González, 1980; 18/19).

After a cautious beginning in 1977–1980, the collectivization was accelerated in 1981–1983, raising the share of CPAs in peasant land from 13% in 1980 to almost 58% in 1983. In 1984 and 1985, the transformation was slowed down, and in the beginning of 1986, about 61% of the private land was collectivized (AEC 1982, 1983; 210; AEC 1984, 1985; 189; Castro, 1986b; 4).

High costs can be blamed for the deceleration in the formation of CPAs. Firstly, the Cuban government has to provide tremendous amounts of capital in order to supply the new production cooperatives with machinery and transportation facilities which are necessary to maintain large-scale production units. Secondly, the collectivization of small peasant holdings requires high urbanization cost (housing, electricity, road construction, social services, etc.) since Cuban peasant farms are not concentrated in villages but scattered throughout the rural areas. Thirdly, to encourage peasants to turn over their plots to production cooperatives, the government provides social insurance benefits for CPA members, i.e., an old-age pension, leading to a high share of pensioners in the CPA labor force.

Farmers who are not willing to give up their farms have been seriously discriminated against, for instance, by the creation of a high tax on peasants' income, which in the meantime, however, has been adjusted to the income tax imposed on the CPAs. But in general, the method used to collectivize the peasant land is reminiscent of the integration policy of the late 1960s when the Cuban government invested large amounts of money to merge private farms with state farms (Gey, 1986). A Cuban official told the author in 1985, that the costs for the formation of CPAs will probably not be covered "even in one hundred years." In many cases, he admitted, the benefits of large-scale, capital-intensive production cooperatives are "more potential than real" due to the scarcity of managerial skill and modern inputs which are required by larger production units. Indeed, CPA presidents complained that they received less than one fourth of the oil necessary to meet the planned goals in rice production, and ANAP president Ramírez encouraged the use of ox carts over tractors when possible (ANAP, 1985, No. 7; 13; ANAP, 1985, No. 12; 11).

The Introduction of Collective Plots for Self-Consumption on State Farms and CPAs

Information on the private plots of state farm workers has been limited up until now. It was known that in the early 1960s state farmers were allowed a vegetable garden for family consumption but these plots were eliminated when the Sino-Guevarist model was adopted in 1966–1970 (Mesa-Lago, 1976; 276/277). It was not before 1984 that Cuban authors gave a description of the non-state agricultural marketing including all categories of landowners such as state, cooperative and private farms as well as small plots and gardens. They reported that in 1981, agricultural workers and former peasants (who had sold their farms to the state), pensioners and other individuals had 64,020 private plots for family consumption and side-line production, covering 2.5% of the total land (Figueroa/García de la Torre, 1984; 39, 42). However, it was not clear when the plots had been returned to the state farm workers who formed the largest group among the "parceleros."

When the above mentioned article was published, it was already obvious that the Cuban leadership had adopted a new policy towards the plots, differing greatly from those in other socialist countries. In October 1985, the Cuban journal "Bohemia" reported under the headline "Adiós al conuco" (Good-bye to the Plot), that since the beginning of the 1980s, individual plots of state farm workers and CPA members had been fused into "collective plots" intended for the self-consumption of state and cooperative farmers and their families. In the sugar sector alone, these areas are intended to provide agricultural products for 1.3 million people, this is 13% of the Cuban population (Bohemia, No. 40, 4.10.1985, S. 28–31). Special brigade teams attend to these collective plots, and their crop output is sold at low prices in internal stores. Although the government intends to sufficiently subsidize the collective production for self-consumption and deliveries to the state, it remains to be seen whether the collective version of the plots will be successful (Gey, 1986).

Artisan and Peasant Markets

Since 1968, private retail trade and free markets had been illegal, but towards the end of the 1970s, the Cuban government began to tolerate private farmers selling their products openly on the street. In 1980, artisan and peasant markets were opened in Havana and other cities where handmade goods and agricultural products (with the exception of beef, tobacco, coffee and cacao) were freely sold. By allowing the farmers to sell their surplus (i.e., output beyond their contractual commitments with the state collection agency "acopio") at the price set by supply and demand, the government intended to eliminate the black market and to improve both the quantity and quality of the national diet (Forster, 1981/1982; 123; Mesa-Lago, 1985; 292/293).

The free markets motivated the small peasants to increase their output since equilibrium prices were much higher than those paid by acopio. The United Nations Economic Commission for Latin America reported that not only did the food supply benefit from an increased flow of goods, but acopio also received greater volumes of products since private and cooperative farmers had to fill their contracts with the state before being allowed to sell on the free market (ECLA, 1982; 185). Cuban authors repeatedly stated that the free peasant markets, among other things (i.e. the reform of acopio prices and improvement in the organization of the acopio system), contributed considerably in mobilizing the productivity reserves of the non-state economy, in reducing the black market, in increasing the peasant income and in satisfying the demands of urban consumers (Figueroa/García de la Torre, 1984; 49–54; Figueroa/Averhoff, 1986; 62/63).

Castro's New "Revolutionary Offensive"
Against the Private Sector

The free play between supply and demand resulted in high prices for both agricultural and artisanal products, in some cases equalling or exceeding those on the black market since the quantities available were still inadequate to meet the demand. Profits were tremendous for those who sold at free prices, while for low-income groups, access to the free markets was difficult. Thus, it was no wonder that the ideologically oriented wing of the party objected to the increased role of the private sector within the economy because they feared it would open the door to private capital accumulation (although profits could not be invested in land or heavy equipment).

President Castro stood at the head of those who criticized the introduction of free markets and the legalization of self-employment in services (e.g. physicians, carpenters, tailors, architects) due to their resemblance to capitalism. In two of his speeches in spring 1982, Castro inveighed against "shady characters" (the middlemen) who were causing "discord" and "chaos" on the free markets. The peasant markets were characterized as a "capitalist formula" which has to be applied as long as the "selfish and inefficient minifundium" has not disappeared. Castro admitted, however, that the agricultural production of the state sector was insufficient and that the state collection system had grave deficiencies (Gey, 1984b; 246–252). Non-agricultural private activities were not excluded from the attack made by the Commander-in-Chief against the "new bourgeoisie with capitalist attitudes," and 250 self-employed were arrested on a charge of "prostitution of the self-employment concept." In spite of the leftist, puritan overtones, reminiscent of the Sino-Guevarist period, these attacks against the private sector were not followed by the overall elimination of the free markets (Mesa-Lago, 1985; 295/296).

In the following years, Soviet-oriented Cuban scholars discussed the economic mechanisms and incentives by which non-state marketing of agricultural products might be encouraged, praising the important role of "personal property" such as plots of state and cooperative farmers and other individuals for self-consumption and supply of food for urban and rural consumers (Figueroa/García de la Torre, 1984). However, at a meeting of more than 1,000 representatives of the CPA and nearly the entire PCC Politbureau and Council of Ministers in Havana, on 17/18 May 1986, Fidel Castro announced that the government, "rushed by the CPA presidents," was basically going to put an end to free marketing of agricultural surplus products (TRAB, 19 May 1986; 1; Castro, 1986b).

Castro said the free peasant markets gave rise to a wide range of middlemen who profited at the expense of others. He showed himself disappointed at the CPAs being highly privileged in terms of purchase prices and input supplies, but falling victim to the challenges of "comercialismo" recently emerging within the country. Castro accused individuals of making 50,000 pesos per annum by cultivating one hectare of garlic (annual average salary in 1984 was 2,230 pesos, see AEC 1984,

1985; 106). "Such an individual," he stated, "might hardly join the cooperative movement, by no means."

Unlike his 1982 attacks against private farmers, middlemen and small businessmen, this speech was directed against the pursuits of profit in general, thus, including the so-called second economy. For example, Castro became indignant with rewarded cane cutters who received a car for 4,000 pesos, and sold it for 20,000 pesos; with CPAs who sold construction materials to private peasants at much higher prices, and with house-owners who made profits by buying and selling houses. Castro announced that the 1985 Housing Law might be checked and revised since "it became a new mechanism for enrichment." This law provided that former tenants could buy their dwellings from the state, and within a year, 500,000 Cubans received the right of ownership (TRAB, 8 July 1986; 1).

The free peasant markets instantly became illegal. (The previous year, in 1985, sales totalled about 70 million pesos, i.e. approximately 1% of the total turnover in Cuba's retail trade, see Castro, 1986b; 3). It is not clear whether self-employment opportunities were ruled out as well or not. Castro's new revolutionary offensive against "comercialismo," reaching appalling puritan and moralistic overtones, has indicated, however, that the economy will continue to suffer from the lack of private activities. That these are badly needed, not only in the service, housing and construction sectors but also in the tourist sector which is expected to blossom as it did before the Revolution, is another part of the story.

A Look at the Economic Approaches in the Second Half of the 1980s

Due to the absence of public discussion in Cuba, an evaluation of the island's forthcoming economic policies becomes a matter of speculation. But since there are no serious indications of a fundamental shift in the economic scheme, it can be regarded as being sure that Cuba will follow the Soviet model over the rest of the decade. Inside the scope of Soviet-type planning, however, a switch to a more pragmatist route is presently less probable then ever. As in the Soviet Union as well, Cuban planners confine themselves to a greater decentralization of decision making and simplification of planning procedures when correcting their problems with the centralized economic model. At the same time, the government enforces a sustained monetarization of the consumer market, on the one hand, and leftist attitudes such as stressing moral incentives and voluntary labor, on the other.

Administrative Decentralization

As could be seen in the first half of 1986, planners obviously concentrate, firstly, on the paperwork, which can be reduced without jeopardizing the functioning of the system of administrative planning as a whole, and, secondly, on obsolete planning procedures which for years have been officially acknowledged as inefficient and, hence, urgently require drastic modifications.

As to the paperwork, higher levels of the administrative apparatus appear to demand, the Cuban press released some interesting figures. At the Havana meeting of representatives of 900 enterprises already mentioned, the director of an agro-industrial complex reported that in his case the managers have to fill out 160 forms, 39 of which are required by the statistical apparatus and 121 by the Ministry of Agriculture and other state agencies. While the managers at the enterprise level have to dedicate considerable time to meet the bureaucratic requirements of the system, the information obviously does not fulfill the needs, since "when somebody needs some information, he directly contacts the enterprise." This remarkable quantity of paperwork, however, does not ensure that the enterprise receives the supplies on time necessary to meet the planned targets, thus, leading to the "marathons of the last hour." As a first step to more manageable data processing, the President of the State Committee of Finance proposed that compulsory information be reduced from 546 to about 150 indicators.

The Minister of the Basic Industry, Marcos Portal, received a round of applause, when he criticized the unnecessary formation of numerous enterprises and agencies. He endorsed plans on economic decentralization leading to the simplification of the organizational and administrative structure. The minister stressed that the autonomy of enterprises is to be improved, avoiding the intermediate authorities between producers and suppliers.

The most striking point of the administrative reform plans is the fact that budgetary financing of enterprises will be cancelled by 1987. From then onwards, losses will not be automatically covered by the state at the end of the year. Hence, after more than a decade of implementing the SDPE, self-financing of enterprises would finally be put to practice, although the rules of the game are not yet clear (e.g. whether or not "development funds," based on enterprise profitability, will be introduced, or unprofitable enterprises will be closed) (TRAB, 27 June 1986; 1, 5).

Monetarization of the Consumer Market

Since the early years of the Revolution, ration books have played the most important role in Cuba's food distribution system, entitling every member of the household to a fixed monthly ration of consumer goods (both foodstuffs and manufactured goods). Prices have been substantially subsidized by the government order to ensure that low-income groups receive at least the basic necessities. In the beginning of the 1970s, when wages were linked to output norms and work quotas, it turned out that the rationing system had been providing poor incentives for those who earned higher wages for harder work, since the selection and quality of rationed goods had remained modest. Although the original goal of equality has not been abandoned, material rewards and private consumption became essential targets in the political and ideological re-education of the workers. This, however, required the reorganization of the country's distribution system (Bach, 1985; Benjamin/Collins, 1985).

In 1971, planners gradually began to shift to equilibrium prices, selling tobacco, cigarettes and liquor freely at substantially higher prices. During the 1970s, the range of surplus products sold at prices reflecting supply and demand, was continuously expanded, including foodstuffs and manufactured goods from domestic and international production. In 1981, the non-ration distribution system was officially institutionalized as "parallel market." Presently, there are 616 parallel market-units, offering foodstuffs and 142 units, selling manufactured goods. The total sales on the parallel market considerably increased from 565 million pesos in 1983 to 931 million in 1985, reaching a share of 14.4% in total retail trade (TRAB, 10 June 1986; 4). On the other hand, the number of non-foodstuffs distributed by the rationing system, was reduced from 150 in 1980 to 68 in 1985 (Castro, 1986a; 3).

The monetarization of the consumer market is likely to continue during the rest of the decade. The parallel market is considered, firstly, to be the "fundamental distribution system" for putting "the socialist principle of distribution according to work" into practice, and, secondly, to be an adequate instrument of fighting excess money in circulation, hence, of giving money a better buying power (TRAB, 10 June 1986; 4). Theoretically, the expansion of the non-ration distribution system can be considered as a pragmatic step towards more rational prices and more balanced internal finances (which had thus far been badly neglected in post-revolutionary Cuba). In practice, however, it might turn out to be a difficult task for Cuban planners since many Cubans have come to see the "libreta" (ration book) as a vested right to buy goods at prices considerably below cost.

Moral Incentives and Voluntary Labor

Material incentives and work quotas, belonging to the basic elements of the SDPE, were supposed to improve both the motivation and discipline of the workers. It turns out that the SDPE has been rather successful in terms of criminal prosecution, raising the number of charges for indiscipline from 9,988 in 1979 to 27,572 in 1985 (TRAB, 5 July 1986; 1), but has obviously not been very effective economically. The scope of illegal practices officially reported ranges from individual absenteeism, indiscipline, irresponsibility and other infractions of the labor code, to collective deals among clever administrators, foremen, workers and other individuals: salaries which do not correspond to the actual work performed since work quotas have been arbitrarily applied in order to get more money or to meet the norm in a shorter time; technical norms are ignored or remain unfulfilled, leading to considerable flaws; doctors hand over unjustified medical certificates, etc. (TRAB, 30 June 1986; 1; TRAB, 5 July 1986; 1).

To fight the problems of labor indiscipline, the political leadership reverted to measures and appeals well known from the Sino-Guevarist period: moral incentives and voluntary labor. Though the party and mass organizations have always paid rhetorical homage to these measures, they were drastically curtailed in the 1970s (Mesa-Lago, 1982; 159). In mid-1986, however, the trade unions stated that "the material stimulus is not as important as the moral" (TRAB, 3 June 1986; 1). Even more noteworthy was Fidel Castro's categorical statement at the final session of the Havana meeting in June 1986, when emphasizing the concept of unpaid surplus labor as represented by the former "micro-brigades." According to Castro, this is to be revitalized, being a "counter-offensive against the apprentices of capitalism who believe more in spontaneous mechanisms than in consciousness" (TRAB, 26 June 1986; 1; TRAB, 27 June 1986; 5).

While the "micro-brigades" are small teams of workers, mainly occupied in house construction, there are so-called "big mobilizations" as well, calling upon the workers of entire sectors of the economy or even the total Cuban population. The latter is the case on "Red Sundays" (Domingos Rojos), when not only the trade unions but also the other mass organizations and the armed forces appeal to their members to perform unpaid labor. In November 1985, among others, 240,000 construction workers, 280,000 sugar workers and 230,000 state farmers were mobilized to do voluntary work apart from their usual job (TRAB, 31 October 1985; 1). Although voluntary labor is supposed to yield net productivity, this is hardly true in the case of the "big mobilizations." All the same, the Cubans have seen a notable renaissance of moral incentives and voluntary labor.

Conclusions

By the mid-1980s, the SDPE had lost a great deal of its appeal to Cuban state and party leaders. As Fidel Castro stated: "After the initial impulse in the implementation of the System of Economic Management and Planning, its completion was not consistently advanced. Initiative was reduced, and there was no creativity necessary to improve the adaptation of a system, which in a good deal was drawn from the experiences of other countries, to our specific conditions." (Castro, 1986a; 7).[10]

Thus, the situation was similar to that twenty years before, when Soviet and Czech planners attempted to apply the Soviet model of central planning with no effort to adapt it to Cuba's developing economy based on agriculture and heavily dependent on foreign trade (Gey, 1985; 265–268; Mesa-Lago, 1981; 14–18). And once more, the Cuban leadership is obviously not willing to make use of market relations or to provide private property rights at least in some segments of the economy in order to make the system manageable. Instead, a combination of measures, which can be attributed partly to the Soviet reform model and partly to the Sino-Guevarist approach, is expected to improve the efficiency of economic activities.

Although Castro's subjectivist approach to solving economic problems notably reminds of the Sino-Guevarist stage of the Revolution, a new radicalization of Cuban economic policies comparable to the "Revolutionary Offensive" of 1968 is not the order of the day. It clearly indicates, however, that the Cuban leadership still tends to moral and puritan attitudes, when criticizing both central planning and market relations as "bureaucratic" and "capitalistic," respectively.

Notes

The author gratefully acknowledges comments and suggestions by Robert K. Furtak and Karl-Eugen Wädekin. He alone is responsible for the contents.

1. Recently, this periodization of systemic changes in Cuba described by C. Mesa-Lago in several of his writings (e.g., 1978; 1–10; 1981; 10–32) was sharply criticized by Cuban authors (Torres/Carballosa, 1985). Following Soviet historiography, they insisted that there has been only one "socialist" stage of postrevolutionary development, following the "popular-democratic" (which ended in 1961). In summer 1970, however, still under the fresh impression of the "search for something new," Fidel Castro was less reluctant to announce that the revolution was entering a new phase, "a much more serious, mature, profound phase" (cited in: Mesa-Lago, 1978; 26). And in his report presented to the First Congress of the PCC (17/18 December 1975), he frankly stated that revolutions do have "their periods of utopia," causing huge wastes of labor and material resources (Castro, 1975; 53–55).

2. It is beyond the scope of this paper to deal with this period in more detail. The internal and external reasons behind the economic failure of the 1976–1980 plan have been examined in Mesa-Lago, 1982.

3. In the beginning of the 1960s, Cuba introduced the methodology of the Material Product System which is usually applied in socialist countries. Thus, the Cuban national income accounting system differs significantly from those of all other Latin American countries which use the System of National Accounts methodology, and Cuban macroeconomic data cannot be directly compared with those of other economies in the area.

4. The aggravating external situation shed light upon the gap between persistent ideological radicalism in the political sphere and enforced pragmatism in the economic field. When in April 1984 the deterioration in the price of sugar and the onerous servicing of the country's hard-currency debt (2,862 million pesos at the end of 1983, see BNC/CEE, 1983; 8) had induced a new round of negotiations with Western creditor countries, Fidel Castro was preparing a vast campaign in favor of the cancellation of the repayment of Third World countries' external debts (GRS, 22 July 1985). The National Bank of Cuba, however, emphasized "the country's strict meeting of its commitments to creditor governments and banks" (BNC, 1984; 30). In the party organ "Cuba Socialista," reference was made to "Cuba's solidity and capacity of debt payment," responding to Western "bourgeois cubanologists" who paid attention to the island's foreign debt (J. L. Rodríguez, 1985; 101).

5. The "bottom up" approach "constructs constant-price quantity index numbers for branches of the economy and combines these indexes into measures of activity at the level of economic sectors and ultimately of the entire economy." Pérez-López admits that by doing this, resulting indexes tend to understate real growth rate since improvements of goods and services and emerging products over a period of time often are not included.

6. About the alimentary industry, it was reported in general terms that in the first half of 1985, only 49 out of 84 enterprises had covered their costs (TRAB, 6 September 1985; 1).

7. Some Western scholars argue that short-term cost-benefit analyses are shortsighted and misleading, since they can not capture the long-term benefits. According to these, socialism seems to have an advantage over capitalism because a socialist state can apply a longer planning horizon and afford greater losses over the period required by the process of technical change. Further, an "empirical test" of the viability of the Cuban development strategy cannot be made before decades will have past (Edquist, 1985; 142/143, 165/166; Fabian, 1981; 25–30).

8. Hence, the average number of workers per brigade in 1985 amounted to 59. The lower limit is set by 50, the upper by 80 workers, including white collar workers. As from 15 brigades, enterprises are required to establish an intermediary level, formed by "production units" (unidades de producción), embracing 3, 4 or 6 brigades (TRAB, 17 June 1985; 6).

9. In contrast to this, Cuban authors reported high increases in land productivity of small farms: While the arable land was considerably reduced from 1972 to 1976, yields increased by 50% in the case of tubers and by 82% in that of vegetables (Figueroa/García de la Torre, 1984; 38). This confirms Western calculations that in the mid-1970s when the collectivization of the small peasants

was decreed, yields were much higher in the private than in the state sector. Even in capital intensive crops such as sugar cane, yields in 1975–1977 were about 17% higher in private than in state farms (Forster, 1981/1982; 115–119; Gey, 1984a; 213/214).

10. Castro also said that the decision was made to establish a National Commission attached to the Executive Committee of the Council of Ministers in order to "revitalize" operations concerned with the SDPE (Castro, 1986a; 9). The National Commission was finally established on 22 May 1986 and is headed by a director who ranks as minister (TRAB, 27 May 1986; 1).

References

AEC: Anuario Estadístico de Cuba, edited by the Comité Estatal de Estadísticas. Havana

ANAP: Asociación Nacional de Agricultores Pequeños (monthly), Official Organ of the National Association of Small Peasants. Havana

Bach, R. L., 1985: Socialist Construction and Cuban Emigration: Explorations into Mariel, in: CS/EC, Vol. 15, No. 2; 19–36

Benjamin/Collins, 1985: Is Rationing Socialist?: Cuba's Food Distribution System, in: Food Policy, Vol. 10, No. 4; 327–336

BNC, 1982: Banco Nacional de Cuba, Informe Económico. Havana

———, 1984: Banco Nacional de Cuba, Economic Report. Havana

BNC/CEE, 1983, 1985: Banco Nacional de Cuba/Comité Estatal de Estadísticas, Cuba. Quarterly Economic Report, December. Havana

Castro, F., 1976: Informe Central del PCC al I. Congreso, Parte II, Desarrollo Económico, in: ED, No. 36; 13–63

———, 1980: Informe Central al Segundo Congreso, in: GRS, 28 December 1980

———, 1984: Discurso en el acto de clausura del Primer Forum Nacional de Energía, el día 4 de diciembre de 1984, in: GRS, 16 December 1984 (supplement)

———, 1985: Discurso en la clausura del VII período ordinario de sesiones de la Asamblea Nacional del Poder Popular, el día 28 de diciembre de 1984, in: GRS, 13 February 1985 (supplement)

———, 1986a: Informe Central al Tercer Congreso del PCC, in: GRS, 16 February 1986

———, 1986b: Conclusiones en el II Encuentro Nacional de Cooperativas de Producción Agropecuaria celebrado el día 18 de mayo de 1986, in: TRAB, 21 May 1986; 3–4

CEP: Cuestiones de la Economía Planificada (four-monthly), edited by the Central Planning Board JUCEPLAN. Havana

CS: Cuba Socialista (bimonthly), edited by the Central Committee of Communist Party of Cuba. Havana

CS/ES: Cuban Studies/Estudios Cubanos (biannually), edited by the Center for Latin American Studies, University of Pittsburgh. Pittsburgh

Domínguez, J. I., 1978: Cuba. Order and Revolution. Cambridge (Mass.)/ London.

Duncon, W. R. 1986: Soviet-Cuban Relations, in: The Kennan Institute for Advanced Russian Studies, Meeting Report of 12 February 1986. Washington, D.C.

ECLA, 1982: Economic Commission for Latin America, Economic Survey of Latin America 1980. Santiago de Chile

———, 1983: Economic Commission for Latin America, Economic Survey of Latin America 1981. Santiago de Chile

ED: Economía y Desarrollo (bimonthly), edited by the Faculty of Economics of the University of Havana. Havana

Edquist, Ch., 1985: Capitalism, Socialism and Technology. A Comparative Study of Cuba and Jamaica. London

Fabian, H., 1981: Der kubanische Entwicklungsweg. Ein Beitrag zum Konzept autozentrierter Entwicklung. Opladen.

Figueroa, V. M./García de la Torre, L. A., 1984: Apuntes sobre la comercialización agrícola no estatal, in: ED, No. 83; 34–61

Figueroa, V. M./Averhoff, A., 1986: Desarrollo de la producción agropecuaria y su repercusión en el mejoramiento del nivel de vida de los trabajadores del campo cubano en veinticinco años de revolución socialista, in: ED, No. 90; 50–68

Forster, N., 1981/1982: Cuban Agricultural Productivity: A Comparison of State and Private Farm Sectors, in: CS/ES, Vol. 11, No. 2/Vol. 12, No. 1; 105–125.

Gey, P., 1983: Cuba's Economy Between East and West. Domestic and Foreign Economic Aspects (in German, English summary), Bundesinstitut für ostwissenschaftliche und internationale Studien, Report No. 47. Köln

———, 1984a: Die Kollektivierung der kleinbäuerlichen Landwirtschaft in Kuba, in: Agrarwirtschaft, Vol. 33, No. 7; 209–216

———, 1984b: Die Stellung des privaten Agrarsektors in der kubanischen Wirtschaft, in: Th. Bergmann/P. Gey/W. Quaisser, ed., Sozialistische Agrarpolitik, Köln; 232–257

———, 1985: Planning in Cuba (in German, English summary), in: P. Gey/ J. Kosta/W. Quaisser, eds., Socialism and Industrialization. Frankfurt/New York; 263–285

———, 1986: Kubanische Agrarpolitik zwischen Sowjetmodell und Castros Utopie, forthcoming in: Osteuropa, Vol. 36.

GRS: Granma Resumen Semanal, Granma weekly review, Official Organ of the Central Committee of the Communist Party of Cuba. Havana

Gutierrez et al., 1984: J. Gutierrez Muniz/J. Camarós Fabián/J. Cobas Manriquez/R. Hertenberg, The Recent Worldwide Economic Crisis and the Welfare of Children: The Case of Cuba, in: World Development, Vol. 12, No. 3; 247–260

Mesa-Lago, C., 1976: Farm Payment Systems in Socialist Cuba, in: Studies in Comparative Communism, No. 3; 275–284

———, 1978: Cuba in the 1970s. Pragmatism and Institutionalization. Albuquerque

————, 1981: The Economy of Socialist Cuba. A Two-Decade Appraisal. Albuquerque

————, 1982: The Economy. Caution, Frugality, and Resilient Ideology, in: J. I. Domínguez, ed., Cuba. Internal and International Affairs. Beverly Hills/ London; 113–166

————, 1985: The Cuban Economic Model in the 1980s: Conflicts between Ideology and Pragmatism (in German, English summary), in: P. Gey/J. Kosta/W. Quaisser, eds., Socialism and Industrialization, Frankfurt/New York; 286–308

Mesa-Lago, C./Pérez-López, J., 1985: A Study of Cuba's Material Product System, Its Conversion to the System of National Accounts, and Estimation of Gross Domestic Product per Capita and Growth Rates. World Bank Staff Working Papers, No. 770. Washington, D.C.

Pérez González, H., 1978: La obtención de la mayor eficiencia posible en el uso de nuestros recursos, in: ED, No. 46; 167–197

————, 1980a: Sobre la implantación del Sistema de Dirección y Planificación de la economía de la provincia Ciudad de La Habana, CEP, No. 2; 9–23

————, 1980b: Discurso de la clausura, in: Junta Central de Planificación, ed., Segunda Plenaria Nacional de chequeo de la implantación del SDPE, La Habana; 3–42

————, 1982: Acerca del Plan de la economía nacional para 1982, in: CEP, No. 13; 22–39

Pérez-López, J. F., 1985: Real Economic Growth in Cuba, 1965-82, in: Journal of Developing Areas (forthcoming)

Proyecto, 1986: Proyecto de Programa del PCC, Part I, in: TRAB, 28 April 1986 (supplement)

Rodríguez, C. R., 1985: Discurso durante el acto efectuado en Cienfuegos con motivo de declararse esta ciudad victoriosa en la batalla por el noveno grado el día 16 de marzo de 1985, in: TRAB, 6 April 1985; 4

Rodríguez, J. L., 1985: Un enfoque burgués del sector externo de la economía cubana, in: CS, Vol. 5, No. 1; 78–104

Torres, M./ Carballosa, R., 1985: Análisis crítico de algunos planteamientos de la cubanología burguesa sobre la economía cubana, in: ED, No. 89; 201–215

TRAB: Trabajadores (daily), Central Organ of the Cuban Labor Confederation. Havana

6

The Crisis and the Reform of the Yugoslav Economic System in the Eighties

Jože Mencinger

Introduction

Three main findings of the essay presented two years ago at the Symposium on "Socialism and Industrialization" (Gey, Kosta, Quaisser, 1985) were (1) that on a medium-term basis the Yugoslav economy would undergo a period of stagnation, increasing unemployment and decreasing standard of living, (2) that the existing system of "contractual socialism" would represent a major obstacle towards a more open and market-oriented economy, and (3) that the ability to change the system, and the relative pragmatism in defining what socialism is would be an important advantage for the development of the Yugoslav economy. While the first two propositions remain valid, the optimism on the third has faded and the future systemic transformation into a market-oriented system appears questionable.

This essay is divided into three parts. The main features of the economic systems and economic performance before the eighties are summarized in the first. The second part describes and comments on systemic changes and economic debates which have been taking place during the turmoil of the eighties, and the economic movements of the eighties are presented in the third.

Two of the most characteristic features of the Yugoslav economy in the eighties, namely inflation, which has acquired some characteristics of hyperinflation, and unemployment together with regional disparities, are analyzed somewhat more extensively.

99

Systemic Changes and
Economic Performance, 1945–1985

Although the Yugoslav economy serves as the one example of a socialist market economy, its institutional setting has not been particularly stable and has often considerably differed from the theoretical blueprints. Systemic development, at least on the ideological level, can be divided into four distinct systemic periods:

- the period of "administrative socialism," or of a Soviet-type economic system (1945–1952),
- the period of "administrative market socialism" (1953–1962), sometimes referred to as the period of decentralization, which gradually lead to
- the period of "market socialism" (1963–1973), and
- the period of "contractual socialism" (1974 on), referred to as the period of income relations.

Table 6.1 presents a summary of their systemic and macroeconomic characteristics.

The periodization is normative, with four post war constitutions (in 1946, 1953, 1963, and 1974) forming the basis; the starting years of the periods are the years in which new constitutions were passed. Such periodization, based on constitutional rules for the functioning of the economy, can be subject to criticism. First, it creates the notion of abrupt changes which did not occur. Second, some far-reaching institutional changes preceded constitutional changes; some followed them in consecutive years. Third, the gaps among the ideologies included in the constitutions, the actual normative setting, and reality, have always been wide. Fourth, some economic policy changes have had much greater impact on actual economic development than systemic changes. The 1965 economic reform, which was dominated by the macroeconomic policy change (Bajt, 1984; Burkett, 1983) has even been considered the turning point between the "more successful" and the "less successful" period of labor management (Horvat, 1971; Sapir, 1980). The same is true for 1980, when the change of economic policy urged by indebtedness caused a similar turning point in all measurable performance indicators. The periodization is, however, closely related to the allocation of decision-making within the economy.

In "administrative socialism," the answers to the basic economic questions, namely *what, how, to whom*, and *when* were to be given by the planner. In other words, valuation, organization of production, income distribution, and saving-investment decisions were to be centrally

Table 6.1 The Overview of the Yugoslav Economic System and Macroeconomic Characteristics, 1946-1985

Period	Role of market/planning	Type of plans	Type of economy	Type of main constraint	Macroeconomic performance Internal stability Growth	Capacity utilisation	Inflation	External stability
1946-1952	Extremely weak/strong	Directive soviet type yearly plans	Centrally planned	Capital resources skilled labor	Slow	Low and unstable	Nil	Relatively high
1953-1962	Increasing/decreasing	Global balance midterm plans	Say's type supply constrained	Capital resources	High	High	Low	High
1963-1973	Strong/weak	Indicative planning and resolutions	Specific Keynesian	Money supply	Moderate	Unstable	Increasing	Low and decreasing
1974-1985	Decreasing/weak	Social planning	Stagflationary supply constrained	Foreign exchange	Decreasing and nil after 1980	Low	Extremely high	Low up to 1980

Source: Synopsis by the author

planned. 1950 can be considered the peak of "administrative socialism," followed by its very rapid disbandment.

After 1952, Yugoslavia started to move away, step by step, from the centralized economic planning by reducing administrative constraints and by giving the enterprises a more independent role in decision-making. While the birth of the new system can be attributed to the Law on Management of Government Business Enterprises and Higher Economic Associations by Workers' Collectives, enacted in 1950, its basic legal and political features were explicitly defined in the Constitution Act of 1953. It is this system which, according to the theory on economic systems, often serves as the one example of a socialist market economy or of a socialist self-managed economy. Up to the early sixties, self-management was rather limited even in a normative setting. In short, two of the basic economic decisions, namely *to whom* and *when* remained under strict government control, while the *what* to produce was to be decided upon by consumers, and independent enterprises were free to decide *how* to organize production and how to combine productive factors.

Although system changes were permanently taking place, two reforms, in 1961 and in 1965, can nevertheless be distinguished. Due to these reforms, the mechanism of economic control was reduced, the autonomy of economic units increased, and a phase referred to as "market socialism" was initiated. With the abolition of wage controls and with the changes in the investment system, the remaining two basic economic decisions *to whom* and *when* were at least formally transferred to independent enterprises.

By the early seventies, important institutional changes were introduced. They started with constitutional amendments in 1970, and were to be the blueprint for the so-called associated labor concept of the self-managed economy. Although, they did not formally question the pro-claimed basic elements of the system, the changes were so far-reaching that the market character of the Yugoslav economy has become questionable. Namely, to a considerable extent, the associated labor concept rejected two components of the market economy: the market as the basic allocative mechanism, and macroeconomic policy and indicative planning as means of indirect regulation of economic activities. It insisted that these were to be substituted to the greatest extent possible by mechanisms of social contracts, self-management agreements, and overwhelming social planning. In short, the question of *who* is to answer basic economic questions became blurred.

The above normative periodization arises the question of what the reasons for systemic changes were. If the rather mystical "development of productive forces" is not accepted, the question is reduced to a

Table 6.2 The Main Performance Indicators of the Yugoslav Economy, 1946-1985

Period	1946-1952(a)	1952-1962	1963-1973	1974-1979	1980-1985
Rates of growth of					
Gross domestic product	2.3	8.3	6.5	3.5	0.8
Industrial production	12.9	12.2	8.6	5.4	3.0
Agricultural production	-3.1	9.2	3.1	2.3	0.3
Employment	8.3	6.8	2.4	3.6	2.4
Exports in US dollars	-3.1	12.0	14.0	11.3	6.5
Imports in US dollars	3.6	10.1	16.6	10.3	-2.0
Fixed investments		11.5	5.3	0.7	-8.9
Private consumption		6.5	6.4	2.2	-1.0
Retail sales prices		3.6	13.0	33.3	48.7
Ratios(b)					
Investment/GDP rate		41.99	38.87	35.21	28.60
Capital/output ratio		2.28	2.23	2.64	2.82
Employment/output ratio(c)		3.87	2.42	1.86	1.84
Unemployment rate		5.01	7.58	13.29	14.24
Export/import rate		64.66	69.44	63.96	74.81

(a) Horvat, 1971
(b) 1974-1984 and 1980-1984 periods
(c) number of employees per 1 million dinars in 1972 prices
Source: Statistički godišnjak, different issues,
Saopstenje SZS 226/1986, Beograd 1986

simpler one, namely whether the reasons (and the goals) of the systemic changes were inspired predominantly by economic or by political considerations. Although it is not easy to answer even such a simplified question, it seems that the political factors prevailed in the abandonment of the Soviet-type, centrally planned system in the early fifties, and in the adoption of the associated labor concept in the early seventies, while the reforms in the early and mid-sixties were prompted predominantly by economic considerations (Mencinger, 1986).

Performance indicators for the periods are summarized in Table 6.2 (i.e. indicators of growth, capital formation, standard of living, employment, price stability, efficiency of production factors, employment balance, and external balance). A sub-period, 1980-1985, is added to the period 1974-1985.

The growth rates in Table 6.2 appear satisfactory when compared to those of developed market economies. The comparison with similar economies, however, suggests that the Yugoslav growth performance was not exceptional except for the agricultural production in the period

1953–1962, which was predominantly a result of the fact that the previous catastrophic policy of collectivization had been abandoned. A much higher industrial performance in the second period compared to the first is evident, as well, although this rapid growth is at least partly due to huge investments into industries with high capital/output ratios and long gestation periods, which started in the first period but added to growth in the second, and which also enabled the pre-orientation to industries with lower capital/output ratios.

The comparison of the growth figures from the two most recent periods with the figures of the comparable group of countries (middle income oil importers) indicates that they are in the same general range. For both periods the average rates of GDP growth in Yugoslavia were slightly lower than for the group (7.0% for 1965–1973 and 5.6% for 1973–1980 period); industrial production growth was slightly higher in Yugoslavia in the first period (8.6% compared to 8.2%) but lagged behind in the second (3.8% compared to 5.4%). Growth of agricultural production lagged in both periods—3.1% compared to 3.4% and 2.7% compared to 2.1% (World Bank, 1985).

The figures on the share of investments in GDP, however, suggest that the cost of growth in Yugoslavia was much higher (Bajt, 1984), and, indirectly, that Yugoslavia, despite all institutional changes, retained the Soviet pattern of development. According to the figures of the World Development Report, the investment share in GDP in middle income oil importers was 22.0% in 1965, 24.9% in 1973, and 26.6% in 1980. The same source reports the Yugoslav figures as 30.2% for the 1965–1972 period, 33.1% for the 1973–1978 period, and 36.5% for the 1979–1983 period.

The same is true for the previous periods. In the period of "administrative socialism," economic growth was achieved by enormous input increases; both, capital/output and labor/output ratios increased rapidly. When rigid planning was abolished and the sovereignty of planners was replaced by that of consumers and the independence of producers in determining the combination of productive factors, the economy became more efficient. In the period 1953–1962, both the capital/output and the labor/output ratios decreased rapidly. Yugoslav economic performance in this period has often been considered impressive (Balassa, 1970). In the third period, the capital/output ratio started to grow again, while the labor/output ratio slowly decreased. The changes in the distribution mechanism, which made relatively abundant labor expensive (the majority of taxes and contributions were levied on wages) and scarce capital a free good (with real interest rates extremely negative), appear to be the main reason for such a development. The situation worsened considerably in the period of "contractual socialism"; the growth rates slowed, capital/output ratio started to increase rapidly, labor/output ratio stagnated and even began to increase after 1980.

Systemic Development in the Eighties

Although the criticism of the associated labor concept of self-managed economy was vigorously refuted as hostile to self-management and socialism, it soon became apparent that the system blueprints were either inoperative or produced undesirable results. This became particularly apparent after 1979, when the net inflow of foreign capital ceased. 1979 can therefore be considered the peak year of "contractual socialism." However, contrary to the situation in 1950, when "administrative socialism" was quickly abolished, the disbandment of the "contractual" system has, at least on the ideological level, been rather slow. On the other hand, more and more government interventions have been required to replace a number of suspended or irrelevant "rules of the game." This has been done through numerous administrative measures and incessant changes in legislation. The actual economic system has gradually regained many characteristics of the administrative system.

The economic situation, which by 1980 had developed into the most severe crisis in the Yugoslav economic and political system, prompted a new reform. It started in 1982 with the "Long Run Stabilization Program" (Savezni društveni savet, 1984) which consists of seventeen documents (over 1,000 pages) dealing with inflation, unemployment, foreign economic relations, infrastructure, agriculture, transport, energy, "small scale" industry, regional development, social policy, changes of the economic and legal system, etc. It was produced by groups of economists, led and supervised by politicians. Although the Program is highly inconsistent in its approaches to different economic problems, one could say that it contains all schools of economic thought, from extreme monetarism to orthodox Keynesian, often nicely cloaked in Marxian terminology; its main orientation is nevertheless clear: the reintroduction of the market and the reduction of a number of institutions introduced in the seventies.

Enormous conceptual differences between the Long Run Stabilization Program, which tried to revive "market socialism" and the Associated Labor Act, which is the cornerstone of the "contractual socialism," have not deterred politicians and some social scientists from applauding both at the same time. The Program has remained the single proclaimed answer to the crisis in most of the speeches at the party and trade union congresses in 1986. This, however, does not mean that all politically relevant social groups in fact accept the premises of the Program or that its goals (which have not been enforced by the IMF) have been readily introduced into the economic system. On the contrary, the future systemic development appears to be less clear in the middle of 1986 than it was in the preceding years.

Another document, The Critical Analysis of the Functioning of the Political System of Socialist Self-management, (Savezni društveni savet, 1985), which appeared at the end of 1985, has been considered an alternative to the Program by most economists. The Analysis, though stressing the need for radical changes and formally appealing to the Program, reopens most of the economic questions it deals with. More importantly, its basic idea is that there is no need for changes to the premises of the economic system. What should be changed, according to the Analysis, is the behavior. Namely, the breakdown of the system and the catastrophic economic results were caused by the inappropriate behavior of the economic units and not by deficiencies in the blueprints.

The actual changes in the economic system are nevertheless permanently occuring. Two quite different directions can be distinguished. Some systemic laws reintroduce the "rules of the game" which restore "market socialism," while others strengthen the transition to "administrative socialism." The new price control law (1984), the law on the banking system (1985), the proposal on the abandonment of the law on compulsory "pooling of labor and resources" of trade organizations with the productive organizations, can be considered examples of the first direction, while the new laws regulating foreign economic relations (1985), the planning law (1985), or the proposals for the regulation of income distribution, strengthen the transition to the administrative system.

The new price control law abolished the Self-managed Associations for Prices (SMA) and the criteria for price formation, and restored the principle of free price formation on the enterprise level without negotiations within the SMAs, and, realistically, the need for government price controls. The law on the banking system re-established banks as independent economic units. On the other hand, the foreign trade system of 1977 (the actual operation of which was enabled by the help of "gray" markets for foreign currency, cloaked by appropriate self-management terminology) was replaced by the administrative system in 1986. The questionable right to foreign currency by those who "created" it and the theoretically inacceptable principle by which imports should equal exports on all levels, were replaced by a principle of socially (administratively) determined import needs. The new planning law, though simplifying the planning system to some extent, retained some social planning characteristics, and regained some from directive planning.

Furthermore, the short-run plan for 1986 (resolution), reinforced direct control in those fields where it existed previously (prices, imports), extended it to new fields (inventory formation), and questioned some of the cornerstones of the Program, such as the "real positive interest rate" and the "real" exchange rate.

The variety of ideas concerning the answer to the crisis has been particularly wide in academic debates; A number of solutions have been suggested and most of the taboo topics have been reopened (Horvat, 1985; Jerovsek et al., 1985). These include, to name a few, recognition of labor and capital markets as indispensable segments of the market economy, the changes in self-management principles (Goldstein, 1985), the questioning of the social property concept and its replacement by the collective property (Bajt, 1986), the mixed economy (Popović, 1984). Although published, most of the ideas have been rejected, or what proved to be more efficient, ignored. The traditional division of Yugoslav economists into "profiters" (Bajt, Horvat, Pjanić, etc.) and "incomers" (Korać, Vlaskalić, Papić, etc.) has continued. It is reflected in the controversies between the Program, supported by "profiters," and the Analysis favoured by "incomers."

The economic reform, which began in the eighties when the counter-reform of the seventies was over, maintains the general characteristics of economic reforms in other socialist countries. It tries to increase economic efficiency by introducing or reintroducing the tools of capitalist market economies. The Program will, therefore, most likely share the fate of economic reforms in other socialist countries; the ideological obstacles and the fear of the unacceptable weakening of the Party's political monopoly will be the final and the most decisive arguments for determining the actual extent of the reforms and their duration. The ability to change the system and to re-evaluate Marxist ideas might, again, push the trade-off between ideology and economic efficiency in favor of the latter. Despite some recent discouraging developments, the final direction of future systemic developments is uncertain. It seems, however, that the outcome will be highly influenced by the present economic situation and its social and political implications. Administrative solutions will be favored for at least two reasons. First, the reintroduction of the market would increase social differences among individuals and regions to unacceptable dimensions. Second, increased efficiency of the economy can only be reached by changing the framework which determines it, i.e. the economic and political systems, and by giving up many "unquestionable" premises on social property, self-management, political monopoly of the Party, etc. This would require radical political changes which are, however, unlikely.

The Limits of the Development, 1986–1990

Although systemic factors are important, one cannot overlook the state of the economy (putting aside its interdependence with systemic changes) and its direct effects on future economic development. The macroeconomic performance in the period of "contractual socialism" is characterized by the break in 1980, dividing the more and less successful sub-periods. The movements in the balance of payment, however, indicate that the success before 1980 was fictitious. The yearly inflows of foreign capital were, namely, greater than the increases in the gross domestic product. Thus, the Yugoslav economy was doomed to stagnate for a decade if there were no foreign capital inflows. When the possibility of development based on foreign accumulation faded and when the accumulated debts required an enormous outflow of capital for debt servicing, the fictitious success dissolved, as well.

Thus, the state of the economy has been determined primarily by foreign economic relations dominated by the need to re-establish an external balance. In the past five years economic policy succeeded in balancing the balance of payments. This is presented in Table 6.3. The "price" for achieving external equilibrium was high. It consisted of stagnation, unemployment, inflation, and increased interregional disparities. The growth of GDP decreased from 6.1% yearly in the period 1971–1979 to only 0.9% in the period 1980–1985. The unemployment rate reached 15.4% at the end of 1985. The average inflation rate increased from 20% in the 1971–1979 period to 40% in the 1980–1984 period, and to 80% in 1985, with a spiraling inflationary tendency similar to that in Latin America. The real wages lowered to two-thirds of those in 1979 and interregional differences increased. The continuation of such trends, therefore, represents economic, social and political threats to the future development.

The Social Plan for the period 1986–1990 indicates that the planners' attention was directed towards ways in which more stable growth could be ensured. According to this plan, "economic development should be based predominantly on the maximum activation and efficient use of the existing capacities and other available resources" (Društveni plan Jugoslavije za razdoblje 1986–1990; 1). As the planners were well aware of the situation, the goals of the plan are relatively modest when compared to previous goals. Even so, two questions remain unanswered, namely, whether the goals are realistic enough and on what changes in the external economic conditions, in the economic system, and in the economic policy are they based.

Table 6.4 enables the comparison of the current goals with the previous ones, and the comparison of the planned rates of growth with the actual rates in the planning periods. It indicates, that Yugoslav planners, on the average, overestimated the development potentials, and that the gaps between the planned and the actual development were increasing. While they were rather exact in predicting industrial production, their ability

Table 6.3   The Balance of Payments, 1975-1985

	1975	1976	1977	1978	1979	1980	1981	1982	1983	1984	1985
Goods											
Exports	4072	4878	5254	5671	6794	8978	10204	10241	9914	10254	10622
Imports	-7697	-7367	-9636	-9988	-14019	-15064	-14528	-13334	-12154	-11993	-12223
Balance	-3625	-2489	-4380	-4317	-7225	-6086	-4324	-3093	-2240	-1639	-1601
Nonfactor Services											
Exports	1984	2051	2267	2380	3771	4334	4509	3616	3513	3397	3581
Imports	-695	-888	-888	-1051	-1624	-1724	-1954	-1428	-1161	-1241	-1064
Balance	1289	1163	1379	1329	2145	2599	2555	2188	2352	2156	2517
Balance of goods and services	-2336	-1326	-3001	-2988	-5078	-3487	-1768	-905	112	517	916
Factor Services											
Net remittances	1327	1415	1327	1714	1710	2280	2042	1828	1227	1189	1001
Net transfers	281	355	303	318	345	362	380	395	467	535	595
Net interest payments	-275	-279	-258	-300	-633	-1084	-1710	-1782	-1532	-1638	-1664
Balance	1333	1491	1372	1732	1422	1588	712	441	162	86	-68
Balance of payments	-1033	165	-1629	-1626	-3656	-1929	-1056	-464	274	603	848

Source: Čičin-Šain, A.: Uravnotezenje platne bilance uz stagnaciju izvoza i smanjivanje uvoza, Aktuelni Problemi Privrednih Kretanja i Ekonomske Politike Jugoslavije, Zagreb 1984; 109.
Bilten Narodne Banke Jugoslavije, December 1985; 67. Beograd 1986.

Table 6.4 Planned and Actual Rates of Growth

Plan	GDP	Industrial production	Agricultural production	Employment	Imports	Exports
1957-1961 planned	9.5	11.0	7.4	4.4	8.0	12.0
actual	10.4	12.6	8.8	7.7	13.0	11.6
1961-1965 planned	11.4	13.0	7.2	6.2	10.0	14.2
actual	6.8	10.5	1.4	4.2	5.9	10.1
1966-1970 planned	8.0	9.5	4.6	2.7	11.0	14.0
actual	5.7	6.2	3.0	1.0	14.8	6.2
1971-1975 planned	7.5	8.0	-	3.0	10.0	12.0
actual	5.9	8.0	2.3	4.4	7.6	5.7
1976-1980 planned	7.0	8.0	4.0	3.5	10.0	14.0
actual	5.2	6.7	2.1	4.1	12.1	13.2
1981-1985 planned	4.5	5.5	4.5	2.5	1.1	8.0
actual	1.1	2.9	2.6	2.4	-6.2	0.6
1986-1990 planned	4.0	4.5	3.2	2.0	5.3	5.7
"actual"	1.9	3.1	1.2	2.3	4.8	2.1

Source: Mencinger, 1985; 37

to predict foreign trade flows was poor. The "ratchet effect", observed in centrally planned economies (Keren et al., 1983) can be seen in the Yugoslav planning practice, as well (Mencinger, 1985). Bearing this in mind, the most likely growth figures, based on planned figures and the previous planning practice, are added for the period 1986–1990 (the last row of Table 4). The planned or "predicted" development does not appear to offer rapid solutions for the severe problems of Yugoslav development manifested in inflation, unemployment, and regional disparities.

Inflation

According to the framework of Vanek's general theory of the labor-managed economy (Vanek, 1970), long-run price stability should be more easily achieved in a socialist market economy than in its capitalist counterpart. The absence of union power to fix wages and the natural reluctance to fire workers should enable prices to sink as easily as they rise. Although Horvat, starting from the same point, i.e. a reluctance to dismiss workers but also stressing the unwillingness to reduce wages, came to the opposite conclusion regarding downward wage rigidity, he found the solution for lower inflation in the absence of class struggle (Horvat, 1972). The arguments do not seem persuasive, and the facts have flatly denied their relevance. The Yugoslav economy has always been subject to considerable inflationary pressures. The rate of inflation was the highest in Europe in the sixties and seventies. It increased considerably in the eighties, when it acquired some characteristics of hyperinflation. The highs and lows of the cyclical movements of the price growth rate have been on higher and higher levels, the periods of increasing rates have become longer and those of decreasing rates shorter. Three interacting factors explain the inflationary movements in the eighties: (1) the systemic factors, (2) the shift in the allocation of macro output, and (3) government interventions. The systemic factors diminish the price responsiveness of the economy and create circumstances in which open or suppressed inflation in form of shortages is unavoidable. The shift in the allocation of macro output required for achieving external balance was also inevitably accompanied by high inflationary pressures. Finally, the onesided and shortsighted government interventions in the price formation caused cyclical movements of price changes and increased inflationary expectations.

Three systemic factors will be briefly discussed: systemic prevention of the entry of efficient economic units, systemic effects on the savings-investments balance, and systemic creation of a monopolistic economic structure.

The agricultural sector provides the most characteristic, although possibly not the most important example, of the relationship between the institutional framework and the standard structural cost push explanation of long-term inflation. The ideological prejudices against family farms, summarized in the maximum land tenure determination, prevent the formation and entry of efficient private economic units which, at given today's technology, undoubtly exceed the constitutionally set maximum of ten hectares. The institutional regulation, on the other hand, favors large-scale socialist farms which are, due to the specific nature of agricultural production, also far from the minimum long-run average costs. The productivity in the agricultural sector is therefore lagging behind technological possibilities, while the growth of agricultural income must follow general income growth in the economy which is possible only if the prices of agricultural products increase faster than they would if efficient units were not prevented the entry.

The systemic factors can also be blamed for the constant inflationary pressures which stem from the nature of saving-investment decisions. This results in the demand for investment resources unmatched by voluntary ex ante savings. Namely, if workers decided on income distribution, one could expect that the largest possible share of enterprise income would be channeled to wages in order to increase private consumption and private savings and not to enterprise funds which would increase social productive assets and the probability of future higher wages. The preferences for channelling savings into social fixed assets are, due to the limited property rights, unlikely unless workers become legal collective owners of the assets. The enterprises which accumulate enough to meet the high investment propensity, increased by the "soft budget constraints" (Kornai, 1984) are therefore exceptions. Although the savings-investment gap could be filled with private savings through the banking system, the socialist environment (restrictions on the ownership of the means of production, relatively high social security, destroyed price structure) increases the propensity to consume or to invest in nonproductive assets. Inflationary financing of investments in productive assets can therefore be considered as a normal replacement of direct forced savings which characterizes socialist countries with suppressed inflation. This implies persistent overall macro excess demand, which before the eighties, was at least partly softened by the inflow of foreign capital.

The inflationary nature of the Yugoslav economy, strengthened considerably in the period of "contractual socialism," which created monopolies also in those fields in which natural monopolies had not existed. Legally promoted price agreements caused the formation of prices which enabled the least efficient producer to survive, the others being satisfied with smaller shares of the market but at prices higher than those at which they would otherwise be willing and able to produce. In the context of Kornai's shortage economy, one could claim that the institutions of the contractual economy considerably softened "soft budget constraints" and reduced price responsiveness.

World inflation in the early eighties and the need to establish an external balance forced inflation in the eighties even higher. Increased shortages of imported materials strengthened monopolistic structure of the economy. The breakdown of the legal system, the need to establish "equilibrium" prices of capital (positive real interest rates) and of foreign exchange ("real" exchange rate), was accompanied by an enormous increase in excess demand, caused by the reduction of the balance of payments deficit. The possibility to balance aggregate supply and demand by external imbalance faded; the domestic demand which reached 110% of the domestic supply in the seventies had to be reduced to 95%. This shift in the allocation of macro output is the most important direct cause for the inflation in the eighties.

Although economic policy cannot be blamed for what happened in the early eighties, it can be blamed for the use of inappropriate devices to curb inflation. The inflation control was reduced to direct price controls which were not even accompanied by wage controls. This policy resulted in incessant switches from relatively liberal price controls to relatively strict ones. The resulting destruction of the price structure caused partial imbalances and increased overall imbalance for a very simple reason; the uncontrolled wages and frozen prices increased aggregate excess demand. Frequent policy switches increased inflationary expectations and prompted responses of the enterprises to expected future price freezes.

Unemployment and Regional Disparities

The economic, social and political implications of the unemployment figures differ from the implications of comparative figures for a developed industrial country in many respects. The labor supply and demand characteristics make Yugoslav unemployment basically a long-term and regional problem which worsened when production began to stagnate after 1980, and no solution similar to the one in 1968 (the exodus of labor) was available. In Yugoslavia labor supply is determined by the developing nature of the country, with relatively high birth rates, high percentage of agricultural population and specific ownership structure, predominant socialist nonagricultural and predominant private agricultural sectors. Rapid industrialization, the spread of technological progress in agriculture, differences in real wages, and economic policy inspired by ideological prejudices caused a quick one-way flow of labor from the agricultural to the nonagricultural sector. Agriculture became the most important source of labor for the nonagricultural sector, and in the period 1968–1973, for the foreign sector, as well. It was also a buffer against the social and political effects of unemployment. On the other hand, the demand for labor was determined by the long-term scarcity of capital which implies a complementary, rather than substitutional relation between labor and capital. This was amplified by underpriced capital which favored capital intensive project selection.

Four categories of unemployment should be distinguished to properly discuss the unemployment problems in Yugoslavia: registered, standard hidden, "internally" hidden (those who are formally employed but do not add to the product), and potential (workers abroad).

The number of job seekers (those registered as unemployed) at the end of 1985 reached 1,080,000, and the unemployment rate was 15.55% (Note that the unemployment rate—the number of registered job seekers/ the number of employees is unrealistically high because of the very narrow employment definition which does not take into account independent farmers and other active persons who do not comply with the official status of employed person).

The category of hidden unemployment does not differ significantly from similar categories in other economies and can be estimated by demographic and employment movements. It is concentrated in the less developed regions and amounts to several hundred thousand people.

Domestic employment in the eighties, which is characterized by an autonomous growth independent of ups and downs in production growth, produced enormous "internal unemployment." This has been an obvious (conscious or unconscious) way of neutralizing the social and political effects of unemployment, by transforming both registered and hidden unemployment into "internal" unemployment in the form of underutilized labor. The estimated number of those who can be considered internally unemployed depends heavily on the methodology used. According to a rather simple estimation, based on monthly labor-output ratios for thirty-seven sectors of the economy and on the Wharton capacity utilization index methodology (Mencinger, 1983), the average "internal" unemployment rate for the period 1971–1983 was estimated to be 9.26%. The average yearly figures are presented in Table 6.5.

The low mobility of labor from the south to the north (due to cultural differences and other factors such as housing) is another specific employment characteristics which relates unemployment phenomena to regional disparities (see Table 6.5).

Although the supply of labor is expected to decrease, mainly due to the age structure of the agricultural population, the demographs (Macura,

Table 6.5 The Regional Development of Yugoslavia

	SFRJ	BIH	CG	H	M	SL	SR	SR proper Kosovo	Kosovo	Vojvodina
Participation rate (1984)	.277	.227	.248	.327	.245	.432	.252	.276	.120	.295
Net participation rate (1984)	.417	.365	.405	.527	.411	.690	.405	.427	.232	.460
Unemployment rate (1984)	.153	.226	.23	.075	.262	.018	.193	.169	.491	.154
Indexes (Yugoslavia=100)										
GDP/capita (1983)	100	69	77	125	65	197	91	99	28	120
GDP/capita (1955)	100	83	77	122	68	175	86	91	43	94
GDP/employee (1983)	100	88	88	100	82	126	99	98	70	110
GDP/employee (1955)	100	87	87	102	100	129	89	85	106	95
Growth rates 1956-1983										
GDP	5.7	5.3	5.9	5.3	5.9	6.0	6.0	5.9	5.7	6.2
Population	0.9	1.2	1.1	0.5	1.4	0.8	1.0	0.8	2.4	0.5
GDP/capita	4.8	4.1	4.8	4.8	4.5	5.2	5.0	5.1	3.3	5.7
Ratios										
K/Q ratio (1983)	2.85	3.44	4.35	2.85	2.85	2.70	2.56	2.44	4.00	2.63
dK/dQ ratio 1971-1983	6.36	7.09	9.52	6.80	6.99	5.62	5.92	5.46	11.10	5.98

Source: Statistički Godišnjak, different years

1986, World Bank, 1983) estimate that the net supply of labor will increase yearly by 2.5% until 1990. A slower growth rate of output and accumulated "internal" unemployment will diminish the capacity of the economy to generate employment even more: The resulting gap can be filled up by increasing "internal" unemployment which has apparent but short-term social and political advantages when compared to registered or hidden unemployment. The economy's capacity to generate employment, which declined sharply as a result of the 1980 break, is not expected to recover in the near future and unemployment will become the most important problem in the second half of the eighties. The changed structure of job seekers (young, skilled people concentrated in industrial centers rather than unskilled workers dispersed in small villages) will affect its social and political dimensions.

The goals of the Program aimed at increasing the labor demand, redistributing it and improving the efficiency of the labor market (i.e. changes in investment policies, in the relative price of capital, creation of an employment fund, promotion of small scale industries, new policy towards private nonagricultural sector, changes in shift work, shifts in the location of industries, and measures for increased inter and intra firm and interregional labor mobility, etc.) can be very useful but cannot solve the problem in the near future. The present state is namely a result of long-term demographic factors and basic development strategies of the past. They were based on cheap capital in an economy where capital was scarce and labor was abundant factor. Ideologically founded constraints have also been important as they transferred private capital (especially from workers abroad) into nonproductive consumption and investments (cars, housing) instead of channeling it into productive investments.

Regional disparities (Table 6.5) have actually increased despite efforts to equalize the development level throughout the country. The GDP per capita rate between Slovenia and Kosovo widened from 5:1 in 1955, to 7:1 in 1983. In addition, the intraregional differences are considerable within all regions.

The increased regional disparities are not a result of the stagnation in the less developed regions (the growth of GDP was rather evenly spread and the growth of productive capital was higher in the less developed regions), although the development strategy, based on capital intensive techniques, can be partly blamed.

There are four main factors affecting interregional disparities with very limited prospects of reducing them: demographic movements, extreme differences in productivity between the modern nonagricultural and backward agricultural sectors, weaknesses in the economic structure, and institutional weaknesses.

The different population growth rates diluted the benefits of similar GDP growth rates and widened the ultimate gap between the less and the more developed regions. While natural growth rates, birth rates, and fertility rates, in the more developed regions, and also in most of the less developed regions, stabilized around 1970, the population of Kosovo continued to grow extremely rapidly. The fertility rate of 5.4 (in 1975) enables the population of Kosovo to more than double in one generation, meaning that even if the fertility rate declines sharply, the working age population would still continue to grow fast for decades.

The disparity between the productivity of the modern nonagricultural and traditional private agricultural sector, within the same region is enormous. Thus, the differences in the participation rates, which indicate the relative size of the modern sector, point to the main source of regional disparity. Furthermore, there are enormous differences in the productivity, even within industries, as indicated by the average and marginal capital/output ratios.

Voluntary transfers of resources and related technology cannot be expected. Direct voluntary investments made by enterprises from the developed regions to the less developed regions are not profitable, partly due to low absorptive capacities, and partly due to the legal determination of social property, which does not protect the investors from loosing both the capital invested and the control over the established enterprises.

Any sizable reduction of regional disparities will therefore be slow and expensive. A gradual reduction of disparities might be accompanied by an extended period of rising unemployment (Katz, 1983) and increased political tensions aggravated by increased nationalism. Massive transfers of resources will continue to be necessary if socially and politically acceptable disparities are to be retained. This appears to be feasible only through administrative movements of resources from the north to the south.

Conclusions

The prospects of the Yugoslav economy for the second half of the eighties do not appear encouraging. The external balance was enforced due to overindebtedness and achieved at the cost of internal imbalance. The possibilities of economic recovery and development will therefore be rather limited. The transformation of the economy, which obtained a large proportion of its disposable product (up to 10%) abroad into an economy where foreign demand increases the productivity enough to offset such losses and to generate the outflow of capital required by debt servicing, can only be accomplished on a long-term basis. Although some results indicate a rather weak and vague transfer to a policy of export expansion and outward oriented strategy, the sole fact that it took half a decade to stabilize the balance of payments, indicates the difficulties of such changes. They will be hindered by the existing economic structure, which render export expansion more difficult, and by the existing economic system.

The adaptation to external balance has, in the eighties, most seriously affected the share of investment in GDP, which means not only a slower growth of productive capacities and employment, but also, a slower introduction of technological changes. This has, up to now, not even been able to substitute for the decreases in labor inputs and to cope with the increased costs of the social and political superstructure.

Minimal growth rates and the prevention of an even worse economic position within Europe (including Western and Eastern countries) appear to be the uppermost Yugoslavia can hope to attain in the second half of the eighties without massive inflow of foreign capital or very radical reforms, not only of the economic but also of the political system. More serious economic reforms, unaccompanied by political reforms, would only increase the inconsistency between the market system, based on competition, and a political system based on the monopoly of the Party, and on "democratic centralism" which can only lead back to an inefficient administrative system.

References

Bajt, A., 1984: Trideset godina privrednog rasta, in: Ekonomist 38, 1–20, (German translation in Sozialistische Theorie und Praxis 13 (1986); 34–62)
――――, 1986: Preduzetništvo u samoupravnoj socijalističkoj privredi, in: Privredna Kretanja 159; 32–46
Balassa, B./Bertrand, J., 1970: Growth Performance of Eastern European Countries, in: American Economic Review (proceedings) 60; 314–320
Burkett, J., 1983: The Effects of Economic Reform in Yugoslavia. Investment and Trade Policy 1959–1976, IIS University of California
Društveni plan Jugoslavije za razdoblje 1986–1990, in: Službeni list, No. 75 (1985). Beograd
Gey, P./Kosta, J./Quaisser, W., 1985: Sozialismus und Industrialisierung. Frankfurt/New York
Goldstein, S., 1985: Prijedlog 85. Zagreb
Horvat, B., 1971: Yugoslav Economic Policy in the Post-War Period: Problems, Ideas, Institutional Developments, in: American Economic Review (supplement), Vol 61, No.2; 71–169
――――, 1972: Critical Notes on the Theory of the Labor-Managed Firm and Some Macroeconomic Implications, in: Economic Analysis, Vol 6; 291–294
――――, 1985: Jugoslovensko Društvo u Krizi. Zagreb
Jerovsek, J., et al., 1985: Kriza. Blokade i Perspective. Zagreb

Katz, A., 1983: Growth and Regional Variations in Unemployment in Yugoslavia 1965–1980, Economic Department, University of Pittsburgh, working paper

Keren, M., et al., 1983: "The Ratchet": A Dynamic Managerial Incentive Model of the Soviet Enterprise, in: Journal of Comparative Economics, No.4 (1983); 347–367

Kornai, J., 1984: Comments on Papers Prepared in the World Bank about Socialist Countries, World Bank. Washington

Macura, M., 1986: Dugoročna Stabilizacija i Problem Zaposlenosti. Beograd (mimeo)

Mencinger, J., 1983: Otvorena nezaposlenost i zaposleni bez posla, in: Privredna Kretanja No. 128; 27–40

———, 1985: Družbeno planiranje—utvara in realnost obvladovanja prihodnosti, in: Gospodarska Gibanja 149; 36–54

———, 1986: The Yugoslav Economic Systems and Their Efficiency, in: Economic Analysis, No. 1 (1986); 31–43

Popović, S, 1984: Ogled o Jugoslovenskom Privrednom Sistemu. Beograd

Sapir, A., 1980: Economic Growth and Factor Substitution; What happened to the Yugoslav Economic Miracle?, in: Economic Journal, Vol. 90; 294–313

Savezni društveni savet, 1985: Kritička Analiza Funkcionisanja Političkog Sisema Socijalističkog Samoupravljanja. Beograd

———, 1984: Dugoročni Program Ekonomiska Stabilizacije. Beograd

Vanek, J., 1970: The General Theory of Labor-Managed Economies. Ithaca

World Bank, 1983: Yugoslavia: Employment Strategy and Manpower Policies for the 1980s. Washington D.C. (mimeo)

———, 1985: World Development Report 1985—Statistical Appendix. Washington D.C.

7

Hungary's "New Economic Mechanism": Upheaval or Continuity?

Andreas Wass von Czege

Economic Development in the First Half of the 1980s

Starting Points and Targets of the 6th Five Year Plan (1981–1985)

High annual rates of inflation, deficits in the trade balance and accumulated foreign debts as well as low growth rates of national income and domestic consumption mark the situation of the Hungarian economy at the beginning of the 1980s. The annual price increase rate was 8.8% in 1979 and 9.1% in 1980, whereas there was an average annual price increase of 2.8% during the period 1971–1975. In 1978, the trade balance deficit in terms of US-$ reached a record high of more than 1.1 billion US-$. Hungary's net convertible currency debt amounted to more than 3 billion US-$, the annual interest payments exceeded the mark of 350 million US-$.

Having limited sources of energy and raw materials, Hungary is a country particularly dependent on international trade. Therefore, it was hit harder than some other CMEA member states by the developments on world markets during the 1970s, such as the increase of oil prices. For Hungary, this meant not only an increase in the cost of vital imports, but also a decrease in exports. In 1978, for example, the Hungarian export turnover increased by only 0.9% instead of the planned 11%, whereas at the same time import expenditures grew by 12.6% due to unfavorable price developments on world markets (Statisztikai Havi Közlemények, 1/1979).

Table 7.1   Growth Rates of Important Indices of Performance in the
            Five Year Plans of the 1971-1985 Period (Percentages)

Index of performance	1971-1975 actual	1976-1980 actual	1981-1985 plan	Annual average
National income	35	17	14-17	2.9
Industrial production	37	18	19-22	3.8
Agricultural production	26	13	12-15	2.6
Private consumption	26	17	7-9	1.6
Exports	57	40	37-40	6.6
Imports	42	21	16-19	3.3
Investment in industry	35	19	35	6.2
Investment in agriculture	3	-2	12.5	2.4

Source: Wharton Econometric Forecasting Associates, Centrally Planned
Economies Current Analysis, June 8, 1982

Hungary's "New Economic Mechanism," established in 1968, proved
to be too inflexible to adapt the structure of the national economy to
changed world market conditions. Thus, the high expectations concerning
this reform were only rarely fulfilled. The continuing deterioration of
the terms of trade, the increasing debt service and the emerging of
protectionism on world markets necessitated a change of economic policy.
Thus, the relatively modest targets of the 6th Five Year Plan reflected
an orientation towards the re-establishment of external balance and the
maintenance of international solvency (Table 7.1). Until the middle of
the 1980s, Hungarian economic policy was focussed on three basic goals:

- Maintenance of the ability to meet international financial commitments,
- Reestablishment of the equilibrium in foreign exchange by increased
  export attempts, thereby reducing domestic absorption and adjusting
  the production structure towards the needs of the world market,
- Maintenance of the standard of living.

The economic development in the first half of the 1980s, however,
indicated very early that only some of these targets could be realized.

The Consolidation of the Balance of Payments

The drastic increase in the international interest level, as well as a
change in the attitude of the international financial world towards CMEA
member states, caused by the fear of possible insolvency, led to a liquidity

crisis in Hungary in 1981/82 which could be resolved only with the help of the Bank for International Settlements and the International Monetary Fund. Due to the increase in interest rates, Hungary was forced to pay 400 million US-$ more than originally expected during the period 1981 to 1985. In order to meet its commitments, Hungary secured a six-month loan of 500 million US-$ with the BIS and received an additional 600 million US-$ from the IMF. Hungary's membership in the IMF and the World Bank not only resulted in new credit sources (the drawing rights were used only partly in subsequent years), but more importantly in the recognition of Hungary's solvency and credit-worthiness thus facilitating access to international financial markets.

Consequently, in the following years, there was an outflow of an increasing amount of Hungary's national income as an attempt to re-establish external balance. The decline of domestic absorption primarily affected the capital goods industry. In 1984, investments had fallen back to the level of 1974. Later, however, private consumption was affected as well.

By reducing imports and reinforcing their export policy, Hungary tried to maintain its solvency and credit-worthiness on international financial markets even if this meant offsetting the decrease in export revenue by an increase in export quantities.[1] In 1985, the imports in ruble trade were about on the same level as 1980, whereas the volume of exports (due to an attempt to offset the continuously deteriorating terms of trade) exceeded that of 1980 by 34%.

With regard to hard-currency trade with non-socialist countries, Hungary could reduce its foreign debt from more than eight billion US-$ in 1983, to less than four billion US-$ in 1985, due to an overall hard-currency trade surplus of 2.5 billion US-$ in the period from 1982 to 1985. This result, however, was achieved mainly by a reduction of imports (Table 7.2). The attempt to increase world market shares of Hungarian products failed for the following reasons: international demand was stagnating, competition became stronger, Hungarian production and supply structures were not adaptable, marketing was insufficient, the revaluation of the US-$ had an unfavorable effect and, finally, the above mentioned import reduction led to a qualitative deterioration of the Hungarian exports.

Stability at the Expense of Economic Growth and Structural Change

The attempts to stabilize the Hungarian balance of payments were costly: subsidizing the unprofitable but necessary exports became an increasing burden to the government budget, the restrictive import

Table 7.2 Indicators of Economic Development during the 6th and the 7th Five Year Plan Period

Index	6th Five Year Plan 1981-1985 (1980=100)		1981	1982	1983 actual values (previous year=100)	1984	1985	7th Five Year Plan 1986-1990 (1985=100)	1986 plan
	plan	actual							
National income	114-117	106	101.8	101.5	100.5	102.9	99.0	115-117	102.3-102.7
Gross industrial production	119-122	110	102.8	102.4	100.8	102.7	100.8	114-116	102-102.5
Gross agricultural production	112-115	105	100.7	108	99.2	103.3	94	107-110	103-103.5
Consumption	107-109	107	102.4	101	100	101	101.5	108-110	101
Consumer price index	122-128	139	104.6	106.9	107.3	108.3	107	128-139	105
Real wage per capita of workers and employees	100	95	101.4	97.9	97.5	97	100	105	100.5
Real income per capita of population	106-107	107	102.2	100.5	100.5	101	101.5	109-111	101.5
Export turnover	137-140	151	106.5	108.4	115.3	110.7	102.6	116-117	103.5-104.5
Import turnover	116-119	137	104.8	103.4	112.4	107.0	105.0	113-115	101-102

Source: Synopsis by the author

policies hampered economic growth and rendered the essential structural change more difficult.

Whereas agriculture proved to be an important pillar of the Hungarian economy (even if the targets of the Five Year Plan could not always be fulfilled due to unfavorable weather conditions (Table 7.2)) industry was forced to cope with a number of problems. Domestic turnover decreased, particularly in the area of capital goods, because of the government's stabilization policy and the related expenditure cuts and investment reductions: In 1985, the overall demand for capital goods in the socialist sector was 22%, the value of production in the building industry (declining since the beginning of the 1980s) was about 10% below the level of 1980. Industrial export turnover was far below expectations, partly because of worldwide stagnation and partly because of a loss of competitiveness in Hungarian export production. This was not only the result of increasing competition from some newly indus- trialized countries, but a consequence of the weakness in the Hungarian export supply structure, which again was influenced by Hungarian economic policy: Due to the barriers set up and because enterprise revenues could not be retained but were centralized, the necessary investments could not be financed. At the same time, the imposition of import restrictions led to bottlenecks in the supply of some important products, so that growth of industrial production in Hungary stagnated in the first half of the 1980s (Table 7.2).

Therefore, the adaptation of the economic structures to the new world market conditions took place with some delay. The performance of the metallurgical industry, for example, actually decreased between 1981 and 1985 by 7%, whereas the sector of machine building reported a growth of 18%. The bulk of the government grants for investment purposes, however, went into import-substituting industries and the energy sector instead of contributing to a better orientation of production structures towards world market requirements.

Drops in the Population's Standard of Living

Very often the maintenance of the standard of living achieved thus far was stressed as an important objective of the economic policy at the beginning of the 1980s. Although statistics indicate that this target was basically met (Table 7.2), a thorough analysis of the development of the standard of living of different population groups shows considerable deviations from the objectives. Thus, actual wages showed a declining tendency between 1981 and 1985 at which point they were about 5% below the level of 1980. Although the cost of living index decreased from 9.1% in 1980 to 4.6% in 1981, it then again increased continuously amounting to 8.3% in 1984. Altogether, the price level in 1985 was 39% above that in 1980 (instead of the 22%–28% planned). Particularly affected hereby were the country's 2.3 (!) million retired who partly suffered negative impacts on their standard of living. On the other hand, the increasing privatization of certain economic sectors and the newly created opportunities for additional income (i.e. in the form of working teams within state-owned companies) led to growing disproportions in the income distribution and the corresponding social tensions. The latter was demonstrated by growing resistance against the "New Economic Mechanism" and its further developments.

The Second Half of the 1980s: In Search of a "New Path of Growth"

Lines of Development of the 7th Five Year Plan (1986–1990)

The seventh Five Year Plan, implemented as a law on 21 December 1985 (Ministry of Finance (ed), 1986a) was not only (and in contrast to its predecessors) the result of an open and controversial discussion, but was developed for the first time in several versions. Already in the preparatory phase, the most important interest groups and organizations (SZOT, Chamber of Commerce, etc.), as well as scientific committees, were included in the planning procedure. Altogether they submitted more than one hundred proposals for amendments, out of which 50% were accepted and an additional 33% were either passed on to special committees for further treatment, or were postponed.

The plan and its targets are based on an expected economic upswing, accelerating in 1987/88, which can be described as follows:

- The main goal over the next five years appears to be the accelerated modernization of the economy by increasing productivity, efficiency and technological progress: At least two-thirds of the increase in production during the next five years should be achieved by improving efficiency, thereby encouraging an improvement in export performance to reduce the external debt.
- The role of economic growth has been relegated to the third position in terms of the government's priorities, thus less essential over the next five years than "modernization" and the reduction of the external debt: The targeted annual growth of national income (net material product or NMP) is in the range of 2.8% to 3.2%. This is virtually the same as in the previous plan, but represents a marked acceleration from the 1.3% actual average over the last five years.

- Industry is to be the main promoter of development; its share in the NMP (produced) is planned to increase by 22–24%, which reflects the expected impact of modernization and increased productivity in this sector.
- Domestic consumption is expected to stagnate in the first half of the period and pick up thereafter, with an average growth rate of 1.6% to 1.9%. The same trend is foreseen in investment spending, which is scheduled to increase at a faster pace after 1987. Domestic absorption and, above all accumulation, will show the first increase in a long time. Gross investment as a share of domestic absorption should again reach 25% in 1990, so that total national assets are expected to increase by 12% to 15%. 60% of the 1,200–1,250 billion Forint planned for investment purposes will be managed by the enterprises themselves. The population will spend, based on their own savings, an additional 300 billion Forint, supplemented by credits and public grants, which will go mainly into the building of houses.
- The demands concerning the ability and willingness to export will be very high for Hungarian enterprises: To meet commitments of intergovernmental agreements in CMEA-Trade, export shares in the food and light industries must be increased. A problem for Hungary in the coming years will be the reduction of its hard-currency income from trade with the Soviet Union, since the Soviets plan to decrease their hard-currency payments for "hard" imports (wheat, meat, etc.) from Hungary. Pressure from the Soviets for "better" and "higher quality" goods appears to be a first step towards announcing fundamental changes in bilateral trade within the CMEA in the next few years. In addition, the Soviet Union is pressing Hungary to reduce its accumulated ruble debts. In the trade with hard-currency countries, for the further consolidation of the balance of payments, during the next five years annual surpluses of 400–600 million US-$ will be needed, whereby, opposed to earlier years, the manufacturing industry should play a major role.[2]
- For the achievement of the growth targets, external resources can be relied upon only to a very limited degree: The import of energy and raw materials from the CMEA will basically remain on the 1985 level in the coming years; the increase of imports from hard-currency countries will be restrained by the amount of foreign exchange earned and the external indebtedness. The consumption of energy may not increase in the next five years by more than 1%, the consumption of electrical energy by not more than 3% annually and the specific material consumption should decrease by 0.5%–

1% per annum. In order to achieve these targets, several "central
development programs" were prepared.

A summary of the most important targets of the new Five Year Plan,
in comparison to the targets and the degree of success of the expired
6th Five Year Plan (1981–1985), is shown on Table 7.2.

The statements and targets of the new Five Year Plan are controversially
discussed even in Hungary. Among others, the following points of the
7th Five Year Plan were critisized:

• The assessment of economic development in Hungary and on world
  markets is too optimistic, which is reflected in an expected domestic
  inflation rate of only 5–6% per annum.
• It remains unclear as to which sources growth should be based on.
• Neither were the incentive structures and institutional preconditions
  established, nor are the worldwide economic conditions such to
  enable the achievement of the very high export targets.[3]
• Uncertainties remain about the treatment of unprofitable enterprises
  because the new bankruptcy law could not be implemented as
  scheduled by the end of 1985. Hence, structural adjustments will
  still be made only with delay and not to a sufficient extent.
• The measures intended to reduce the huge income disparities in
  some sectors of the economy and to improve the living conditions
  of retired and other disadvantaged groups are insufficient.

Altogether, the critical discussion of the 7th Five Year Plan indicates
that two conceptional problems have not yet been resolved: (1) the
version of the Five Year Plan legally implemented did not sufficiently
satisfy the expectations of all interest groups; (2) it could not be
guaranteed that resources, in the quantities needed for the achievement
of the targets, would be available. The burden to fulfill the plan lies
mainly with the industry and the success will depend on its international
competitiveness. But currently several industrial sectors, i.e. coal mining
and metallurgy, are experiencing major adjustment problems. Last but
not least, the results of 1985 and 1986 do not indicate an end to the
economic crisis in Hungary so that there is no concrete reason to consider
the new Five Year Plan as an example of realistic planning.

Lack of an Upswing in the Years 1985–1986

The optimistic expectations of Hungarian economic policy-makers,
reflected in the figures of the 7th Five Year Plan, cannot be founded
on the most recent economic development. The 1985 results were already

quite dissatisfying. As the data indicate (Table 7.2), the 1985 growth rates of almost all the performance indices were lower than in previous years. Energy consumption and usage of productive resources per unit of output showed an increase for the first time in years. The trade surplus in convertible currency was half that of the previous years and Hungary's net indebtedness on international credit markets increased after a two year period of reduction (Wass von Czege, 1986).

The unfavorable development in 1985 continued at the beginning of 1986: In the first three months industrial production rose by only 1% instead of the 2.8% planned and the increase in productivity was only slightly above that. Nevertheless, wages and salaries increased at a rate of more than 8%, which was considerably higher than in the previous year and the index for the cost of living remained above 7%. Furthermore, the development of the balance of payments was again disadvantageous: On the one hand, imports in convertible currency increased very dynamically (+24%), whereas exports in terms of hard currencies rose only slightly. The reason for this only partly lies in the unfavorable development of the terms of trade.[4] One major cause of the economic downswing with regards to the new Five Year Plan is the Hungarian Economic Mechanism and the strategies used by enterprises as a result: again in 1985 the enterprises succeeded in increasing their profits as compared to the prior year despite their poor performance and unfavorable economic development, whereas the budget deficit of the government increased more than planned. While profits increased by 6% in 1985, up to almost 232 million Forint (mainly due to additional public grants to unprofitable enterprises and sectors) the public deficit reached a record of 16 billion Forint instead of the 2.5 billions planned. These figures indicate a very questionable redistribution of income from the strong and profitable enterprises to the weak and unprofitable ones who receive government subsidies. The system set up to regulate enterprise income causes the enterprises to strive for maximum wages and premium payments and, accordingly, to neglect long-term investment.[5] Thus, Hungarian enterprises are more oriented towards the administration authorities than towards market events.

The developments in 1985 and 1986 and the difficulties in fulfilling the targets of the new Five Year Plan, caused the Hungarian economic policy-makers to focus again on the consolidation of the balance of payments and the maintenance of price stability. Thus, Hungary was the first CMEA member to lower the targets of its plan and correspondingly to take some temporary measures, partly to restrain the financial scope of the enterprises,[6] and partly to stimulate exports to western countries.[7]

Hence, the rise in competitiveness of Hungarian export products on world markets is the basis of a future economic upswing and the fulfillment of the new Five Year Plan. The preconditions for this, however, are far-reaching changes in the economic mechanism leading to a long-term structural improvement and an increase in efficiency.

Hungary's "New Economic Mechanism"— Crisis-Handling or a Third Way to Socialism?

The Reform Concept of 1968—Pretension and Reality

The main principles of Hungary's "New Economic Mechanism" (NEM), established in 1968, were, in short:

1. Economic organizations decide what and in which quantities they want to produce and on which markets they want to sell or buy. Thus, the choice of partners as well as the choice among different forms of transaction remained in the domain of the enterprises.
2. Macroeconomic planning is separated from autonomous enterprise planning. Enterprises participate in macroeconomic planning only by providing information and proposals but are not obliged to fulfill any quantitative targets broken down from the macroeconomic plans to the enterprise level. The annual as well as the medium term National Economic Plans set the major objections of economic development, define the means of their implementation and prescribe the obligatory direction of economic control activities by the Council of Ministers and other governmental bodies. Although compulsory for the government, the approved plan figures serve only as guidelines for the economic organizations.
3. Economic organizations as well as households coordinate their plans and activities on markets, which are basically controlled by the government according to macroeconomic plans. Government activity, however, may not substitute or replace these market forces and relations.
4. The implementation of the objectives defined by the National Economic Plans is to be achieved by central regulation of the economy. The latter is the result of the joint impact of income regulators such as taxation, credit terms, creation and utilization of funds and other instruments of fiscal and/or monetary policy. Direct intervention and administrative rules are used only exceptionally as means of economic control and management.

In practice, this reform concept could be realized in the 1970s only to a certain extent. The reasons for this were of a complex nature.

The worldwide economic conditions, strongly rising prices for energy and raw materials, stagnating demand and increasing competition on Hungary's most important export markets as well as its foreign indebtedness reaching the solvency limits, made short-term stabilization targets more urgent than (long-term) institutional reforms.

The shifts in spheres of influence and reorganization of communication and coordination procedures related to the reforms were heavily resisted by the organizations concerned. This phenomenon is generally referred to as "organizational barriers towards innovation" by behavioral scientists.

Imperfections and inconsistencies in the reform concept made indirect management of the conduct of economic organizations more difficult. Therefore, administrative interventions by government bodies in the market mechanism were necessary. Such conceptional errors were, among others:

- confinement of the measures of the reform to the system of economical planning and management without the accompanying re-organizational measures, which could have abolished the inflexible and hierarchical coordination structures;
- the renunciation of a precise definition and limitation of government intervention into the management of enterprises. This led to very frequent interventions on the part of the administration, disturbing independent entrepreneurial activities;
- the orientation of "economic regulators" towards annual profits of enterprises, although enterprises' decisions and actions are, in practice, often more determined by other factors, for example, "expectations" of ministries, size of wage funds to be received, travelling opportunities of management.

Therefore, the limited autonomy was again removed from the enterprises in the 1970s as a result of stabilization-policy restrictions (import, wage and price controls, investment freeze and withdrawal of liquidity), or because of a lack of efficiency of the indirect management system. Moreover, enterprises very often did not exercise their rights because of existing uncertainties, a lack of incentives and/or failing entrepreneurial mentality. Even if market relationships were admitted in principle, they could not be developed because governmental interventions were still too dominant. The traditional, hierarchically structured forms of interaction between government and enterprises remained the same, but were now executed, because of the lack of institutional and legal bases, mostly via informal, and therefore uncontrollable channels.

The lack of efficiency in this interventional economic policy in the 1970s led to a major change in the reform policy, initiated by a decision of the central committee in April 1978.

The Reforms in the First Half of the 1980s—
Principles and Results

At the core of the reforms of the economic mechanism implemented in the early 1980s were changes in the organizational system of the economy, which were consciously avoided in the reform policy before due to the given power structures. A distinction can be made between:

- redistribution of functions and competence within the government administration,
- changes in the field of interaction between government administration and economic organizations.

The reforms within the government administration were aimed at reducing the influence of the branch ministries in favor of the more functional and not branch-dependent organs of economic policy (Ministry of Finance, National Bank of Hungary, State Price and Material Office etc.). Among the most important measures in this area were:

1. the organizational merger in 1981 of three branch ministries into one Ministry of Industry with half the number of employees;
2. the expansion of functions and reinforcement of competences of the National Bank responsible for supplying the economy with liquidity (right of co-operation in the development of the economic plans, formation of economic policy and execution of the "guide-lines for credit policy" determined by the Council of Ministers (Law Decrees No. 25/1984 and 26/1984, Magyar Közlöny, 31 October 84);
3. the extension of the range of instruments for fiscal policy in the Ministry of Finance i.e., introducing new tools,[8] and the rein-forcement of its influences on market organization and regulation (Ministry of Finance, ed., 1985a);
4. the transformation of the State Price and Material Office (OAAH) from an authority responsible only for price control and manage-ment of materials to one in charge of market supervision (very similar to the German "Bundeskartellamt") and having far-reaching competences concerning market organization and regulation.[9]

Closely related to the redistribution of functions and competences within the central administration of the economy was the institutional reshaping of relationships between these central planning authorities and the single economic organizations. In this area as well, the reforms carried out in the early 1980s were aimed at strengthening the influence of monetary and fiscal policy on the economic process, and at the same time at reducing direct interventions into business activity of enterprises. This was accomplished, e.g., by:

- measures to deconcentrate;
- new organizational and legal forms for small-scale production;
- delegation of property rights from the government to the enterprises;
- extension of monetary and credit relationships, creation of opportunities for the promotion of market coordination and establishment of competition between enterprises.

The deconcentration of Hungarian industry, which has one of the highest degrees of concentration within Europe to date,[10] was primarily intended to create competitive market relationships between enterprises by increasing the number of market participants. On the other hand, it was meant to create a sound structure among large-scale, medium-scale and small-scale enterprises, as well as to reduce the number of hierarchic management levels by an almost complete abolishment of the trust organizations which had monopolistic positions in most of the sections of the economy before (Keveváry, 1980). Between 1980 and 1985, the number of trust organizations decreased from 24 to 9 and more than 400 new and independent economic organizations were created partly by dissolution of these trusts and partly by division of enterprises. At the same time, the extension of the scope of administration for the economic organizations led to the foundation of more than 200 subsidiaries mainly in the form of small enterprises and about 400 small cooperatives. The possibility of small-scale production, newly created in 1982 (also on a private or half-private basis), further increased the number of suppliers where particularly the "working teams within enterprises" reported a dynamic development. At the beginning of 1986, the number of these working teams was about 23,000, in which 262,000 workers achieved an annual production turnover of about 16 billion Forint.

Nevertheless, the result of the executed measures of deconcentration and the increase in organizational forms within the industry did not completely fulfill the expectations. Most of the newly created enterprises have a labor force of 800–1,500 employees, so that small and medium-sized companies, which could stimulate competition, are still almost non-existent. Among the 460 sub-sectors in the Hungarian industry, there is not a single one, in which the largest supplier has a market share of less than 51%, and there are only a few markets in which the two largest suppliers together have a market share of less than 75% (Figyelö No. 2, 9 January 1986).

Up until now, competition has developed only in borderline areas (i.e. some consumer goods) and the expected increase in efficiency and the qualitative improvement of supplies has not yet occurred. This is due to the continuance of traditional management and coordination structures, the seller-orientated situation which still exists on almost all product markets and the lack of entrepreneurial potential.

The delegation of property rights to state-owned enterprises took place step by step during the last few years: Between 1981 and 1985, 140 enterprises were newly entitled to independently execute foreign trade activities, so that the overall number reached 270 at the beginning of 1986. Furthermore, the organizational scope of state-owned enterprises was enhanced by modifications which considerably extended the possibilities of institutionalized, intercompany cooperation, made the foundation of subsidiaries possible and changed the Company Law, which in turn enlarged the scope of legal forms for a company. Already at the beginning of the 1980s, the obligation of production enterprises was loosened by a legal act according to which enterprises may make up to 30% of their overall turnover without special permission in addition to their normal business activities stipulated in their statutes.

Finally, the competences concerning the choice of activity and employment of top managers were extended and even some of the rights of public employees, e.g. the selection and sanctioning of deputy directors and department heads, was delegated to the enterprise level. The bulk of directors' posts of state-owned enterprises was publicly tendered from 1983 onwards and the positions were filled in cooperation with the enterprises concerned (Figyelö No. 34, 23 August 1984). A decisive step in this development was made in 1985/86 with the introduction of the so-called "New Forms of Management," based on the enterprises' rights of self-management, which had been already exercized in the frame of the cooperative movement.[11]

In most of the state-owned enterprises operating in the "competitive sector," the control and management by supervisory authorities were replaced by two new forms of management: The enterprise-council and, in smaller organizations, the general assembly, or the assembly of employee delegates. According to preliminary estimates, the implementation of these new forms will affect about 75% of all state-owned enterprises. Excluded are public utility companies and economic organizations, working mainly for other CMEA-countries or national defence purposes.

A common feature of these two forms of management is the collective nature of all decisions concerning problems related to enterprise strategy.[12]

The enterprise-councils (EC) exist in all companies with a labor force of more than 500 people and are composed of management representatives and of elected workforce delegates, the latter representing not less than 50% of the EC members. The general manager, who is elected for a set period by the EC, is also a member, but not necessarily the chairman, of this strategic decision-making body. The management representatives in the EC are appointed by the general manager, who will also autonomously control the enterprise in the future with full responsibility within the framework of strategic decisions made by the EC.[13] In case of smaller enterprises (with a labor force of less than 500 people), the board of directors must be elected and the activities are controlled by an auditing commission, composed of employee delegates.

The autonomy of enterprises can be extended in both of the new forms of management by the fact that the enterprise's organization and activities are controlled entirely by its collective (even including the decision to cooperate with another enterprise). The increasing autonomy also manifests itself in the fact that, by transferring the rights of the employer, over the general manager to the collective (or to an institution), the supervision of the enterprise will be replaced by the exertion of the founder's rights and by legal supervision. The rights of the founder (implemented by the organ which founded the enterprise) affect matters of basic existence (e.g. the liquidation of an enterprise), the preliminary consent to the election of the general manager, and finally, to extend instructions on the implementation of production or service tasks which cannot be enforced in any other way (Decree No. 23/1984 of the Presidential Council, Magyar Közlöny, 31 October 1984).

The separation of entrepreneurial activity from central economic planning established by the "New Forms of Management," correspondingly requires an independent representation of the interest of enterprises towards the government. This role will be taken over in the future by the "Hungarian Chamber of Commerce" which, in the frame of the most recent economic reforms, obtained a number of new functions and competences in the field of interaction between enterprises and the central economic planning bodies (Beck, 1985; 11; Lantai, 1986a; 8–10; Pacsay, 1986; 8).

The significance of the institutionalization and articulation of group interests in the process of economic policy decision-making was clearly recognized in Hungary. Reforms in this area, however, are very often rejected by the party and the unions, which are "primary" organizations within the society, thus not subject to legal supervision, and function as representatives of the "Common Interest." Although until now, these organizations strongly influenced decision-making on all levels of the economy, this was very often not institutionalized or legally regulated. Within the frame of the new reform concept, however, their tasks and competences are openly discussed, specified and based on legal regulations. The unions' influence must be redefined, particularly in the area of the "New Forms of Management."

Of particular importance to the reform concept in the 1980s are the measures for strengthening "indirect" economic management with the help of economic regulators. A significant step in this direction was the transformation of banks from administrative organs, or agents, of central economic management to independent and profit-oriented partners of enterprises. In order to realize this transformation, the number of banks and credit institutions was increased by way of reorganizational measures within the banking system. At the same time, the creation of new institutions was made easier and their credit scope was enlarged (Timár, 1984; 1041–1046; Ministry of Finance, 1985b). By facilitating inter-company credits, e.g. in the form of trade credits, bills of exchange business, emission of obligations or transfer of development funds for the execution of joint investments, the base of a rudimentary capital market was formed. The utilization of these new forms of financing, however, was relatively low in the first half of the 1980s. The possibility of emission and purchase of obligations established in 1983 was used only very hesitantly and enterprises were more interested in emitting than in purchasing obligations. Up to the beginning of 1986, obligations worth 4 billion Forint were sold (Lantai, 1986b; 10; Pacsi, 1986). Even the other forms of intercompany credit in Hungary were accepted slowly. Thus, only 331 bills of exchange, worth 3.7 billion Forint, were sold to the Hungarian National Bank. Even the financing of investment credits play a minor role in Hungary: In 1985, for instance, only 26 out of the total 190 billion Forint invested were financed by credits.

The emerging interbank competition as well as the decentralized flow of credits and capital between enterprises and sectors, open up new possibilities for central economic management. Thus, the liquidity of enterprises as well as the size and direction of monetary flows can be influenced, according to macroeconomic objectives by a flexible interest and exchange rate policy on the one hand, and by measures of regulation in the banking system and the minimum reserve policy newly established in 1985 on the other hand.

The promotion of market coordination and the creation of competition between enterprises was carried out using a number of measures established in the 1980s concerning market organization and regulation. Market organization and regulation are elements of the so-called market surveillance, a term which was used for the first time in 1980. Precisely, this means "the continuing and organized observation, evaluation and influencing of *domestic* markets; particularly the development of supply and demand, prices and the factors which can influence the former on a *short-term basis*" (Resolution of the Council of Ministers No. 1060/ 1980, in Magyar Közlöny, 21 December 1980; empathized by the author).

One of the instruments of market organization is the possibility of influencing the size and development of concentration of enterprises (the State Price and Material Office obtained co-operative rights concerning decisions about foundations, reorganization or liquidation of enterprises and has the authority to launch related initiatives). Another instrument consists of the planning and execution of centralized programs for economizing material and energy (Bakonyi, 1986; 1–8; Sziksay, 1986; 5–10). Changes in the price system and in price regulation, an increase in the possibility of administrative intervention in business activities and the extension of the "intervention fund," however, serve the purpose of market regulation more effectively.[14]

The legal basis for market creating and regulating measures is the law concerning interdiction of dishonest economic activity, giving the authorities a wide range of possibilities to sanction the illegal conduct of enterprises.[15] Unique about this reform concept is the *active* influence which the organs of central economic management have on market organizations and on competition: Instead of leaving the creation of markets to the spontaneity of decentrally coordinated economic processes, interventions are intended to create possibilities of market coordination. At the same time the organization of markets and the intensity of competition are to be influenced according to the objectives of the overall economic plan.

The OAAH's increase of power related to this form of economic control, is controversial in Hungary particularly because the branch ministries, which already suffered from a loss of power within the frame of other reforms, fear the emergence of a new "super-ministry," at though other branch ministries besides the OAAH can exert market supervision in their area of responsibility; the Ministry of Industry, for instance, in the area of energy production and consumption, the Ministry of Transport in the area of transport and traffic and the Ministry of Domestic Trade in the area of trade with consumer goods. The branch ministries, however, want to participate at least in the decisions regarding the distribution of the "Intervention Fund." Therefore, the government stresses that the emphasis of the OAAH's future activities lies in avoiding market disturbances by market-oriented measures and in establishing a corresponding information system. The strategic decisions remain in the competence of the Plan Commission, or the Economic Commission, of the government, whereas the influence of the OAAH is limited to short-term measures concerning market processes.

The Reform Package for the Period 1986-1990

The further development of the Hungarian Economic Mechanism is aimed at the improvement of the working conditions of enterprises and the expansion of their earning opportunities. Therefore, the decision-making process with regards to labor, previously in the hands of the public economic administration and the enterprises, will be changed and the appropriation capacities of capital goods are to be expanded in favor of the enterprises. The 7th Five Year Plan, in its paragraphs 74–92 determines the direction of further reforms in detail.

Based on these and other statements, the most important reform measures in the years ahead are:

- the transformation of the transitional period to the so-called "New Forms of Management" in state-owned enterprises, which began in 1985 and is scheduled for completion by the end of 1986;
- the strengthening of interest in property and/or capital assets on the part of economic agents by increasing their appropriation capacities with regard to state-owned capital goods;
- the delegation of central competences for decision-making to (regional) councils, including more complete financial independence for the latter (Ministry of Finance, 1986b);
- the strengthening of the market's control function through further liberalization of the wage and price system, the promotion of competition between enterprises, the creation of new markets and the termination of unprofitable activities with the help of a new bankruptcy law (Népszabadság No. 269, 16 November 1985; 5);
- the execution of a comprehensive tax reform, including the establishment of a unified income tax system by 1987/88. In addition, the taxation of enterprises is to be modified so that the strongpoint of taxation lies in the sphere of turnover and not in the sphere of production (Figyelö No. 46, 7 November 1985; 11–14; Népszabadság No. 262, 12 November 85; 21; Heti Világgazdaság No. 46, 16 November 1985; 53);
- the further development of the capital market, which was partially established at the beginning of the 1980s by the creation of a share market. And later, the transition to a double-phase banking system and the attachment of major importance to credit policy in the frame of economic control;

- the development of new mechanisms for the balancing of interests among different economic groups.[16]

Although these reform objectives indicate a strong emphasis on market coordination and an increasing recognition of consumer sovereignty, as well as the plurality of interests in the Hungarian economy, this still does not mean that the basic socialist principles of the Hungarian economy have been abandoned. This is stressed in the individual sections of the new Five Year Plan, where, i.e., the following issues are mentioned:

- The continuation of a central price policy (§78);
- The maintenance of direct central decisions, primarily concerning the structural development of the economy (§81);
- The prevention of "dishonest economic activities" with the help of reinforced central price control (§83);
- The maintenance of central quota determination and inventory control concerning single groups of products (§89).

It will heavily depend on the conduct of the agents of economic policy in these tense areas, as to how far the above mentioned reform ideas can be realized and, therefore, whether the export trade can be maintained, which is vital to the fulfillment of the new Five Year Plan and the mastering of the current economic crisis.

Particularities, Tendencies and Limits of
the Hungarian Reform Model

The Hungarian attempt to utilize the information, incentive and coordination functions of the "market," while maintaining the basic principles of a socialist economy (common property of capital goods, primacy of planning, leading role of the party), is not a deviation per se from similar reform attempts in other CMEA countries. Characteristic for the Hungarian reforms, however, is the existence of a comprehensive conception, the dynamic and intense execution of amendments (as compared to other CMEA countries) and the inclusion of sensitive areas, such as the organization of the organs of central economic planning, the banking system and the organs for the representation of the interests of different social groups.

The continuity in the development of the Hungarian reforms, which began in the middle of the 1960s (only at the beginning of the 1970s were there some tendencies towards recentralization)[17] indicates that the intention of the reforms is not a form of crisis-handling on a short-term basis. In spite of the critical economic development in Hungary at the end of the 1970s, the resolution of the MSZMP Central Committee (Hungarian Socialist Party) in December 1978 and their statement on 17 April 1984 concerning the tasks of further developing the economic mechanism, both reflect the continuation of the basic concepts of the "New Economic Mechanism" established in 1968.

The shifts of power experienced among the individual organs of central economic management, and between these and the enterprises, as well as the consequently recognized plurality of interests and their permanent institutionalization, might lead to a conflict of interests, which can be destabilizing for the political system. Potential areas of conflict result from instabilities within the society induced by the reforms due to a decrease in job security and an increase in income disparities which are diametrically opposed to the socialist objectives of guaranteed full employment, stability of the price levels and equal incomes. Here, the fundamental conflict between socialist ethics and system-neutral thinking, in terms of efficiency, arises (Kornai, 1980). Finally, the Hungarian enterprises lack the financial means necessary to take full advantage of the additional leeway created by the reforms. This applies in particular to the high performing enterprises. The short-term target of the maintenance of domestic and external balance in Hungary still dominates the reform attempts on a long-term basis. Thus, in Hungary, as opposed to other CMEA countries, reforms and economic crises are pitted against one another. In the long run, the reforms should facilitate a flexible adaptation to the economic crisis, or better still, avoid them. In the short run, however, the existence of such crises and the related measures of economic policy, impede a realization of the reform objectives.

The areas of tension and conflict mentioned above, however, do not only jeopardize the realization of a reform concept in Hungary, but even impede the communication of these reform ideas to other CMEA countries, where even the basic conditions responsible for the relative success in Hungary are lacking.

To be mentioned here is the unique structure of the Hungarian party which, based on the experiences made in 1956, has continuously moved towards a system of decision-making which is flexible and open for criticism and experiment. The party, or essential forces within the party, are presently the pillars of the Hungarian economic reform. The party's power has never been doubted and the present conditions do not indicate that this might change in the near future. The small size of the country and the high degree of organizational concentration in Budapest lead to close personal relations among the leaders of the party, the government and the economy. This, along with the ethnical, lingual and cultural homogeneity of the population assure a domestic stability which does not exist in other CMEA countries. This stability enables a relative tolerance towards activities in the second economy and other activities. It also allows a relatively unlimited flow of information within and particularly beyond the bounds of the system. This in turn facilitates the formation of "human capital" which is a precondition for, and at the same time, result of the Hungarian reforms.

However, the information flow across borders and the resulting contact to partners in, and particularly outside, the socialist world have political implications which are carefully observed by the Soviet Union who fears an infiltration of damaging ideas causing destabilizing effects. Thus, other less stable CMEA countries are not very eager to imitate the Hungarian reform concept.

Hungary's type of socialism (unique in the Eastern Bloc, particularly in the field of economics) is limited due to Hungary's integration in an economical, political and military bloc. Thus, the scope of any possible reform is determined, as in all CMEA countries, by the "four S's: *Security, Soviet domination, Stability,* and *System compatibility*" (Hans-Hermann Höhmann). Although the contents of these terms clearly need interpretation, which is influenced by where and when this is done, the act of interpretation is traditionally reserved to the Soviet Union who therefore determines the scope of reforms in any CMEA country.

Notes

1. The loss in export income due to a price decrease in Hungarian export products during the period 1981 to 1985, is estimated at more than 110 billion Forint (overall exports in 1985: 424.6 billion Forint). If only the 1985 food exports alone were to be carried out at 1981 prices, export revenues would increase by 600 million US-$ (the trade balance surplus, in terms of US-$, amounted to 303 million US-$ in 1985).

2. The plan for 1986–1990 forecasts an increase of 35–40% in hard-currency exports of machine-building products, whereas the effective increase was only 20% from 1981–1985.

3. The worldwide upswing in the coming years is expected to take place mainly in the Pacific area, as compared to Western European countries, who are the main importers of Hungarian products. At the same time the competition from Third World countries is growing steadily.

4. The drastic fall of the oil prices in the first half of 1986, for instance, will lead to a clear reduction of export revenues for the Hungarian oil refinery, which turned out to be one of the large foreign currency profit-makers in the past years: According to estimates, the reduction of hard-currency exports will amount to 100–200 million US-$.

5. Moreover, wage payments above plan in 1985 and 1986 were made out of amortization funds. This was made possible by the fact that the funding system and the creation of funds were liberalized at the beginning of 1985. The

management of enterprises are forced to increase wage payments because of their increasing dependency on the (qualified) personal, which is still insufficient. This deteriorated even further after the most recent reforms.

6. These measures include the raising of corporation income tax from 35% to 40%, a wage freeze for a number of unprofitable enterprises, stricter price controls and cuts in subsidies.

7. For the promotion of hard-currency exports, the Forint was devaluated, export-promoting investments were exempted from accumulation tax, and leasing facilities were created. Apart from this, exporting enterprises were offered special credit lines and easier access to the necessary import licenses.

8. Thus, a 10% payroll tax, a 3% property tax and an "accumulation tax" determined annually according to the economic needs, were established and put into effect on 1 January 1985. For more details on the Hungarian tax reforms see also Ministry of Finance (ed): Income Regulation System of the Hungarian Enterprises as valid from 1985 onwards, Public Finance in Hungary No. 22, Budapest 1985.

9. See Decree No. 37/1984 (MT) of the Council of Ministers on market surveillance, published in Magyar Közlöny 5 November 1984.

10. In the 1960s, Hungary experienced a wave of concentration initiated by the central administration, which led to a decline in the number of state-owned industrial enterprises from 1,368 to 840. After the economic reform, this trend continued at a slower pace, this time initiated by the enterprises themselves: In 1970, 812, and in 1979 only 702 state-owned industrial enterprises were reported. Concerning the development of the concentration of Hungarian industry and its consequences, see I. Schweitzer, A vállalatnagyság, Budapest 1982.

11. See Law-Decree No. 22/1984 on the modification of the Act No. VI/1977 on State Enterprises as well as Decree No. 33/1984 (MT) of the Council of Ministers on the implementation of Act No. VI/1977 on State Enterprises, both published in: Magyar Közlöny, 31 October 1984.

12. For the similarities and differences between enterprises managed by an enterprise council or by a general assembly, delegate meeting, and for the characteristic features of the new forms of management in general, see Ministry of Finance (ed): Introduction of New Forms of Management in State Enterprises, in: Public Finance in Hungary No. 21, Budapest 1985.

13. The EC's range of authority includes, among others, the selection or recall of the general manager, the reorganization of the enterprise (e.g. union with or separation from other enterprises), the establishment and change of the organizational and business rules, the approval of the medium and short-term plans as well as of the balance-sheets and the declaration of the principles of income distribution within the enterprise.

14. The intervention fund, financed by the central budget, was directed up until now by the government's economic commission which used the money to influence market processes.

15. Cf. Law No. IV/1984 concerning the Interdiction of Dishonest Economic Activity and the Decree of the Council of Ministers No. 31/1984 concerning

the Detection of Dishonest Prices, both published in Magyar Közlöny, 31 October 1984.

16. Among the reforms in this area are the institutionalization of special organs for the representation of the interests of previously unorganized groups within the society (senior staff, working teams within state-owned enterprises, etc.), as well as the strengthening of the competences and influence of existing interest organizations, such as SZOT (National Council of the Unions) and the Chamber of Commerce.

17. Thus, in the resolution of the MSZMP central committee, on 2 November 1972, it was agreed to grant special preferences to large-scale enterprises and in the Plan Law of 1972 the competences of the National Planning Office (Országos Tervhivatal) were considerably extended. Cf. Law No. VII/1972, published in Magyar Közlöny, 22 December 1972.

References

Bakonyi, A., 1986: A gazdaságos anyag elhaználásra irányuló program három éve, in: Ipargazdaság, No. 3/1986; 1–8

Beck, T., 1985: Neuer Status der Ungarischen Handelskammer, in: Ungarische Wirtschaftshefte, No. 4/1985; 11f.

Kevevári, B., 1980: Some General Problems of Trust Organizations in Hungary, in: Acta Oeconomica, Vol. 24, No. 1–2/1980; 125–137

Kornai, J., 1980: The Dilemma of a Socialist Economy: The Hungarian Experience, in: Cambridge Journal of Economics, No. 4/1980; 147–157

Lantai, A., 1986a: Die Ungarische Handelskammer wird aktiver, in: Wochenbulletin No. 8, 21 February 1986; 8–10

————, 1986b: Erfahrungen mit Obligationen in Ungarn, in: Wochenbulletin No. 7, 7 February 1986; 10f.

Ministry of Finance, ed., 1985a: Scope of Authority and Duties of the Minister of Finance, in: Public Finance in Hungary No. 25, Budapest

————, 1985b: Act on Public Finances, in: Public Finance in Hungary, No. 23, Budapest

————, 1986a: Act on the 7th Five-Year Plan, in Public Finance in Hungary, No. 29, Budapest

————, 1986b: The Management of Councils, in Public Finance in Hungary, No. 26. Budapest

Pacsi, Z., 1986: A kötvények három éve, in: Népszabadság No. 6, 8 January 1986

Pacsay, V., 1986: Interessenvertretung von Direktoren der Unternehmen, in: Wochenbulletin, No. 9, 28 February; 8

Schweitzer, I., 1982: A vállalatnagyság. Budapest

Szikszay, B., 1986: Az anyagforrások ésszerü hasznosításának tapasztalatai és feladatai a VII. ötéves tervben, in: Ipargazdaság, No. 1/1986; 5–10

Timár, M., 1984: Az anyagi eröforrások áramlásának és a bankrendszer továbbfejlesztésének nehány idöszerü kérdése, in: Közgazdasági szemle, No. 9/ 1984; 1041–1046

Wass von Czege, A., 1986: Ungarn 1985/86—Mit Startschwierigkeiten in das neue Planjahrfünft, in: K. Bolz, ed., 1986: Die wirtschaftliche Entwicklung in den sozialistischen Ländern Osteuropas zur Jahreswende 1985/86. Hamburg; 289–336

8

The Chinese Economic Reform: Approaches, Results and Prospects

Jiří Kosta

The Struggle for the Economic Reform

The outset of the economic reform in China is usually seen as coinciding with the 3rd Plenary Session of the Party's 11th Central Committee, which took place in December 1978 (Ma, 1983; 26). It has been a gradual, prolonged process, starting with the defeat of the Leftists ("Gang of Four") in the Fall of 1976 and reaching its temporary peak with the decision on the "Reform of the Economic Structure," taken in October 1984 (Decision, 1984).

The approach to the new system, based on a combination of planning and market elements, was by no means rectilinear (Kosta, 1983; 60–67/Lin, 1985; 66–69/Schram, 1984; 431–437). The first break-through in 1978, and the following ups and downs of the reform course, can be traced back primarily to the power constellation within the leadership. The more the group close to Deng Xiaoping gained ground, the further the reform advanced. In order to uphold the alliance with his orthodox combatants (Chen Yun and others), Deng did not hesitate to brake the speed of the reform while eliminating the old vanguard step by step. A temporary weakening of the reformers' position, from 1981 to 1983, was the reason for some setbacks.

Looking back at the history of the People's Republic, the interplay between politics, ideology and economics has always been obvious. This interrelationship has become particularly distinct through the economic disaster of the Great Leap Forward (GL: 1958–1960) and the stagnation of the Chinese economy during the Cultural Revolution (CR: 1966–1976). It was the utopian concept of the leftist group which caused the collapse of the economy in both cases, and it was this crisis which

145

contributed decisively to the victory of the pragmatic wing under Deng (Kosta, 1985b; 229–238).

After 1978, the interdependence between economics and politics appeared in a somewhat modified form. When the reform measures entailed distinct successes, then the reformers' position within the leadership was strengthened. The best example for this phenomenon were the excellent results in agriculture after the "responsibility system" was introduced (Quaisser, 1986). This logic is also conversly true: all difficulties which arose during the implementation of new measures appeared to be a support for the Conservatives. This was the case when inflationary tendencies, unemployment, corruption, etc. arose. In such cases, the weight of the "Old Ones" increased, who pleaded for more planning, centralization and political education (battle against "Spiritual Pollution") (Kosta 1982/84/85).

The debates on the decentralization of the Chinese industry, however, went on after 1978. Notwithstanding the ongoing controversy between the plan and the market-orientation in the urban economy, it was rather the market-oriented reform concept[1] which was gradually implemented in the agricultural sector (Quaisser, 1986). Between 1979 and 1983, partial reform measures were only sluggishly implemented in Chinese industry. Before 1984, the factual situation in a Chinese industrial enterprise did not differ too much from that in any other country where Soviet-type planning was applied. In one aspect the Chinese system was even more rigid than in Eastern Europe, i.e. in the field of labor allocation; here the principles of imperative assignment and job tenure were practiced (Kosta 1985a; 137).

The reform chances improved with the gradual loosening of the political and ideological atmosphere in 1983 (Schram, 1984; 436–438). A State reform commission prepared a document which intended to formulate a comprehensive reform concept for the urban sectors. No doubt, the final reform decision which was passed in October 1984 (Decision, 1984) was the result of many foregoing controversies, not only among the experts, but also, as mentioned above, within the political leadership.

The contents of the October Document show, in spite of some compromises, a break-through towards a market-oriented reform (see also Group, 1985). However, this does not mean that the conflict between the protagonists of the market concept (see note 1) and their opponents, has come to an end (Hang, 1985).

The Main Features of the Reform Concept, 1984–1986

Decision Structure, Plan and Market

The crucial point of the decision structure in socialist economic systems is the position of the enterprise vis-à-vis the "upper institutions," such as ministries, planning offices and regional bodies. Moreover, the role of the Party in economic decision making under "real socialism" cannot be excluded.

The Leading Role of the Party: Although there is not much concrete evidence in Chinese sources on this subject, it does not appear that there has been an obvious weakening in the traditional "leading role of the Party" within the economy. Nevertheless, a certain tendency towards a clearer distinction in decision making can be observed, namely between Party organs on the one hand, and State or economic institutions (enterprises included) on the other. Emphasizing the weight of expertise and qualification, in its consequence might reduce the discretionary competence of the Party Committee in plants and other economic units (Kosta, 1982/84/85).

Strengthening the Independence of the Enterprise vis-à-vis the Upper Bodies: It is the explicit objective of the reform to "separate government from enterprise functions," in other words to release enterprises from their former dependency on superior institutions such as ministries, regional departments, etc., and to "invigorate" them to "become producers of, and in, commodities, responsible for the own profit and loss" (Decision, 1984; 8–12; 19–24). The intention was to reduce the number and size of the giant bureaucratic institutions of the past and, at the same time, to reshape a good part of the administrative bodies into economic organizations or associations. Some doubts can be articulated as far as the realization of this idea is concerned.

Workers' Participation in Decision Making: One should bear in mind that Mao's "mass line," with its absoluteness of workers' rule ignoring expertise discredited the principle of workers' control in general (Kosta, 1984; 115–117). This might be the reason why the democratization of decision making did not play a greater role in the reform concept. The emphasis placed on managerial and technical competence at the enterprise level, being an understandable reaction to the former leftist practices, might have counteracted to a rehabilitation of real participation. True, there were appeals and recommendations to develop and strengthen the workers' conferences to participatory bodies within the enterprises, to organize elections of managers, etc. (Decision, 1984; 8–12, 19–24). But it seems that such democratic procedures are rather the exception than the rule in China today.

Property Rights: The main change regarding the ownership of production means refers to the quasi-privatization in the agricultural sector (Quaisser, 1986). In the urban industries (including services), the rise of small scale, one-man or family-owned shops, sometimes private enterprises employing a certain number of workers, is a new phenomenon appearing to a larger extent in recent years (Kraus, 1986; 1–18). According to official statistics, the number of "individual laborers" in cities and towns increased from 150 thousand in 1978 to 1,130 thousand in 1982 and to 3,390 in 1984 (SYCh, 1985; 235). The majority of these deal with retail trades and catering. Another source (Liu, 1986; 19–20) indicates that 11 million households, with 16 million members, undertake private business (in September 1985) throughout the country; this includes 2.6 million households with 3.6 million members in the urban area. However, the country-wide share of their output in total industry (in 1984) represented only 0.2%, whereas the proportion of private retail trade (including catering) in the national trade turnover amounted to 9.6%. Chinese comments on this "heritical" tendency is, of course, more pragmatic than ideological: both supply difficulties and employment problems will be overcome easier, it is said, in this way (Decision, 1984; 29).

Another feature of the reform is the shift in the proportion of collective to state owned property (Tang/Ma, 1985; 633–637). It is more the transformation of state to collective enterprises (many of which were formerly collectively organized) than the foundation of new collective units that has lead to this development. In 1984, the proportion of industrial output was about 3:1 (state to collectively-owned industry); the proportion in retail trade about 1.15:1.00 (Liu, 1986; 20).

It is worthwhile to mention that some steps towards a "democratization" of property rights can be observed in issuing shares for employees (Liu, 1986; 21–22). Yet it seems to us that this approach does not mean a radical change: by selling shares to workers, it is intended to give them the feeling of co-ownership rather than to use these monetary means in a capitalistic sense, i.e. to consider shares being negotiated at a stock-exchange.

Plan/Market: The system of decision making is not solely dependent on the institutional set-up of the decision making bodies and individuals. All forms, methods and instruments of planning, guidance, and stimulation must be regarded as parts of the decision structure in a broader sense.

In the summary of a case study on the changes in two of 6,600 pilot enterprises, worked out by Chinese and World Bank experts in 1984, it is stated:

First, the dominant influence on both firms has been the market, not directive plans. Second, financial incentives and planning systems are both, weak and manipulable at the enterprise level (Byrd et al., 1984; X).

This characterization might have applied more or less to other experimental firms as well.

There is other evidence that, after 1978, the role of the market mechanism did increase slowly but surely. The following quotation illustrates this process:

In the case of consumer goods, direct retail sales by industrial enterprises accounted for over 17% of the total value of retail sales of non-agricultural commodities in 1983, compared with 14% in 1980, under 11% in 1979, and considerably less in earlier years. . . . In the case of producer goods, the share of output distributed outside the framework of directive planning and the administrative allocation has increased though unevenly across different types of commodities. Machinery and electrical equipment are a particularly salient example, where direct marketing by producers became common in 1979/1980 as orders for many types of machinery through the state plan declined sharply. In 1980, direct sales outside the state plan accounted for 46% of total sales by enterprises under the First Ministry of Machine Building (compared with only 13% in 1979) and one-third of sales by all machinery producers. Many enterprises in this industry, including some of those in our sample,[2] have become responsible for virtually all of their sales. Direct marketing of raw steel outside the plan accounted for only 3.6% of total national production in 1979, but 10.6 percent in 1980 and a peak of 19.9 percent in 1981 (Byrd, 1985; 1–2).

Besides the progress, some obstacles must also be mentioned which prevented further reform achievements. The traditional sellers' market could not be replaced by a buyers market, which alone could bring about a radical improvement in efficiency. The impediments consisted of (Kosta, 1982/84/85):

- the administrative monopolization and hence a lack of competition;
- the dominating soft budget constraint because of different financial support by governmental authorities;
- little chance to close down enterprises although a new bankruptcy law—yet for trial implementation—was passed in Dec. 1986;
- false price signals.

Prices

The former debates on the use of the law of value (Kosta, 1983) again raised the question of an appropriate price formula after 1978 (Krug, 1986; 12–18). Patterned according to Marx' reasoning on the transformation of values into prices under capitalism, different price types were suggested (based alternatively on the value of labor, of capital, or of both) (Social Sciences, 1/1984; 152–176; 2/1984; 55–82). Only in the course of time, did the opinion gain ground that, following the logic of market mechanism, prices should reflect scarcities, i.e. "to assure balance between supply and demand to bring about the rationalization of industrial structure" (Social Sciences, 4/1985; 177–194). Taking the scarcity of resources into account, more flexible pricing had to be envisaged. In other words: The traditional principles of price formation, according to a certain formula (fixing prices at the central level and maintaining these for years) had to be questioned (for details, see also Xue, 1981; 135–162).

Another pricing principle taken over from the traditional Soviet model was rejected, namely keeping the price level of certain goods and services consciously below costs, i.e. producer goods, basic food stuff, housing, transportation, etc. This entailed a huge burden for the state budget. Further negative consequences of this principle consist in the waste of production factors, disregard of maintenance, and false signals for structural and technological changes (Xue, 1981; 135–162).

Taking the weaknesses of the old price system into consideration, it is only understandable that the 1984 reform document primarily postulates: "We should readjust irrational price ratios on the basis of the exchange of equal values and changes in the relation between supply and demand, lowering or raising prices as the case may be" (Decision, 1984). Let us look at the concrete reform measures that have been taken in the respective fields.

The gradual increase in input prices, combined with dual (or even multi-level) pricing implemented after 1979, attempted to correct the most striking distortions. Two examples might illustrate the respective measures:

1. The level of purchasing prices increased because "above quota prices," negotiated prices and free prices (besides the traditional "state quota prices") had been introduced.
2. Prices of basic materials were raised in the following manner: coal: +32% (1979), natural gas +60% (1982), iron ore +49.1% (1980) and +47.1% (1984); timber +30% (1980) and +10 up to 20% (1983); rolled steel (small profiles) +20% (1979); soda ash +50% (1983); plate glass +47% (1983) (Chai, 1985; 26).

A much more difficult task was, and still is, the price adjustment of scarce consumer goods, including basic food stuffs. After the rationing of such goods (sold at suppressed prices) had been almost completely abandoned a total decontrol of prices would lead, no doubt, to galloping inflation, severely affecting the living conditions of the population. To cope with this problem, the government pursued three strategies:

Firstly, conditions which would induce manufacturing enterprises to substantially cut down inputs ought to be created so that the increased production costs, resulting from the higher price of production factors, could basically be offset (Decision, 1984; 18).

Secondly, they maintained price control by the coexistence of different price categories such as (1) fixed prices controlled by the State, (2) floating prices with the State setting upper and lower price limits, (3) negotiated prices agreed upon between selling and purchasing enterprises, (4) free prices, fixed by the retailer according to market prospects, yet at the same time controlled, by the authorities (Chai, 1986; 22–25).

Thirdly, a negative impact from price increases to the development of real income ought to be avoided by appropriate wage adjustments.

Monetary Management and Control

By monetary management at the macroeconomic level we mean, to put it in Western terms, both, monetary and fiscal policies. Let us start with fiscal reforms and then continue with the new approaches in the banking and credit policy.

The main changes in the fiscal field were implemented under the headings of "profit remittance" (or "retention") in 1978, and "income tax payments" during the early 1980s, implemented under the slogan "Substitution of Tax Payments for Profit Remittances" (Donnithorne, 1986; 1–3; Ho, 1986; 1–29; Lee, 1986; 45–71).

The main goal of switching "from a situation in which the (enterprise income) residue went to the State to one in which the residue goes to the producers" (Donnithorne, 1986; 1) consisted in the extension of the enterprise's discretionary power.[3] The producing unit is to dispose of financial means not only current costs, but also bonuses, welfare facilities and investments. This will create incentives which are hardly needed to invigorate the formerly sluggish work collectives. The introduction of taxes, instead of the previous profit surrender, should create a certain yardstick of work performance and guarantee a more secure source of revenue for both the enterprise and the government. Simultaneously it should counteract inflationary pressures.

At present, taxation remains more an ad hoc instrument than a yardstick because, besides a uniform income tax (as a rule 55% on profits), so-called regulatory or adjustment taxes on excess profit, are being levied. This tax is basically negotiated between the fiscal authorities and the enterprises. This practice covers not only taxation, but also sharing "after tax profit in excess" between the state and the enterprise. One has to agree with the critical remark of a Western scholar who characterizes this problem in the following way:

The trouble with these measures was that they were all cumbersome and liable to abuse, depending as they did on a process of negotiation between each enterprise and the State, with the scope that gives to irregular pressures and inducements (Donnithorne, 1986; 4).

Once the amount of the enterprise's profit after taxation is known, the proportion to be divided among three funds, the "development fund" (for investments), the "social welfare fund," and the "bonus fund" (Bohnet, 1985; 79–80; Ho, 1986; 5–7) is set. Although the proportion of the three funds did not seem to be uniform (up to the end of 1985) in all enterprises (Kosta, 1982/84/85), a source points out that as "a general principle" any retained portion of an increase in profit is to be allocated (among the three funds) in the ratio 5:2:3 (Ho, 1986; 17). One can certainly agree with the opinion of Chinese economists that the income tax scheme (incl. sharing after tax) is unfair in that it favors less efficient enterprises and punishes more successfull ones (Ho, 1986; 10).

In taking over the Soviet model, the Chinese introduced a sales tax in the 1950s named the "Industrial and Commercial Tax" (Donnithorne, 1986; 5–6). As this was more or less a substitute for scarcity prices, hundreds of different tax rates were fixed mainly to balance the short supply of consumer goods against excess demand. (True, this solution counteracts one of the well-known diseases of non-market prices, namely ill-adaptation of the product-mix to consumers' needs.) Moreover, one of the purposes of the tax was to absorb excessive purchasing power.

Again, similar to the income tax, the absence of uniformity implies the lack of an efficiency criterion since profitability no longer depends on market performance alone. It is true that the industrial and commercial tax has recently been changed into various new taxes, such as product tax, value-added tax, salt tax and business tax (Donnithorne, 1986; 5–6; see also Ho, 1986; 17), however the rates are not yet uniform.

Some other taxes (resource tax, construction tax, tax on bonuses, etc.), which cannot be described within the scope of this essay (Donnithorne, 1984; 4–9), are all intended to save resources and/or to absorb excess liquidity.

Regardless of these and other weaknesses in fiscal policies, on the whole the new measures corresponded to the logic of the reform concept by decentralizing the competence of the enterprises with regard to the use of budgetary means. This also applies to monetary policies which we will discuss in the following paragraphs.

Under the reform, the bulk of investments, independent of whether they are still performed according to plan targets or to market demand, is financed to a lesser extent by budgetary grants than by credits. Bank loans create the firms' budgetary base. To name a few examples:

Bank loans to industrial enterprises more than doubled from 1979 to 1984 (SYCh, 1985; 526).[4] In 1978, the state budget was used for 83.3% of all investments in capital construction, and in 1979, 80.0%; this share decreased to 58.2% in 1983 and to 54.4% in 1984; the remainding "outside state budget" funds came from credits and self-financing (SYCh, 1985; 420).[5]

Some experts recommend using interest rates as the price of money, i.e. to equate by this rate the demand and supply of money (Kosta, 1982/84/85). But with regard to the inflation rates in recent years, the given interest rates for bank credits, though higher than in the past, are still lower than the inflation rate.

Under the old system, the Bank of China, together with its local branches, assumed all banking functions, such as money emitting, monitoring all currency flows, controlling financial operations of enterprises according to the financial plans, organizing loans and credits, etc. The Peoples' Bank now maintains the tasks of a central bank (in a Western sense). However, commercial activities, which became crucial under the reform, were then devoted to specialized banks (such as the "Industrial and Commercial Bank," the "Agricultural Bank," the "Construction Bank," the "Bank of China," the "Chinese International Trust and Investment Corporation" and the "Investment Bank," see: Donnithorne, 1986; 19–24; Beijing Rundschau, 23/1985; 18–20).

The institutional splitting of the banking system is, in our opinion, a step forward in terms of a market reform. By specializing the banks, they will better meet the various functions of a monetary controlled economy. To fulfill their numerous tasks with regards to efficiency, however, a competitive structure would presumably be more appropriate. Moreover, some practices of the new banks are reminiscent of being "still mainly a passive conduit for budgetary funds" on behalf of the State Planning Commission (Donnithorne, 1986; 21).

Incentives

A scheme of eight wage grades for workers (and a similar one for officials) existed in China for more than three decades (Lee/Chow, 1986; 4–5). Yet, under the Leftist rule, one did not make use of the wider margins provided by this scheme, nor were bonuses (out of the scheme) or piece-rates granted. Another weakness consisted in freezing the wage rates at one level for many years. The reform measures started, therefore, with six wage hikes (1977, 1978, 1979, 1981, 1982), the criteria of which referred to individual competence, performance and qualification.

Above all, this implied a salary adjustment for particular professions, such as teachers, medical personnel, technical and administrative staff and the like.

Yet, the increases, it is true, were partially set off by price increases. Whereas monetary wages of workers and staff in state-owned enterprises grew by 44% from 1977 to 1983, real wages (regarding the increase in the costs of living) went up by only 22% (Lee/Chow, 1986; 18).

Recently, the eight-grade wage scheme has been losing its decisive role in determining a worker's income. However, it is not clear yet whether the grade system has already been completely abolished, while the wage bill is becoming more and more linked with the enterprise's performance.[6]

Although by 1985, the wage bill did not seem to be consequently linked to the results that an enterprise achieved, the bonus fund has been allotted from retained profit in many enterprises since early 1980. Bonuses have been used to a larger extent since 1978.[7] With the new arrangements in the field of self-financing mentioned above (profit remittance, taxing), the role of the bonus fund and of individual bonuses has increased. At the same time, the increase in individual bonuses and the growth of the work force contributed to the inflationary pressure within the Chinese economy. To counteract this tendency, a bonus ceiling, fixed by an equivalent of two and a half months of wages, was set in 1980 and replaced in 1984 by a highly progressive tax on the increase of bonuses.[8]

As a result of two decisions made by Chinese leadership in May and October 1984, the discretionary competence of allocating manpower, (the assignment of a worker to a certain place of work, up and down grading, and, to a certain extent, dismissing workers) was shifted from the upper authorities to enterprise management (Bohnet, 1986; 93–94). True, the individual choice of job has not yet been totally realized. But with regard to experts some steps in that direction have been taken, and last but not least the door for private activities has been opened.

The labor contract system within Chinese industry best expresses the new approach in urban areas (Lee/Chow, 1986; 11–16). Following older arrangements on seasonal and temporary work, which were exercised in the years before the Cultural Revolution, the system was started again in 1980 with pilot programs and 120,000 industrial workers were employed temporarily under the contractual rules. This settlement represents the counterpart of the hitherto exclusively existing fixed employment system giving life-tenure to workers. The labor contract system has spread since 1983 but there is no evidence, to our knowledge, about the actual scope of its realization.

The description of reform measures in the field of work incentives and employment policies has shown that the changes in favor of market stimulation have been remarkable. There are, however, still considerable remainders of "iron rice bowl" practices.

Development Strategies

A strategy of balanced growth was not duly considered from 1976 to 1979. The rate of accumulation, which amounted to 22.7% between 1963 and 1965, increased permanently between 1976 and 1979 (30.9% in 1976; 32.3% in 1977; 36.5% in 1978; 34.6% in 1979); only since 1980 can a slight decrease be seen (Dong, 1982; 88).

Yet balanced growth did not mean merely a balance between accumulation and consumption. It implied the coexistence of different sizes and technological levels of enterprises as well. It was not clear, in this sense, whether the "Walking on Two Legs" would mean a simultaneous promotion of large-scale, up-to-date enterprises on the one hand, and small units, based on rather traditional, labor-intensive work processes (located predominantly in the rural area) on the other.

It took some time before the idea was fully accepted by the reformers. For many reasons, both types of enterprises have their raison d'être: employment difficulties, limited opportunities for income improvements, problems with consumer goods supply, bottlenecks in skill, transport and communication, which all support the existence of the traditional small-scale sector, while modernization could not be realized without an advanced large-scale industry (Kosta, 1982/84/85).

With regard to the employment question, one of the most pressing problems in China was the surplus of labor stemming from the explosive population growth. Notwithstanding former attempts to stop this increase (Kosta, 1985a; 106–122), the burden resulting from the huge work force potential can be illustrated by the following figures:

China's population increased from 552 million in 1950 to 963 million in 1978, surpassing the limit of 1 billion inhabitants in 1981 (Kosta, 1985a; 107). The share of the population in the working age rose from 49.5% in 1964 to 54.9% in 1982 (Kosta, 1985a; 103). The proportion of persons employed in agriculture decreased from 83.6% in 1952 to 75.9% in 1979, and to 68.4% in 1984.[9] The excessive labor potential called for the creation of new jobs without delay[10] and, in the long run, for limiting the demographic explosion.

To reduce the population growth rate, different instruments and measures were used. Under the motto "one-child-family," moral and material incentives and disincentives were (and still are) practiced, such as campaigns, public announcements, rewards and penalties, etc. (Kosta,

1985a; 127–128). China finally succeeded in reducing birth rates in the last few years (from 11.5 per mill in 1981 to 10.8 per mill 1984 (SYCh, 1985; 186). It is not yet clear whether the official goal of not surpassing the 1.2 billion mark of total population by the year 2000 will be fulfilled (Kosta, 1985a; 130).

It should be mentioned that there is a migration from rural to urban areas. But the political authorities exercise strict control over the moval to large towns for obvious reasons.[11] There is, on the other hand, good reasons for developing smaller cities throughout the country (compare a series of articles in Beijing Rundschau 14/1985; 25–28; 17/1985; 22–23, 29; 22/1985; 24–26). With this policy, China wants to kill numerous birds with one stone: the threat of unemployment, the migration towards large cities and the bottlenecks in the service sector throughout the country (including trade, commerce, transport, communication, housing, etc.). Moreover, the use of market forces requires additional interlocal and interregional links, which will be established more easily within this pattern of urbanization.

Open-Door Strategy

In order to take leave of the closed-door policy a notable increase of the hitherto underdeveloped extent of foreign trade was first be made. Opening the national economy to international markets has its consequence on the commodity composition of imports and exports as well. Import substitution, i.e. protecting domestic branches from competitive goods, imported from abroad by producing them all at home, is considered as only a temporarily tolerable means of encouraging the take-off in an underdeveloped economy (Teng, 1982; 175–178). It is, above all, Western technology (including, of course, Japanese) which the Chinese consider to be indispensable for the envisaged modernization (Beijing Rundschau 10/1986; 18–21). Chemicals and other more sophisticated products must also be imported, yet the import of raw materials and semi-products have to be gradually reduced, though a radical change in this direction is not expected to occur in the foreseeable future (DIW 41/1985; 472).

On the export side of the balance of trade, it is intended to change the pattern of many Third World countries, namely replacing primary goods exports by manufactured products. Although there was never an extensive stop on exporting typical industrial items produced in China, such as textiles, porcelain, special food stuff and the like, at present, an expansion of both traditional exports and the export of more sophisticated manufactured articles, is strived for (DIW, 1985; 472).

As to the regional direction of China's foreign trade, the domination of the advanced Western economies has become obvious. The break between Beijing and Moscow in the late 1950s explains the drop of the socialist countries' share in Chinese foreign trade turn-over, from 66% in 1960 to 30% in 1965, to 23% in 1970 and to only 16% in 1974 (Kosta/Meyer, 1976; 158–159, 195). The decrease continued in the following years and reached the rather low figure of about 7% in the early 1980s (DIW 41/1985; 474). This decline was not only a consequence of the political clash with the USSR, but was increasingly a result of the Soviet's inability to meet China's demand for modern equipment and other desirable goods.

The OECD countries' share in Chinese foreign trade turnover amounted to 47% in 1970, 56% in 1975, and about 60% in the first half of the 1980s. The OECD import share alone was nearly 75% of the total imports to China in 1980, and oscillated around 68 to 70% in the first half of the 1980s (DIW 35/1975; 283; 30–31/1976; 290; 4/1985; 475). Looking at the most significant import item, i.e. technological equipment, it is obvious that the advanced economies play the most decisive role: namely Japan, the US, West Germany and France; these four countries are the forerunners with regard to the number of contracts and the value of technology imported in 1985.[12]

The need for imported machinery, expressed by Chinese planners, has brought about a permanent danger for the country's balance of payments. The former Maoist aversion against credits from the capitalist world vanished, to be replaced by a spreading interest in Western products, not only for machinery, but also for consumer goods such as electrical equipment, cars (for organizations only), etc.

The decision to open the economy to the outside world was taken but the goals connected to this strategy could not be pursued without changes being made in the trade institutions. The old rigid structure of the import and export organizations, being fully isolated from the domestic economy, had to be loosened (but a sudden and total abandonment was hardly feasible).

One arrangement concerned the extension of export and import authorizations in addition to the existing national foreign trade corporations. A considerable number of enterprises and other organizations are now entitled to enter foreign trade transactions though under the supervision of central bodies; in some cases, besides the Ministry of Foreign Economic Relations and Trade, provincial authorities and other ministries have also been authorized to participate in the respective trade decisions (Chan, 1986; 1–8).

Some institutional changes in China go far beyond the reform practice in the Soviet-bloc countries. This concerns different forms of foreign investment on a regional and enterprise level, which can be described as follows.

One of the most startling steps in this direction was the establishment of four Special Economic Zones (SEZ) in 1980, among them Shenzhen (the largest and quickest growing), Zhuhai and Shantou in Guangdong province, and Xiamen in the province of Fujian. With the establishment of the SEZ it is intended

- to attract the foreign capital that is lacking in view of the ambitious modernization goals,
- to introduce technical and organizational know-how by importing advanced technology from the West,
- to lay the foundation for inducing exports of more sophisticated articles,
- to create a field for observing the problems connected with Deng's call for "One Country, Two Systems."[13]

Some success can be registered as far as the first two points are concerned: the expansion of foreign investments (albeit, mainly through the participation of Hong Kong entrepreneurs and other foreign compatriots) the corresponding growth of production, a rapid development in infrastructure, all of which can be documented by abundant data (see e.g. Beijing Rundschau 39/1985; 4–5, 25; 8/1986; 14–18; 13/1986; 24–26). And moreover it is indeed very impressive to the foreign visitor (Kosta, 1982/84/85). One should not ignore, however, the significant difficulties which have become manifest in the SEZ: the export has not developed to the desired extent; serious ecological problems which by no means have yet been mastered; extreme income differences within the zones and between these and the mainland might create threatening social tensions; black markets and corruption also seem to be spreading (Gehrmann, 1986; 19–20; Kosta, 1982/84/85).

In summary we feel that the positive effects, stemming from the enormous dynamics of the SEZ, outshine negative concomitants.

The opening of fourteen coastal cities (Shanghai, Tianjin etc.) and some other regions, for foreign capital does not show a development comparable to the zones. Here, the problem is primarily one of the balance of payments and of limited capacities to absorb huge quantities of imported technology in a short time.

The open-door policy finds another expression in the expansion of enterprises with foreign participation. Three types can be distinguished: (1) sole foreign proprietorship, (2) joint ventures, (3) looser forms of cooperation between Chinese and foreign companies (DIW 41/85; 468–471; Kosta, 1982/84/85).

By the end of 1985 there were only 120 enterprises in the first category, i.e. enterprises belonging exclusively to foreigners; this shows the hesitation of these entrepreneurs who might fear the risk of the undertaking. The second type, joint ventures, are obviously the most appropriate form with regard to the aims envisaged. From 1980 to 1985 about 2,300 joint ventures were licensed. The third type, representing different forms of cooperation between domestic and foreign companies are more numerous; yet the alleged number of 3,700 cooperative enterprises is not very informative because there are no accurate rules or definitions (BR 22/1986; 4,7; BR 35/1986; 4–5).

There can be no doubt that the open-door policy significantly contributed to the dynamics of the Chinese economy. Yet this advance should not be traced back to the institutional changes alone. Another point that furthered the comparative advantages of external economic relations is the human factor, which has been applied consequently in the past years: thousands and thousands of experts, in particular young people, were sent abroad and are now contributing to the positive results.

The Outcomes of the Reform Period

Two Methodological Notes

It can be assumed that the outcomes of economic development, expressed in terms of growth, efficiency and of social indicators, are to a high degree a consequence of the given (or changing) economic system and the respective measures of economic policy. This assumption would be particularly plausible in a period of systemic changes, such as occurred in China after 1979, first in agricultural and later in the urban sectors. Asserting that the reform has a distinct impact on economic performance on the national scale does not imply that there are no other factors of an extra-systemic nature (such as developments on international markets, weather conditions, natural disasters, etc.) which also affect economic results. But we do not consider these non-systemic factors as having the same weight as the reform measures. The following empirical investigation will be carried out under the assumption that it is the economic system itself (and its changes) that first determines the outcomes.

The second remark concerns Chinese statistics. During the CR, the statistical apparatus was almost completely destroyed. The first Statistical Yearbook after the defeat of the Leftists was not published until 1983. Since then, official data have been giving a better and more comprehensive picture of economic development than one could obtain from the figures sporadically published before that. But a proper analysis is still faced with lacking, fragmentary, often vague and not always well-defined data. This is why broad tendencies rather than precise figures and corresponding conclusions are proposed in the course of the following investigation.

Table 8.1   Average Annual Growth in China

Indicator	Total 1953-1978	1979-1984	Per capita 1953-1978	1979-1984	(1979-1985)
National income produced	6.0	8.3	3.9	7.0	(9.1)
Gross industrial output	11.3	8.9	9.1	7.6	(10.9)
Heavy industry	13.6	6.6	11.4	5.3	(9.9)
Light industry	9.1	11.7	7.0	10.3	(12.1)
Gross agricultural output	3.25	9.4	1.2	8.1	(10.9)

Source: Statistical Yearbook of China 1985. Beijing; 12;
in parentheses: DIW Wochenbericht 23/86; 290

Successful Outcomes

We will turn first to a comparison of growth rates in two periods, namely (1) the prolonged period (1953–1978) under the old system (neglecting the different policies under short-term viewpoints) and (2) the phase of economic reforms (1979–1984). By recording not only the growth of national income (total and per capita), but also the contribution of the main sectors, the results of the readjustment policy can be identified (see Table 8.1).

The acceleration of growth in the reform period is particularly distinct for the national income per capita and the agricultural output per capita; in the latter case (although there might be a "rosy" statistical bias), the success was enormous. The upswing in agricultural production and the faster growth of light industry, compared with that of heavy industry, are proof of the successful readjustment policy.

One of the explicit intentions of the reformers was to overcome inefficiencies that are typical of the Soviet-type planning system. Namely the waste of resources which is expressed by slower increase in productivity. Let us look at the development of both productivity of labor and of capital (see Table 8.2).

We cannot calculate consistent productivity indicators. The reasons for this shortcoming are the following: the national income produced (the numerator for both indicators) contains the output of the material sectors only, yet the size of the labor force is recorded in the Chinese statistics for the total economy (i.e. it is not split into material and the non-material sectors). Moreover, there are no data on capital stock (the denominator for productivity of capital), but only on investments. This

Table 8.2 Efficiency in the Use of Resources, Annual Average Change

	1953-1978	1979-1984
(1) National income produced	6.0	8.3
(2) Investment in fixed assets of state-owned units	11.1	10.0
(3) Efficiency in the use of investments: (1):(2)	-4.6	-1.5
(4) Labor force employed in national economy	2.55	3.0
(5) Labor productivity: (1):(4)	3.4	6.2
(6) Labor productivity in industry	5.5	4.7
(7) Labor productivity in agriculture	1.2	7.6

Source: Statistical Yearbook of China 1985. Beijing; 12, 14, 213, 382, 416

is why neither a "clean" indicator for labor productivity nor one for capital productivity can be determined. Thus, we had to settle for "unclean" indicators, which still let us formulate some conclusions on the different efficiency tendencies in the pre-reform and in the reform period.

It turns out that the growth of labor productivity within the economy was faster under the reform than before due to progress in the agricultural sector. A slight acceleration of labor productivity in industry did not influence the general trend. As far as "capital productivity" is concerned, a partial answer can be given by looking at the indicator on the efficiency of investments in fixed capital: under the reform, the negative trend could nearly be stopped.

Taking the picture illustrated by Table 8.2 as a whole, the productivity trends do not appear to be too successful. The use of resources might be even less efficient when regarding the waste of energy and other primary goods (here the lack of data is particularly regrettable).[14] One should keep in mind, however, that the achievements in the increase of labor productivity in the agricultural sector are obvious, and only here did the reform progress notably.

The figures in Table 8.3 show a rise in the living standards in the reform period under a global perspective. Yet, the increase of the consumption rate, from 63.5% in 1978 to 68.8% in 1984, does not give a complete picture. Considering the years before, only in the course of the GL did the share of consumption drop below 60% (56.2% in 1958 and 60.4% in 1959) (SYCh, 1985; 552). During the first Five-Year-Plan (1953-1957), this indicator amounted to about 76%, in the early 1960s it jumped up to over 80% and during the CR (1966-1976) it oscillated between 66% and 79% (SYCh, 1985; 36); the proportion

Table 8.3 Indicators for Living Standards in China I

Indicator	Unit	Year (Period)		Year (Period)	
(1) Share of personal and public consumption in national income available	%	1978	63.5	1984	68.8
(2) Average annual growth of personal consumption of: all residents	%	1953-1978	2.2	1979-1984	7.9
peasants	%	1953-1978	1.8	1979-1984	9.3
others	%	1953-1978	2.95	1979-1984	4.1
(3) Average annual growth of incomes of: peasants	%	n.a.	n.a.	1979-1984	15
workers and staff	%	n.a.	n.a.	1979-1984	8.2
(4) Average annual growth of expenditure of: peasants	%	n.a.	n.a.	1979-1984	13.2
workers and staff	%	n.a.	n.a.	1979-1984	7

Sources: (1)-(3): Statistical Yearbook of China 1985. Beijing; 36, 551, 552
(4): Beijing Rundschau 29/1985; 17

of personal to public consumption was roughly constant at 9:1 during the past three decades (SYCh, 1985; 38).

To assess the change in living standards, the growth index of personal consumption is more relevant than its share in national income. Here our data show an enormous increase in the reform period, particularly concerning peasants' consumption (see also Beijing Rundschau 29/1985; 17–22; 52/1985; 27–28). Comparing both the share of consumption and its growth index, some doubts as to the latter's exactness must be mentioned. This also holds true of the growth of figures concerning the incomes and expenditures of peasants and workers, given in Table 8.3. However, in spite of all inaccuracies, the general tendency of a distinct improvement in the population's welfare is clear particularly with regard to the data shown in Table 8.4.

Table 8.4 shows that the level of nutrition, which was certainly rather low before 1978, was substantially raised during the six years of reform. The supply of manufactured consumer goods distinctly improved as well. The Chinese population suffers extremely from the shortage of living space since housing construction has been sorely neglected in the past. In spite of the care given to the housing sector under the reform, the limited space of 6.3 square meters per capita in the urban area (1984) is even smaller in big cities such as Shanghai, Tianjin, and others (Lau, 1986; 8–12; see also footnote 11).

The increasing attention devoted to education and health in the recent years should be appreciated as well. The educational system is also one of the areas where the omissions in the pre-reform years can hardly be compensated for in the short run. The situation is clearly better in the area of medical care.[15]

Taking the indicators of living standards as a whole, an impressive improvement after 1978 can be observed, which of course is much more striking in the rural than in the urban areas. Nevertheless, the general level of the population's welfare is still rather low when compared to other countries.

Problems in the Reform Course: Inflation
and Unemployment

To complete the picture of the economic outcomes during the course of the reform, at least two problems remain to be discussed: inflationary pressure and underemployment.[16] We will first look at different price indexes for an indication of the inflationary tendencies (see Table 8.5).

Since 1979, all price indexes have gone up, which is clearly a consequence of the steep rise of purchasing prices in agriculture (in reality

Table 8.4 Indicators of Living Standards in China II

Item	Unit	Year (Period)		Year (Period)	
Annual consumption per capita:					
Grain	jin(a)	1978	391	1984	503
Edible vegetable oil	jin(a)	1978	3.2	1984	9.4
Pork	jin(a)	1978	15.3	1984	26.0
Cloth	chi(b)	1978	24.1	1984	32.5
Durable goods per 100 persons/households:					
Bicycles per 100 persons	piece	1978	7.7	1984	18.8
TV sets per 100 persons	piece	1978	0.3	1984	4.6
Wrist watches per 100 households	piece	1981	240.76	1984	282.95
Sewing machines per 100 households	piece	1981	70.41	1984	77.52
Washing machines per 100 households	piece	1981	6.31	1984	40.13
Refrigerators per 100 households	piece	1981	0.22	1984	3.22
Living floor space per capita:					
in urban areas	sqm	1978	4.2	1984	6.3
in rural areas	sqm	1978	8.1	1984	13.6
Social indicators:					
University students per 10,000 persons	person	1978	8.9	1984	13.5
Doctors per 10,000 persons	person	1978	10.8	1984	13.4

(a) 1 jin = 1 pound
(b) 1 chi = 1 foot

Source: Statistical Yearbook of China 1985. Beijing; 551, 565

Table 8.5 General Price Indexes, 1951-1984 (Annual Averages)

	1951-1976	1977-1978	1979-1984
Retail prices(a)	1.1	1.4	2.8
Cost of living(a) (staff and workers)	1.3	1.7	3.1
Purchasing prices of farm and sideline products(b)	2.9	1.8	7.4
Retail prices of industrial products in rural areas	0.4	0.1	1.3

(a) Incl. list prices, negotiated prices and market prices;
(b) Incl. list prices, negotiated prices and increased prices for above-quota purchase of farm and sideline products
Source: Statistical Yearbook of China 1985; 530

the price increase might be even higher than the official statistical data indicate).

The inflationary tendencies should not be seen apart from the strong work incentives connected with the price increases, and hence with huge growth rates in agricultural output (Table 8.1). At the same time it should be noted that the priority given to agriculture had gradually widened the gap between the prices for agricultural and industrial products. This, of course, had its social consequences. With the extension of free markets and a partial decontrol of pricing, the government had to respond to social tensions which arose in Chinese cities in connection with price increases. The policy makers reacted with extra payments in the urban area to compensate the losses caused by growing expenditures for meat and other food stuffs (Beijing Rundschau 16/1985; 21/1985; 4).

A way out of this dilemma was shown by the authorities in Guangdong province (Kosta, 1982/84/85). Here a radical decontrol of list prices on the fish market first led to a considerable price increase. However, this phenomenon entailed, as a consequence of growing profits achieved in fish-hatching, an enormous expansion of fish production, and subsequently, because of the expanding supply, a gradual lowering of the prices. In our opinion the opposite solution, i.e. to uphold the price levels of food, manufactured consumer goods and small-scale services by state subsidies, would not contribute to a lasting invigoration of the Chinese economy.

Another problem is the chronic underemployment in China (Kosta, 1985a; 130–135). It is impossible to give a precise picture of employment when comparing the situation before and after 1978. The Chinese did not record figures on unemployment (the official term: "jobseekers") before the start of the reform. Yet one cannot ignore that under the old system the enterprises tended to hoard labor, in other words, to overstaff. It is almost impossible to estimate the extent of this hidden unemployment. Since 1978, the Chinese sporadically record the number of persons "seeking jobs" and, simultaneously, regard the figures on new jobs created by the employment policy.

According to figures published in China, the number of "job seekers" in cities and towns has dropped from 5.3 millions in 1978 to 3 million in 1982 (Kosta, 1985). Western estimates of unemployment go beyond the Chinese figures. However, it can be assumed, on the whole, that the Chinese have succeeded in providing millions of new jobs during the past few years.

Another question might be whether actual unemployment is a result of the reform policy. The answer is definitely negative. The deficit of jobs compared with job seekers is, above all, a result of the demographic development: the stream of young people, who reached the working age in the early 1980s, together with those who have crowded back from the country where they were "sent down" during the CR (Kosta, 1985a; 109, see also footnote 9).

It is true that the drive for increased productivity caused by the reform might counteract the latent unemployment. The solution would not lie, however, in dampening productivity growth. A strategy started in rural areas proved successfull: it consisted in the expansion of all types of side-line productions, creating in this way an enormous number of new jobs. In the cities and towns a dual employment policy might be promising: it includes the promotion of both modern, capital-intensive technologies and traditional, labor intensive work processes.

To conclude the investigation on the economic outcomes: up until now, the positive results have undoubtedly prevailed during the reform period.

On the Prospects of a Market-Oriented Reform in China

There is no doubt: old dogmas of Marxist-Leninist ideology, in China often in the guise of specific "Mao Zedong Thought," have deep roots. However, the flexibility in the interpretation of this doctrine, in a reform-minded sense, has often been remarkable (see e.g. Su, 1985). Conflicts between the requirements of the economic reforms and the remnants of the old dogmatics will certainly continue with the increasing urgency of new solutions, such as the individualization of property rights, new regulation on capital allocation, etc.[17] Up to now, the barriers of ideology seemed to be surmountable.

The conflict is of a political nature, arising between the importance of economic efficiency and the power interests of old functionaries. True, Deng succeeded in reducing the influence of the more orthodox cadres on both central and provincial levels (Scharping, 1986). Yet, many members of the middle and lower bureaucracy are still present. Some of them might have gone through a learning process and would support the reform line. But a good many might either hold the new course rather formally or even counteract it (perhaps in a more hidden way) wherever they can.

Moreover, it is by no means certain that the rank and file will support the reform measures. The demand for higher performance may be accepted by a great majority of the workers if this leads to higher incomes. If difficulties were to arise (stagnation of real income because of high inflation rates, persisting unemployment and the like), large parts of the working population could then support anti-reformists within the apparatus.

Looking at the official documents, it is not yet clear which course the Chinese reform system will take in the long run: whether it will maintain essential elements of the old central-directive planning model while market mechanisms would be rather restricted, or whether it will end in a socialist market economy, relying basically on market forces which are regulated by indirect means of economic policies.

All of the experiences gathered in China and elsewhere teach us that systemic changes have been widely dependent on political determinants. It is the concept of the respective leadership that determines the development of the economic system.

There are some circumstances in China which point to a market-oriented solution similar to the Hungarian model, such as:

- success achieved in the agricultural and some other sectors (small services, etc.) where the reform has proceeded in a market direction
- the far-reaching learning process of leading economists, who have drawn this conclusion from the past in China and in the Soviet countries as well
- the pragmatic approach of the Dengist leadership and its consequent reform-minded political steps, including the replacement and rejuvenation of apparatchiks at all levels of the hierarchy.

On the other hand, one should not ignore, some relevant factors which could countervail those which appear to promote the market solution, i.e.:

- actual economic difficulties mentioned above. True, the positive results have prevailed up to now; however, the distinct upswing of the Chinese economy could meet its limits before long
- some ideological barriers could arise once new solutions are in sight. It is not certain whether the communist leadership will be courageous enough to then give up the old dogmas
- the process of economic reform might sooner or later run up against the monolithic political system; it is an open question whether, in the long run, an economic system based on market regulation is compatible with a political system characterized by a well-known power monopoly.

Thus a definite answer as to the prospects of the Chinese reform model cannot yet be given.

Notes

1. A market-oriented reform concept does not mean a laisser-faire solution. It implies, according to the Chinese economists, the use of market mechanisms within the limits of mainly indirect regulation ("guidance planning").

2. The sample under investigation comprised 20 enterprises of different branches and regions.

3. "In changing profits into tax, it is necessary to guarantee that the state gets a big share, the enterprise a medium share and individuals a small share," stated a governmental notice (Ho, 1986; 2).

4. Unfortunately, Chinese statistics do not allow giving separate figures on credits for investments and for current expenses.

5. The splitting of the residual shares into both parts (credits and self-financed investments) is again not possible because of a lack of separate data.

6. This has been postulated by Prime Minister Zhao Ziyang, who promised in the Winter of 1984/85 that the eight-grade wage system will be abolished before long (Beijing Rundschau, 1/1985, 14–15)

7. 25% of the growth of the total wage bill was due to the increase of bonuses from 1978 to 1982 (Lee/Chow, 1986; 23).

8. The tax rate is 30% if the annual bonus lies between a two and a half month's wage and a four month's wage. In case it exceeds a six month's wage, the rate amounts to 300% (Bohnet, 1985; 92).

9. The return of young people from the country to the cities contributed to the excess labor supply; the youngsters were "sent down" during the CR (Kosta, 1985a; 123)

10. In coping with these problems some success was registered: between 1977 and 1981 about 5 million new jobs were created annually (Kosta, 1985a).

11. Probably the most pressing problem is that of housing : "the per capita housing floor space in Tianjin, Chonqing and Harbin was still (1982) below 3 square meters" (Lau, 1986; 8).

12. Japan ranked number one with 174 contracts for a value of 550 million US-$, followed by the United States (137 contracts/ 690 million US-$), West Germany (123 contracts/790 million US-$) and France (36 contracts/320 million US-$); in value terms obviously the West Germans were in the lead (Beijing Rundschau 10/1986; 18)

13. This slogan expresses the intention to integrate Taiwan and Hong Kong into a united "Peoples Republic" while maintaining the there existing economic system of market capitalism (Deng, 1985; 30–34, 41, 42).

14. A considerable waste of basic materials and energy is a problem wellknown to Chinese economists. This came out during all our visits to China (Kosta 1982/84/85)

15. The two social indicators shown in Table 8.4 give a very rough picture of the levels of both systems, that of education and of medical care.

16. Critics of "to much market" incline to interpret phenomena such as cheating and corruption as an inevitable result of abandoning planning; we would hold, by contrast, that this reproach might be overdone (since market bargaining is being confused with cheating) and, if the charge proves to be legitimate, such encroachments can and should be, in a market economy, prosecuted by legal means.

17. Reluctance towards the reform, resulting from ideological dogmas and (as pointed out in the next paragraphs) from functionaries and some workers, is a well known phenomenon in Eastern Europe (for China see also Kloten, 1985; 43–45).

References

Beijing Rundschau, German edition (weekly), 1981–1986. Beijing

Bohnet, A./Jaehne, G., 1985: Reformen des Planungs- and Lenkungssystems in der Industrie der VR China. Grundprinzipien, aktueller Stand and Perspektiven, in: Schüller, A., ed., 1985; 63–104

Byrd, W., 1985: The Role and Impact of Markets. Paper prepared for the Conference on Chinese enterprise management, August 27–30, 1985 (mimeographed). Beijing

Byrd, W./Tidrick, G./Chen, J./Xu, L./Tang, Z./Chen, L., 1984: Recent Chinese Economic Reforms. Studies of Two Industrial Enterprises. World Bank Staff Working Papers No. 652. Washington D.C.

Chai, C. H., 1986: Reform of China's Industrial Prices, Hong Kong Conference (see below), Paper No. 36

Chan, T. M. H., 1986: Reform in China's Foreign Trade System, Hong Kong Conference, Paper No. 22

Decision, 1984: China's Economic Structure Reform—Decision of the CPC Central Committee. Beijing

Deng, X., 1985: Build Socialism with Chinese Characteristics. Beijing

DIW, 1975/1976/1985: Wochenberichte des Deutschen Instituts für Wirtschaftsforschung (DIW), No. 35/1975, No. 30–31/1976, No. 41/1985, No. 23/1986

Dong, F., 1982: Relationship between Accumulation and Consumption, in: Xu, D. et al., 1982; 79–109

Donnithorne, A., 1986: Banking and Fiscal Changes in China since Mao, Hong Kong Conference, Paper No. 31

Gehrmann, W., 1986: Kapitalismus im Labor, in: Die Zeit, No. 25; 19–20. Hamburg

Gey, P./Kosta, J./Quaisser, W., ed., 1985: Sozialismus and Industrialisierung. Die Wirtschaftssysteme Polens, Jugoslawiens, Chinas and Kubas im Vergleich. Frankfurt/New York

Group, 1985: Group for the Comparative Study of Economic Structures: On the Model for the Reform of China's Economic Structure, in: Social Sciences in China, No. 1; 9–33

Hang, Z., 1985: Symposium on Restructuring China's Economy: A Summary, in: Social Sciences in China, No. 3; 9–20

Ho, H. C. Y., 1986: Distribution of Profits and the Change from Profit Remission to Tax Payments for State Enterprises in China, Hong Kong Conference, Paper No. 35

Hong Kong Conference, 1986: China's System Reform. International Conference. Centre of Asian Studies, University of Hong Kong, March 17–20, 1986. Hong Kong

Kloten, N., 1985: Der Plan-Markt-Mechanismus Chinas. Das Koordinationssystem in Theorie und Praxis, in: Schüller, A., ed., 1985; 11–61

Kosta, J., 1983: Debates on the Economic Reforms in China: A Comparison with East European Experiences, in: East Asia, Vol. 1; 59–71

————, 1984: Wirtschaftssysteme des realen Sozialismus. Probleme and Alternativen. Köln

————, 1985a: Beschäftigungsprobleme and Beschäftigungspolitik in China, in: Schüller, A., ed., 1985; 105–140

————, 1985b: Die chinesische Volkswirtschaft vom "Grossen Sprung nach vorne" bis zur gegenwärtigen Wirtschaftsreform, in Gey, P./Kosta, J./ Quaisser, W., ed., 1985; 229–247

————, 1982/84/85: Information obtained on research stays in China (twice in 1982, then in 1984 and 1985)

Kosta, J./Meyer, J., 1976: Volksrepublik China. Ökonomisches System und wirtschaftliche Entwicklung. Frankfurt/Köln

Kraus, W., 1985: Wirtschaftsreformen in der Volksrepublik China, in: aus politik and zeitgeschichte, beilage zur wochenzeitung das parlament, B 39/85; 3–16

————, 1986: Private Enterprises in the People's Republic of China—Official Statements; Implementations; Further Prospects, Hong Kong Conference, Paper No. 16

Krug, B., 1986: Preisreform in China, in: Berichte des Bundesinstituts für ostwissenschaftliche and internationale Studien, No. 7

Lau, C. C., 1986: Urban China in Transition: The Impact of System Reforms and Urban Policy, Hong Kong Conference, Paper No. 15

Lee, P. N. S., 1986: Enterprise Autonomy in Post-Mao China: A Case Study of Policy-making 1978–83, in: The China Quarterly, No. 105; 45–71

Lee, P. N. S./Chow, T. H. S., 1986: Incentive System in Chinese Factories: Continuity and Change in the Post-Mao Era, Hong Kong Conference, Paper No. 11

Lin, C. Z., 1985: Chinesische Wirtschaftsreformen heute, in: Europäische Rundschau 4/1985; 53–75

Liu, G., 1986: Über einige Fragen der Eigentumsverhältnisse in China, in: Beijing Rundschau, No. 19; 17–21

Liu, G. et al., 1986: Economic Restructuring and Macroeconomic Management— A Review of the International Seminar on Macroeconomic Management, in: Social Sciences in China, No. 1; 9–35

Ma, H., 1983: New Strategy for China's Economy. Beijing

Quaisser, W., 1986: see the contribution in this Volume

Scharping, T., 1986: Chinas Reformpolitik auf dem Prüfstand. Die Delegiertenkonferenz der KPCh vom September 1985, in: Berichte des Bundesinstituts für ostwissenschaftliche and internationale Studien, No. 9. Köln

Schram, S. R., 1984: "Economics in Command?" Ideology and Policy since the Third Plenum 1978–84, in: The China Quarterly, No. 99; 417–461

Schüller, A., ed., 1985: China im Konflikt zwischen verschiedenen Ordnungskonzeptionen. Berlin

SYCh, 1985: Statistical Yearbook of China 1985, Compiled by the State Statistical Bureau, PR China, English edition. Oxford

Su, S., 1985: Prospects for Socialism as Viewed from China's Experience and Lessons, in: Selected Writings on Studies of Marxism, No. 2. Beijing

Teng, W., 1982: Socialist Modernization and the Pattern of Foreign Trade, in: Xue, D. et al., 1982; 167–192

Wang, B., 1986: Über die Durchführung des Staatshaushaltsplans für 1985 and den Entwurf des Staatshaushaltsplans für 1986, in: Beijing Rundschau No. 20; VI–XII

Xu, D., 1982: Transformation of China's Economy, in: Xu, D. et al.

Xu, D. et al., 1982: China's Search for Economic Growth. The Chinese Economy Since 1949. Beijing

Xue, M., 1981: China's Socialist Economy. Beijing

9

The New Agricultural Reform in China: From the People's Communes to Peasant Agriculture

Wolfgang Quaisser

After more than two decades of experiments with collective agriculture, in the 1980s the new Chinese leadership dissolved the people's communes and reestablished peasant agriculture. At the commencement of the new agricultural policy in 1977/78 no one, and probably not even the Communist Party, might have been imagined how far the reform would go. Of course, at the end of the 1970s the political situation favoured a reform: the influence of the left-wing Maoist party group waned and Deng Xiao Ping and the so-called "revisionists" gained power. This party group had always called for a more realistic policy and it was predictable that some pragmatic modifications of the commune system would be implemented.

The reform as finally introduced was spectacular not only for China. Whereas in Poland and Yugoslavia attempts to collectivize agriculture were soon abandoned for political reasons, all the other communist countries socialized the farm sector. Some modifications were introduced later, but none of them, even the reform in Hungary, jeopardized the predominance of collective or State ownership. China is the first case where an socialist agricultural system was decollectivized in practice.

This chapter deals with the outlines of the new Chinese approach in agricultural policy. Part one analyzes the facts which caused the drift to modernization and agricultural reform. Part two deals with the main steps in the reform and part three describes the problems and results of the new policy. Finally, part four draws some conclusions about the significance of the agricultural policy to the economy as a whole.[1]

The Reasons Behind Modernization and Reform

China is still one of the poorest countries in the world, although basic needs are satisfied. When compared with the situation before 1949 and compared to many developing countries today, even this modest level of average nutrition standards represents a great achievement. But, the generation growing up in post-revolutionary China judges the results of socialism on the basis of their own expectations and according to the promises of the political leaders. Here a great gap developed between the proclamations of socialism and its reality. The following points summarize the most important of the developments which led to modernization and reform.

Production: In twenty years between the mid-1950s and the mid-1970s the gross value of agricultural output grew at an annual rate of 3.2%. Included in this figure are items as subsidiary processing, the share of which in the total rose constantly. If one takes the value of crop output alone, the rate declines to 2.2% while food grain output increased at a rate of only 1.87% per year. Perkins and Yussuf stress that in a historical perspective (compared to the pre-revolutionary era) agricultural growth has been impressive, but in an international contemporary perspective "not particularly noteworthy" (Perkins, Yussuf, 1984; 31). At nearly the same time (1957–1977) the population increased by 1.9% annually. The crucial point is that per capita production of food grain (based both on total population and the number of persons employed in agriculture) in fact declined (Perkins, Yussuf, 1984; 31–35). But it must be noted, that many production teams, especially in poor areas, distributed grain before fulfilling mandatory quotas. This "hidden grain" was not included in the official data on agricultural production so that total grain production was underestimated (Chan, Unger, 1982; 455).

Nutrition: With the exception of the early 1960s, agricultural production was able to feed the rapidly increasing population. But the decline of per capita production indicates that nutrition did not improve in quantity or quality. Whereas per-capita consumption of major items increased from 1952 to 1957, the following two decades saw little change. Within this 20-year period, after the Great Leap Forward, a sharp decline of agricultural production between 1959 and 1964 provoked a food crisis, which resulted in a great deal of human suffering. It has been estimated from new Chinese data that about 30 million people died of starvation and that 33 million miscarriages or belated births occurred. No other known famine has ever had such disastrous consequences. Although the nutrition situation was stabilized in the mid-1960s, it was not before the mid-1970s that the consumption again reached the level of the late 1950s (World Bank, 1983; 54–55; Piazza, 1983; III; Smil, 1986; 112, 114).

Rural poverty: Although basic needs were satisfied, malnutrition and poverty, especially in rural areas, were not overcome until the end of the 1970s. Despite ideological declarations, the disparity in incomes and nutrition between rural and urban areas increased during this period. Lardy pointed out that between 1957 and 1978 average national cereal consumption declined by 3.2% (Lardy, 1983; 157). Rural consumption rose by 10.5%. At the end of the 1970s official announcements openly admitted, that the annual food grain consumption of 200 million peasants was less than 150 kilograms. This means that these people were living in the state of semi-starvation; only government loans and transfers averted mass starvation. Estimates show also that during this time farm income grew only very modestly and that in the poor districts there was no growth at all. Even in 1977 22.5% of the districts reported an average per capita distributed income below the Chinese poverty level of 50 yuan per year. In contrast to the rural areas, income in the urban areas rose significantly during the same period (Lardy, 1983; 157, 163, 166, 171, 186).

Disguised unemployment: Although the share of the population engaged in agriculture declined from 81.1% in 1957 to 74.4% in 1977, the total number of employees and their dependents in this sector increased in this period from 532 to 790 million. The agricultural system and strict reglementation of the labor force provided work for all these people and to a large extent prevented rural-urban migration. But Chinese officials nowadays admit that disguised unemployment existed on a large scale. It was estimated that at the beginning of the 1980s about 30 to 40% of the agricultural labor force was redundant. This problem became even more pressing in the 1980s as large numbers of young people entered the work force. Higher incomes and technological advances in agriculture are inevitably connected with labor outflow out of this sector. Massive migration to urban industrial centers is, however, impossible. Therefore one of the great tasks of economic policy in the future will be to provide jobs outside the agriculture in rural areas and in the so-called middle and smaller towns (Heberer, 1985; 44; Ishikawa, 1982; 104, 105).

Sources of growth: Growth of agricultural output was achieved exclusively through an increase in land productivity (output per ha of cultivated land). Yields of rice per unit of sown area doubled nearly from the mid-1950s to the mid-1970s and are now as high as in the most advanced producing countries. Land productivity was raised by a higher multiple cropping index (area of sown land divided by arable land area) and by increased yields per ha of sown land. Whereas the size of agricultural labor force increased rapidly, the area of land under cultivation declined and, as a consequence, the land-man-ratio (cultivated land per agricultural worker) decreased sharply from 0.63 ha in 1957 to 0.40 ha in 1977.[2] Under such conditions (high supply of labor and shortage of land and capital) technological change and agricultural growth had to pursue the path of intensification by using the most abundant production factor—the labor force—for capital formation. In the early periods, labor was used in collective mass campaigns for the so-called work accumulation. Although there was a lot of waste, especially in the Great Leap Forward, labor-intensive measures extended the irrigation system. The hydrological innovations became the key factor in the increasing output. In the second half the 1960s and in the early 1970s, labor force was diverted to producing chemical fertilizers and agricultural machinery in rural industries. In the mid-1070s it was becoming clear that only additional inputs, primarily those produced in modern industries, could make any essential contribution to modernization and further growth (Ishikawa, 1982; 108, 109; Reisch, 1982; 178; Wädekin, 1984).

The Main Steps in the Reform

After the Cultural Revolution had peaked, some pragmatic changes in economic policy could be observed at the beginning of the 1970s. For agriculture this implied a greater emphasis on the production of industrial inputs for agriculture. But a more distinct shift to modernization was announced by Zhou En-Lai in 1975. The so-called "Four Modernizations" of agriculture, industry, military defense, science and technology were to lead China to new period of economic development (Menzel, 1980; 4–5).

The modernization policy did not envisage institutional changes. The "Dazhai" brigade with its collective work organization and income distribution at a higher level remained the model for agriculture. Even after the death of Mao and Zhou in 1976, the agricultural policy continued to be a compromise between different party groups. It was not before Deng Xiao Ping and his team had neutralized the "Gang of Four" politically that a new pragmatic policy and institutional changes could be considered (Maxwell, 1979a/b; 41–95).

Introduction of the "Responsibility System"

The first and essential step in the new rural policy was the reform of the agricultural management system. In 1978 agricultural policy experimented in several, mostly poor regions with the so-called "responsibility system." This kind of farm management was not created by the reform policy. It had been used before, during the 1950s, in agricultural producer cooperatives. During the first years of the reform various forms of the responsibility system were introduced mainly in the production teams. The various models for the system differed in the content of the contracts (contracts linked to special tasks or to general output or deliveries), in the contracting parties (production teams, smaller responsibility groups and individual households), and in the method of accounting or paying off (working points or residual proceeds). These variations are not described in detail in this paper. This has been undertaken by several other authors[3] and most of the various forms play only a marginal role today. Step by step, especially in 1981 and 1982, the liberated form of the contract system, the "output contract with the household," was spread all over the country. This implied that farm land was divided among the individual households and that they were responsible for their own production. Ultimately this policy was firmly established with the publication of Party Central Committee Document No. 1 in 1984. A historical step, as Kueh stated, "no less spectacular than the land reform of 1949–1952, when land was confiscated from the rich for redistribution among poor peasant families" (Kueh, 1985; 122).

The main features of the new farm management system of the mid-1980s, which was similar to a tenure system, can be summarized as follows:

Land distribution and property rights: Initially, agricultural land was allocated according to the number of labor force. Contracts were signed for 3 or 5 years and later, in 1984, enlarged to more than 15 years. Introducing such long-term contracts made it necessary to modify the mode of land distribution because the previous mode would have affected the contracts with other peasants.[4] Up to the present the household has the right only to use the land which still belongs to the collective unit (brigade, production team or a new cooperative). Furthermore private plots, which are not included in the contracts, were enlarged and many restrictions on their use were relaxed. In 1983 and 1984 gradual land concentration was allowed. When a household under contract is unable to till the land or wants to turn to other work, it may give it back to the collective or transfer it to another person through negotiation. The duration of the contract signed by the household may not be changed. Under these conditions a household may accumulate contracts and, important for structural change, improve land use and technology. But privately owned plots and the contractual plots cannot be purchased, sold or leased (Document No. 1, 1984; III; Interview, 1984; 6; Gey/Kosta/Quaisser, 1985; 13; Kueh, 1985; 128; Walker, 1984, 788).

Production and delivery quotas and agricultural tax: Peasants are free to farm their land in the manner they choose. But until 1984, they were obliged to deliver a certain amount of agricultural products, mainly grain, to the state. These production quotas are comparable to the mandatory deliveries of the 1950s. The deliveries included a levy paid to the collective unit in order to maintain certain services, the welfare fund and water supply. In addition to fulfilling the quota, the household has to pay the agricultural tax. There are no exact data concerning the total share as volume of the quotas. Chinese sources mention that about 13 to 15% of the total income of a household is delivered to the collective, including a 5% tax which is collective by the state. The quota and the tax calculations are based on the land area and the average yields of the last 3 years. But in recent years the administration has tried to keep the quotas constant. Consequently the peasants gained a greater decision making latitude in choosing the production structure. Once the contracts are fulfilled, the household may consume the rest or sell it on the free market. In 1985 the contract system was gradually changed. This change will be described in the final section (Interview, 1984; 9, 10; Kosta, Quaisser, 1984; 9, 10; Watson, 1983; 717).

Inputs and services: Not only traditional inputs (animals, tools etc.) but also small machines and transportation facilities were divided among the peasant households. In some cases draft animals might be shared among several families. Only more important tasks (organization, construction of irrigation systems, motor pumps, larger machines and infrastructure) were left to the collective units (teams, brigades and communes) or their successor organization. These inputs are still distributed by the team or brigade and special teams within the brigade are responsible for services (plowing, herbicides and pesticides). The quantities of fertilizers to be supplied to the peasant household are also fixed in contracts. The household must pay for the inputs and services received. Sometimes families also agree to provide a number of days of free labor to maintain certain collective assets (Gey, Kosta, Quaisser, 1985; 28, 29; Lu Yun, 1984; 20, 21; Wädekin, 1984b; Watson, 1983; 71).

The type of responsibility system was very attractive for the peasants because it guaranteed enough space for self-management. In 1982 nearly all responsibility systems were transformed to conform with this model and in 1983 it was used by 99.8% of all teams. In fact, it reestablished familiy farming within the framework of socialism. Aubert underlines that the rapid extension of peasant farmer shows in retrospective how fragile the equilibrium was between the centrifugal forces of family interests and the political power in the communes (Aubert, 1984; 5; Huang Xiang, 1985; 17).

Today family farming appears to most Chinese officials to be the arrangement best suited for agricultural production. Peasant farming is considered to create highly motivated individuals and flexibility in adjusting to changing natural conditions. Luo Hanxian, a Chinese agricultural economist, expressed it in the following words: "In fact, household farming with the household as the unit of management engaging in diversified economic activities may be considered China's national form of farming" (Luo Hanxian, 1985; 143). It is stressed, however, that family farming is integrated into the socialist system by the collective ownership of land, by contracts and by the remaining collective management and cooperatives (Luo Hanxian, 1985; 173–174).

This strong bias for private agriculture is also underlined by the reform implemented in the state agricultural sector which controls about 4,5% of the cultivated land. At the outset of the reform, the responsibility system was introduced in subunits of the state farms too. Later on, some farms also handed over land to individual peasants by implementing the household responsibility system. From 1979 until 1985 about one million households were established as basic production units in state farms, and in Inner Mongolia, 60% of all state farms practiced this system. Thanks to this reform (and assisted by higher prices) state farms started to make profits (CD, 3. 10. 1985; CD, 10. 2. 1986; Woodward, 1982; 231–251; Chung Ming Pang, De Boer, 1983; 657–660).

The Reform of the Organizational Structure

The introduction of the responsibility system was accompanied by organizational changes in the countryside . In the previous system the communes had been the basic unit of administration organization in rural areas. The communes were established in the late 1950s and remained until the beginning of the 1980s. The communes had three levels of administration: the commune, the brigade and the production team. The production team was the basic accounting unit. At each level economic, administrative and political tasks were integrated in the same organization. The main steps of the administrative reform, which started in 1978, are summarized as follows:

1. Economic and political tasks were divided at each level in the administrative structure. At the commune level special county committees or governments were created to carry out administrative functions. Up to the spring of 1985 nearly 80% of the communes had been organized in this way (Kosta, Quaisser, 1984; 10; Widmer, 1986; 139).

2. In recent years the economic departments of the communes were transformed into agro-industrial or trade cooperatives. So called regional or territorial cooperatives were set up at the brigade level; they took over most of the tasks of the previous brigade. But they are no longer subordinated to the former communes (Gey, Kosta, Quaisser, 1984; 14; Widmer, 1986; 140). The production teams were for the large part dissolved. Therefore the lowest administrative unit is now the brigade or the new regional cooperative. Because the land is not nationalized in China, these organizations are the owners of the land. The regional cooperative is therefore responsible for land management and contracting the peasants. In fact every peasant is by law a member of such a cooperative (Interview, 1984).

3. "Specialized" companies and cooperatives were also created for special tasks (breeding) and to provide peasants with inputs, services, and technical assistance. They are often very small and some of them have been formed voluntarily by the farmers themselves. More detailed information on this topic will be given in the next chapter. The state trade organizations have also been transformed into the old marketing and credit cooperatives which had previously existed in the 1950s. This was considered to be an essential step in the reconstruction of the rural economy. At the end of 1985 nearly 80% of the peasants had bought shares in such cooperatives and they have spread all over the country (Aubert, 1984; 11, 12; CD, 16.12.85; Interview, 1984; 2,6,7; Widmer, 1986; 140).

China is a huge country and one has to stress that all these changes are part of a gradual evolution. The situation differs from one region to the next. In an interview Wu Len, one of the top agrarian experts, commented on the confusing situation in the countryside with a Chinese proverb: If you have seen the spot of a leopard it does not mean that you have seen the whole leopard (Interview, 1984; 6).

Specialized Households and New Cooperatives

Chinese studies define specialized households as a family business based on individual households which are mainly engaged in "commodity production." They concentrate on one activity in which most of their labor and funds are invested. Some research studies define them mainly based on the so-called commodity rate (percentage of the total production directed to the market). Others stress the proportion of total family income earned from specialized production or the quantity of commodities produced. The concrete criteria for definition may vary widely;

only a few counties and regions have their own locally standardized definitions for specialized households (Zhou Qiren, Du Ying, 1984; 53). One can distinguish between two main categories of specialized household, based upon their origin and their development perspective (Song Linfei, 1984; 118, 119; Zhou Qiren, Du Ying, 1984; 50–51).

Contractual specialized households: Such households sign contracts with the production brigade or its successor organization. They take over specialized operation which were previously carried by collective units. To fulfill this contract the household uses the land, facilities and equipment of the collective. In most cases the households also contract farmland for their own consumption. The household is paid for the production or is allowed to retain all that is produced above a certain quota. Some of these households are responsible mainly for production, while the collective is totally or partly responsible for capital, raw materials and marketing.

Self-managed specialized households: These emerged from the family-based sideline occupations in the countryside. These households manage their own labor and capital and undertake their own production, marketing and supply. They are responsible for their own profits and losses. Generally, these households started with traditional types of sideline production, which were suppressed during the period of the left-wing predominance in policy-making. Often, some members of the households use their special traditional skills. Step by step, and in line with general economic progress in any given rural area, more and more labor and capital is redirected to specialized production, which becomes the main source of income for the families affected. Some of these households coordinate their activities or join together in cooperative ventures.

24.83 million specialized households had come into existence at the end of 1983, roughly 15% of all rural households in China. National data on the distribution among the several types are not available, but field studies show that most of them are self-managed. Chinese investigations stress the distinction between these types tends to become blurred. Enlarging their specialized production, contractual households invest their own labor, tools and funds. On the other hand, self-managed specialized households ever more frequently entering into contracts with new collectives (e.g. animal raising) so that some collective means of production augment the self-managed household operations (Yuang Chongfa, 1984; Zhou Qiren, Du Ying, 1984; 52).

Specialized households engage in various types of farming and other activities, which are often linked with agriculture. Some of them are specialized in grain production. These households generally have more labor, capital and land under cultivation and exhibit a higher marketing ratio when compared to the average household. The prerequisite for such a process of concentration is an improvement in the mode used for contracting farmland. This means that farmland is not only distributed according to the number of persons of labor force in a household but also according to the skills and abilities of the peasants. Many specialized households concentrate their production in animal husbandry (ducks, chicken, rabbits, etc.), and horticulture (vegetables, seedlings, medicinal plants) and only a few in forestry. The non-agricultural activities vary from handicrafts (embroidery, weaving, handbags etc.) to labor service (construction, transportation, commerce) and services (restaurants, hotels, etc.). The general trend in recent years has been that many households have turned to non-agricultural activities and the number of households engaged in grain production has decreased. But this depends largely on local conditions. Chinese investigations show that the importance of specialized households depends on the development process in an area. More specialized households have been created in regions with higher development levels than in less developed parts of the country (Huang Huan-Zhong, 1983, 27–31; Song-Linfei, 1984, 119; Zhou Qiren, Du Ying, 1984; 54).

In fostering the spread of specialized households, agricultural policy aims to promote the modernization of agricultural and commodity production in rural areas. The main process will be the following: with the stabilization and expansion of non-farming operations, more and more households are to give up (or sub-contract) their land to become non-farming peasant households. This should promote structural change: labor resources will leave agriculture without migrating to big cities. At the same time the land will be given to households which are engaged solely in farming and which will specialize their production in staple crops (grain, cotton, cash crops) and animal husbandry. Several measures are envisaged and have in part been put into practice to promote land concentration and to provide better technical equipment in such households. For example, households specialized in grain production can obtain more land from the collective. In addition they are supplied with better and more inputs and services (Lin Zili, Tao Haili, 1983; 3–7; Song Linfei, 1984; 124, 125; Zu Weiwen, 183).

New forms of cooperatives or economic associations, sometimes also called new combines, are considered to be a further step in the development and structural change in rural areas. They are formed voluntarily by the peasants themselves for their mutual benefit and they are responsible for their own profits and losses. The property rights of the individual household are not changed upon joining a cooperative and the peasants can leave it on their own will. Field studies show that most of these undertakings are on a small scale and seasonal in character. They are not only engaged in activities directly associated with agricultural production but also in manufacturing, processing, transportation and services. The size and membership in these cooperatives can vary a great deal. Some are established by several families, like the familiar form of mutual aid teams pooling land and labor and sharing the results equally. Others are formed by taking out shares or by combining shares, skills and labor in several forms. The new cooperatives are usually formed on an equal basis by independent households. But some of them, especially those requiring land, are joint ventures where the production team or the collective unit supplies some of the resources and the households provide the skills and organization. Finally, payments to the participants take various forms, according to the type of cooperative or association. They involve various kinds of wages, payments according to the contracts, or a dividend on the capital invested. All this clearly indicates that these new organizations must be distinguished from the cooperatives of the 1950s (N.J.W., 1983; 11–14; Shang Li, 1985; 21–22; Watson, 1983; 722).

Reform of Agricultural Planning and Prices

At the beginning of the agricultural reform, important elements in centralized production planning remained, although fewer targets were handed down to the provinces and the number of mandatory targets was reduced. In 1980, the province of Sichuan was the first to experiment with a relaxation of production quotas, and other provinces followed in the same year. In the following years, based on the introduction of the responsibility system, a shift towards a more indirect method of planning could be discerned. Similar planning methods had existed during the first years of the Peoples Republic (1949–1955 and 1957) and reemerged in the beginning of the 1960s (1961–1965) (Erling, 1984; 222–223; Walker, 1984; 785).

Indirect planning by no means implied that the national or provincial plan was not initially conceived in explicit quantitative figures, also expressed in terms of production targets. But more and more targets for sown area and production were being replaced by targets referenced to the state's acquisition of major products. Up to and including 1984 this applied in the responsibility system in which the households were required to fulfill procurement targets for certain products in quantitative terms. But peasants were relatively less constraint by indirect planning (manipulating prices, credits and taxes) than by direct planning (quotas) since procurement prices were set with the objective of stimulating the delivery of such products. Greater freedom for the production units and the full acceptance of rural peasant markets enlarged the scope of the market mechanism and hence the role of indirect price planning. Farmers were engaged more and more not only in fulfilling the central targets, but in maximizing with relative few constraint their net revenue as well (Lardy, 1983; 18, 19, 88; Walker, 1984; 785).

The first and essential component in the new policy was a substantial rise in procurement prices for the mandatory deliveries or production quotas. Because the prices for manufactured goods increased only slowly, the terms of trade enjoyed by the farm sector clearly improved. At the same time, agricultural policy consciously used price incentives as one policy instrument to achieve desired changes in cropping patterns. Although centralized control still determined on a wide scale the production structure, adjustments in relative farm prices exerted an ever expanding influence on the production decisions made by the peasants. Agricultural policy also provided stronger incentives for marketing. As early as 1070, the state had initiated uniform 20% premium payments for deliveries of grain above the basic "quota deliveries." This premium, which was fixed for a period of several years, was raised to 30% in 1972 and in 1979 to 50%. In 1979 this system was also expanded to cover other products (cotton, oilseeds). Additionally, the state established a fourth price category for cereals purchased, the so-called negotiated prices, which also had been used in the 1950s. Once a producing unit has made its mandatory deliveries and met the purchasing targets beyond the quota, it may sell additional products at prices determined by mutual agreement with the state. Negotiated prices appear to be closely related to market prices. Last but not least, the full political legitimation of peasant markets and the policy concerning them had an important impact on rural marketing. The rapidly increasing production under nearly constant production or delivery quotas led to a greater share of free marketing. This was stimulated by higher free market prices. Hence, the scope of market forces was enlarged in rural areas (Lardy, 1983; 18, 19, 88; Skinner, 1985; 405–409; Walker, 1984; 784–786).

In 1985, agricultural policy embarked upon a further liberalization of the rural marketing system. The leadership clearly recognized the obstacles of the old system. Its primary goal had been to secure a basic production of grain for nutrition. With the high agricultural growth rates which occurred after the reform, this became less important. On the contrary, the quota system with its price structure fixed by the state hindered the sorely needed diversification of agriculture. The increasing volume of state purchase also overloaded the state marketing system, especially with respect to transportation and storage. Similar to other socialist countries, the macroeconomic price system is characterized by a decoupling of producer and consumer prices. Higher state procurement prices and increasing purchasing volume provoked a substantial rise in subsidies directed to agriculture. Hence, a macroeconomic price and wage reform became the key question of the whole economic reform in the mid-1980s (CD, 1. 2. 1985; Du Runsheng, 1985; 17).

The main elements of this reform can be summarized as follows:

Elimination of the production quotas: The quota system for the main agricultural products, and especially for grain, was abolished. Now the peasant sign contracts with the cooperatives, setting the amount of their deliveries before the harvest begins. In some regions the peasants can pay money instead of contracting products and in the future it will be possible to pay the agricultural tax in cash instead of grain. This new system will lead to a greater flexibility in state intervention and to a gradual extension of free marketing. But the state will not refrain from intervening in the market when necessary (price stabilization). It is expected that more state interventions will be necessary at the beginning and less later on, when the price structure becomes more rational. With the expansion of private activities and greater freedom for small scale industries, the procurement of inputs has become more flexible for the peasants. They can now buy inputs directly from such sources (CD, 24. 1. 1985; CD, 6. 2. 1985; CD, 11. 2. 1985; Gey, Kosta, Quaisser, 1985; 49).

New contract prices: The state will now purchase at the former fixed quota price about 30% of the contracted quota for the main products (rice, wheat, corn) and 70% at the higher preferential price. Farmers are allowed to sell their surplus at whatever price they can get on the market. But if the price falls below the low quota price, the state will purchase whatever amount the peasants wish to sell at that price (CD, 6. 2. 1985).

Liberalization of price controls: Price controls (producer and consumer prices) are gradually being relaxed on such products as pork, vegetables and fish. The floating price and the new price rations will give the farmers the correct signal with respect to demand. The consumers were compensated in the first year (1985) with additional payments. Price liberalization was first implemented successfully in Shenzhen and Guangzhou. In the special economic zone of Shenzen all prices were deregulated and all food and oil coupons were abolished. This is to be extended, step by step, to the other parts of the country (CD, 6. 2. 1985; CD, 11. 2. 1985; Cheng Zhiping, 1985; 15, 16; Gey, Kosta, Quaisser, 1985; 48, 49).

Reform of the marketing organization: Although the planning administration has still a wide scope of controls in agriculture, the state monopoly in agriculture marketing has for all practical purposes been abolished and replaced by a diversified system. As mentioned in section II.2., the state marketing organizations were transformed into cooperatives in which farmers can hold shares. Private trading in agricultural products is now also allowed over long distances. More and more farmers are involved in transporting agricultural and sideline products to peasant markets. In addition state, collective and private enterprise are entitled to buy and to sell products on the open markets and to engage in various economic activities (CD, 24. 1. 1985; CD, 11. 2. 1985; CD, 7. 5. 1985; CD, 6. 11. 1985; Yuan Ruizhen, 1984; 23-26).

Achievements and Problems of the Agricultural Reform

The agricultural reform was the first and most successful step in the overall economic reform and an important test of the pragmatic policy of Deng Xiao Ping. This great success is clearly reflected by the production results: Total gross agricultural output (current prices) grew annually from 1979 up to 1984 at an average rate of 15.6% (from 1966 to 1978 by 8.5%). Although the sown area allocated to grain decreased in favor of other crops, grain production from 1979 to 1984 increased by 4.9% annually, which indicates a substantial rise of average yields per sown ha. In 1985, due mainly to weather conditions, grain output fell, but total agricultural production nevertheless increased. The shift in sown area from grain to other crops reflects improvements in diversification of agricultural production which was an essential aim of the new policy. This trend together with higher yields increased the production of the main industrial crops. Between 1979 and 1984 the production of cotton grew annually by 8.5%. Significant increases in livestock production were also achieved, which is reflected by an average growth rate of meat output of 10.2% per year (current prices) although this sector remained small, backward and inefficient during the first years of the reform (Table 9.1).

The rise in per capita production had a strong positive impact on living conditions in rural areas. From 1978 to 1984 per capita rural consumption of grain increased by 7.2%, cooking oil by 102.3%, meat by 87.7% and fish and shrimps by 106.5%. More diversified production and the allowing of private markets and trade sharply improved nutrition in rural and urban areas. The substantial rise in per capita peasant income (nominal) from 134 Yuan in 1978 to 355 Yuan in 19984 enabled the farmers to buy more industrial consumer goods such as synthetic fabrics, bicycles, wrist watches, sewing machines, radios, etc. (Table 9.2). But due to the scarcity of industrial consumer goods and inputs, the peasants invested a large amount of their savings in housing construction.

However, the agricultural policy is currently confronted with the following problems and challenges:

State and collective investments: The Chinese are concerned about the decrease in longer-term investments and in some cases about the

Table 9.1 Major Output Indicators for Agricultural Production

	Absolute figures			Annual growth rates	
	1965	1978	1984	1966-78	1979-84
Gross agricultural output(a)	537	1,567	3,755	8.5	15.6
Grain(b)	19,505	30,477	40,731	3.5	4.9
kg per capita	272	318	395	0.2	3.7
Yields(c)	1,628	2,528	3,396	3.4	6.0
Oil crops(b)	362.5	521.8	1,191	2.8	14.7
Meat output(b)	551.0	856.3	1,540.6	7.6	10.2

(a) Value in 100 Mill RMB (current prices);
(b) In 10,000 tons;
(c) Average yields kg per ha
Sources: China 1985; 8, 33, 35, 36; Statistical Yearbook 1984; 153

Table 9.2 Income and Consumption of Peasant Households (a)

	1978	1984	1984 (1978=100)
Average per capita net income (Yuan)(b)	133.57	355.33	266.0
Per capita consumption			
Grain (kg)	248	266	107.2
Edible oil (kg)	1.97	3.96	202.3
Meat (kg)	5.75	10.62	184.7
Fish and Shrimps (kg)	0.84	1.73	206.5
Consumer goods(c)			
Bicycles	30.73	74.48	242.4
Sewing Machines	19.80	42.57	215.0
Radios	17.44	61.13	350.5

(a) Sample survey
(b) Nominal
(c) Average year end ownership of durable consumer goods
per 100 peasant households
Source: China 1985; 102, 103, 104

neglect of collective property, which occurred after implementing the household responsibility system. This was accompanied by a decline in state budgetary investments in agriculture, forestry, water conservation and meteorology, which decreased by 33% from 1978 to 1984. It is estimated that the other important source of capital formation—the so-called work done by collective labor—has also decreased. Hence the responsibility for investments in water conservation and in the irrigation system, both essential to further agricultural development have not yet been taken over to an adequate extent by new organizations (e.g. county governments). However, these problems are typical for a transitional period in which the rural institutions are being reorganized. The Chinese are fully aware of this and there is no doubt that state and collective investments in the rural economy will still have a high priority in future economic policy-making. In stabilizing the new institutional setting, collective functions will be partly realized in new organizations (companies, specialized households and service centers). Reflecting the monetarization of the economy, the period of "work accumulation" has ended and collective investments will have to be financed by taxes and other levies. At the same time, opportunities are required for private capital formation and the government has just started to reorganize the banking system in rural areas (Walker, 1985; 800–801; Heberer, 1985; 37).

Private investments and mechanization: At the beginning of the reform, rising farm incomes were directed mainly to consumption and housing construction (Walker, 1985; 800, 801). This was due to the fact that the supply of industrial inputs (small tractors, small pumps, chemical fertilizers, etc.) could not satisfy the peasants' demand. The farm machinery industry concentrated above all on producing large implements for big production units. In addition, parcellization of land had an adverse effect on mechanization since the existing technology was not appropriate for the household level. It has on occasion also been mentioned that as a result of the decentralized management of collectively owned machines, many agricultural machine centers which had provided plowing services etc. have been closed (CD, 7. 1. 1986; Lu Yun, 1984; 18–21). But first steps have been made in adjusting the machinery industry during the last years. Greater emphasis has been put on the production of small tractors, while the output of larger equipment (i.e. combine harvester) has been reduced (CD, 30. 12. 1985). At the same time, the sale of tractors to individual households increased from 38000 in 1980 to 2.1 million in 1983. But tractors are often used for transportation, because there is a lack of small lorries. Mechanization is further stimulated by the possibility to buy and sell machines on free markets. But it is also stressed that collective machine stations contracting peasants households must be further promoted to provide peasants with an adequate machinery service (Lu Yun, 1984; 18–21).

Inputs and ecological problems: Further expansion of agricultural land and irrigated area will not contribute very much to agricultural growth in the future. On the contrary: state policy is urgently challenged to implement strict land planning and ecological measures in order to prevent an enlargement of deserts, salted area, erosion and land used caused by urbanization (CD, 30. 1. 1985; CD, 11. 11. 1985). Further agricultural growth will essentially depend on higher inputs per sown area, based on the use of fertilizers and inputs for herbicides and pesticides. The fragile ecological balance of the highly intensive Chinese agriculture can, however, be endangered by too many inputs of this type and by inadequate training in their application. This requires a smoothly functioning extension service and a careful combination of modern and traditional inputs (CD, 21. 12. 1984). At the same time water pollution and the shortage of energy can destabilize the ecological situation in rural areas. The Chinese are quite aware of these problems and have begun to set up service centers. Programs for soil conversation and afforestation have also been started. But this is only the beginning and ecological problems in future will be a great challenge for state regulations and investments. Alerting farmers to ecological problems is also needed (Schinke, 1985; 152, 153; Šmil, 1986; 121).

Agricultural prices and marketing: Although important reform steps in agricultural planning have been taken, the price and marketing system is far from being rational. Price policy has not by any means been based on accurate information. Relative prices, especially in animal husbandry, are often illogical. The new contract system has certainly made state intervention more flexible and the relaxation of the prices for pork, fish and vegetables resulted in a greater adaptation of supply to demand. This is clearly indicated in the Guandong province, where the floating prices affected the supply situation positively: the peasants expanded their production in response to higher prices which, due to market mechanisms, ultimately brought about lower prices. In other parts of the country, especially in big cities, prices rose drastically. Due to natural and marketing constraints, the supply of agricultural products did not react quickly enough. Hence, compensation payments could not cover the price increases and people were discontented. Pork rationing was reintroduced in February of 1985 to cope with an insufficient supply of meat. And neither are input prices by any means rational, in the sense of equilibrium prices, and the problems of high subsidies for consumer products has not yet been solved. At the same time, agricultural policy cannot use price mechanisms effectively, because the marketing system is characterized by an inadequate infrastructure. Major investments are needed to improve transportation, storage and processing facilities as well and to install a marketing information system. Recently, the Chinese have begun setting up wholesale markets for agricultural products (CD, 7. 2. 1987; CD, 29. 11. 1985; CD, 11. 11. 1985; Walker, 1984; 801).

Income distribution and rural poverty: Rural incomes rose substantially due to higher farm prices and increasing production above all in cash crops and sideline products. The available Chinese data indicate that the rural-urban income gap narrowed: From 1978 to 1984, per capita income in rural areas increased by 15% a year, whereas in the same period the urban per capita income rose by only 8% annually (CD, 11. 7. 1985). Especially in poor areas the income situation improved sharply. But in 1984, 5.1% of the peasant households were still earning less than 150 Yuan (nominal) per year, which is below the Chinese poverty level. It is also estimated that in 1984, 11% of the rural population did not have sufficient clothing and nutrition (Smil, 1986; 119). Hence special investments and programs to help the poor are envisaged and have in part been implemented. In poor area government also allowed more private activity and migration out of such regions was recently admitted (CD 20. 11. 1985; CD 22. 1. 1986). In general the available data, based on surveys, indicate that the increase in rural incomes did not widen the income disparity among peasant households (Widmer, 1986; 144, 145). But inter-regional and intra-village disparities may widen in the future and it is obvious that not every peasant can establish a specialized household. It is difficult to predict in which way deeper income disparities will provoke social tensions as well as party resistance in the future. Official policy is currently supporting private accumulation and rich peasants are presenting as shining examples. But on the other hand, the Chinese press has published reports about rural party cadres who are pressuring or even blackmailing rich peasants (CA, June 1984; CA, January 1984; 18). To secure the success of the reform in the long run it will be necessary to break the resistance of lower and middle-level cadres to the new policy and to implement new laws and improve guarantees for private property.

Population and employment: Some were afraid that in distribution land according to the number of members of a household, the responsibility system might counteract state efforts for strict family planning. It was argued that peasant families tend to have more than one child because they wanted to enlarge the labor force of a household and to provide old-age security. As C. Aubert shows, this fear is unfounded. The apparent increase in births in 1981 was caused mainly by statistical adjustments (Aubert, 1984; 26). However, the new mode of land distribution and special contracts for family planning, including incentives and penalties, will strengthen birth control in rural areas (Ren Tao, Yue Bing, 1983; 21). But it is obvious that family planning in rural areas is far more difficult and is sometimes dealt with more flexibility than in urban areas (CD 6. 12. 1985). Nevertheless, China's population will increase by about 400 million people from the mid-1980s to the year 2000, due mainly to the large percentage of young people entering the child-bearing age (Qian Xinzhong, 1984; 19). Disguised unemployment and structural change will aggravate the employment problems in agriculture. Hence, peasants are to turn nonagricultural jobs, above all in small-scale industries, in the rural handicraft and service sector, or in small and middle towns. For that reason, many private initiatives are being allowed and it is expected that part-time farming will expand (Fei Xiaotong, 1985; 25; Kosta, 1985; 127, 132–135). In addition state initiatives in professional training as well as consistent growth and structural policies are needed to secure employment opportunities for upcoming generation.

Conclusions

China's new agricultural policy is essentially a market-oriented reform. The agricultural structure and the property use rights have been transformed to reestablish peasant farming without abolishing collective land ownership. Also, the organizational structure and the institutions in rural areas have been changed fundamentally: the people's communes have been dissolved and political, administrative as well as economic responsibilities have been divided at each level of the administration structure. At the same time, different types of collectives, cooperatives and private initiatives are allowed. Finally, agricultural planning was gradually transformed from direct to indirect price planning, giving wider scope to the self-regulating market mechanism. Although all theses measures may not be implemented in all parts of the country on the same scale, the general bias towards a market-oriented reform is clearly visible.

The reform in rural areas was not only a great success for agriculture, but also an essential precondition for the economic reform in general. Individual motivation, which was suppressed in the collective system, is now being stimulated to increase agricultural and rural sideline production. This helps to overcome traditional bottlenecks and macroeconomic disequilibria in consumer goods markets for food, which has an additional positive impact on the price and wage reform. Furthermore, increasing rural incomes are strengthening the demand for industrial inputs and consumer goods. The intensifies the pressure to change the traditional development strategy in favor of a diversified and more consumption-oriented strategy. Last but not least, the expanding scope of the market mechanism in rural areas requires the reform of the planning and allocative mechanism in the whole economy. But, in turn, the agricultural reform has reached a stage at which its further success depends primarily on important steps towards the economic reform in general.

A solution to or even diminution of the problems which inevitably occur during a transitional period will depend basically on the consistent and ongoing implementation of the reform. But a market-oriented reform by no means implies a laissez faire policy but necessitates a consistent economic policy to create the institutional setting and the qualifications required for proper functioning of the market. Also natural and ecological constraints, as well as the grave demographic situation, require state regulations and initiatives. Finally, the reform is endangered by political constraints, which are typical for socialist societies and widely known. The Soviet model and the left-wing policy of the Cultural Revolution have, however, been deeply discredited. At the moment, it looks as though the party leadership, even against some resistance in its own ranks, will continue the reform, because it is evident that there is no other way to master the problems and to modernize the Chinese economy towards the year 2000.

Notes

1. I would like to thank the members of the Economic and Agricultural Institutes of the Academic of Social Sciences in Beijing, Shanghai and Guangzhou. During my trips to China in 1984 and 1985 they kindly answered many questions concerning the agricultural reform, providing invaluable assistance in preparing this paper. Many thanks also Dr. H. Bechtold, Mr. R. Gerhold, Dr.Dr. P. Gey, Prof. J. Kosta, Prof. E. Schinke, Prof. K.E. Wädekin and Mr. B. Venohr who offered useful comments on the original draft of this paper. I also wish to express my most sincere appreciation to Mr. Zhai Xianglong, researcher at the Institute for Study of World Economy at the Shanghai Academy of Social Sciences, who translated several Chinese language articles for this paper. Mr. Zhai is also co-author of chapter about the specialized households and new cooperatives.

2. As American satellite pictures show, agricultural land is about 40 million ha larger than the official date indicate, because production teams did not report new area but they never failed to report land losses (Chan, Unger, 1982; 454).

3. The different models for the responsibility system are described by Heberer, 1985; Lin Zili, 1983; Watson, 1983.

4. Sometimes a part of the land is retained by the collective for reallocation when the contracts are changed.

References

Aubert, C., 1984: The New Economic Policy in the Chinese Countryside. Paper of the Seventh International Conference on Soviet and East European Agriculture. Grignon

Bergmann, T./Gey, P./Quaisser, W., ed., 1984: Sozialistische Agrarpolitik. Vergleichs- und Einzelstudien zur agrarpolitischen Entwicklung in der Sowjetunion, Polen, Ungarn, China und Kuba. Köln

BR, Beijing Rundschau

BR, 29. 1. 1985: Über die Reform des Preissystems

CA: China Aktuell

CA, January 1984: Wan Li über die Situation auf dem Lande

———, June 1984: Kader gegen spezialisierte Haushalte

CD: China Daily

CD, 21. 2. 1984: Centres to Boost Agriculture across the Country

———, 24. 1. 1985: State Monopoly on Food to be Lifted

———, 30. 1. 1985: Conservancy of Land is Urgent Issue

———, 6. 2. 1985: Price Reforms

———, 7. 2. 1985: Ministry Explains Rationing of Pork

———, 11. 2. 1985: State Monopoly in Rural Areas Must Move with Times

———, 7. 5. 1985: Price Policy Leads to Free Market Boom

———, 11. 7. 1985: Farmers Earn More Faster than City Folk

———, 3. 10. 1985: State Farms Diversify and Cut Losses

———, 6. 11. 1985: Free Market Flourishing

———, 11. 11. 1985: Experts Urge New Land Rent System

———, 11. 11. 1985: Price Rise Fears: "Look at the Bigger Picture"

———, 20. 11. 1985: State Adopts Migration Plan to Help the Poor

———, 29. 11. 1985: Price Changes "Some Showing Benefits"

———, 6. 12. 1985: Birth Policy Continue with Gradual Relaxation

———, 16. 12. 1985: Rural Co-operative Exhibit their Wares

———, 30. 12. 1985: Output Leap for Farm Machinery

———, 7. 1. 1986: Agriculture is Crying out for Machinery

———, 22. 1. 1986: Poor Areas Want Flexible Policy

———, 10. 2. 1986: State Farms Thrive under New System

Chan, A./Unger, J., 1982: Grey and Black: The Hidden Economy of Rural China, in: Pacific Affairs, No. 55; 452–471

Cheng Zhiping, 1985: Preisreform in China, in BR, No. 16 (24 April 1985); 15–17

China, 1985: China a Statistical Survey in 1985 (compiled by State Statistical Bureau Peoples Republic of China). Beijing

Chung Ming Pang/De Boer, A. J., 1983: Management Decentralization on China's State Farms, in: American Journal of Agricultural Economics, November 1983; 657–666

Document No. 1, 1984: Rural Economic Policies in China. Text, as transmitted of the CCP Central Committee's circular on rural work in 1984, in: Documents of the World Bank, January 14, 1984

Du Runsheng, 1985: Der zweite Schritt in der Reform des ländlichen Wirt-
schaftssystems, in: BR, June 25, 1985; 16–19
Erling, J., 1984: Reformen in der chinesischen Landwirtschaft, in: T. Bergmann/
P. Gey/W. Quaisser, ed., 1984; 214–231
Fei Xiaotong, 1985: Arbeitsbeschaffung für überschüssige Arbeitskräfte auf dem
Lande, in: BR, Vol. 22, No. 22 (4 June 1985); 24–26
Gey, P./Kosta, J./Quaisser, W., 1985: Protokolle einer Reise in die VR China
vom 27. 8. bis 16. 9. 1985, in: Arbeitspapiere des Forschungsprojektes "Krise
und Reform sozialistischer Wirtschaftssysteme," Heft 1
Heberer, T., 1985: Zur Problematik der gegenwärtigen Landwirtschaftsreform
in der VR China, in: Osteuropa-Wirtschaft, Vol. 30, No. 1
Huang Huan-Zhong, 1983: Discussion of Some Questions Concerning "Spe-
cialized Households" in Rural Areas (chinese), in: Nongye Jingji Wenti, No.
12 (1983); 27–31
Huang Xian, 1985: Über die Reform des chinesischen Wirtschaftssystems, in:
BR, May 21, 1985, Vol. 21, No. 20; 15–21
Interview, 1984: Talks in Beijing (September 13, 1984) with representatives of
the Research Centre for the Development of Rural Areas subordinated to the
State Council (most of the questions were asked by Dr. Ulrich Menzel, the
answers were mainly given by Prof. Lu Wen; typescript)
Ishikawa, S., 1982: China's Food and Agriculture Performance and Prospects,
in: E. Reisch, ed., 1982; 89–143
Kosta, J., 1985: Beschäftigungsprobleme in China, in: A. Schüller, ed., 1985;
105–140
Kosta, J./Quaisser, W., 1984: Reiseprotokolle der Reise in die VR China vom
8. 2. bis zum 27. 2. 1984, in: Arbeitspapiere des Forschungsprojektes
"Sozialismus und Industrialisierung," Heft 10
Kueh, Y. Y., 1985: The Economics of the "Second Land Reform" in China, in:
The China Quarterly, March 1985, No. 101; 122–131
Lardy, N. R., 1983: Agriculture in China's Modern Economic Development.
Cambridge/London/New York/New Rochelle/Melbourne/Sydney
Lin Zili, 1983: On the Contract System of the Responsibility Linked to
Productivity—A New Form of Cooperative Economy in China's Socialist
Agriculture, in: Social Sciences in China, Vol. IV, No. 1; 53–104
Lin Zili, Tao Haili, 1983: A New Important Progress in the Renewal of Agricultural
Mode of Production (chinese), in Nongye Jingji Wenti, No. 9, 1983; 3–7
Luo Hanxian, 1985: Economic Change in Rural China. Beijing
Lu Yun, 1984: Das Verantwortlichkeitssystem auf dem Land (VI). Einfluss auf
die Mechanisierung der Landwirtschaft, in: BR, Vol. 21, No. 47, November
20, 1984; 18–21
Maxwell, N., ed., 1979: China's Road to Development. Oxford/New York/
Toronto/Sydney/Paris/Frankfurt
Maxwell, N., 1979a: The Tachai Way. Part I: Learning from Tatchai, in: Maxwell,
ed., 1979; 41–70
———, 1979b: The Tachai Way. Part II: The Fourth Mobilization, in: Maxwell,
ed., 1979; 71–95

Menzel, U, 1980: Chinesische Agrarpolitik in der Periode der technischen Transformation, in: Yu Cheung-Lieh, ed., 1980; 3–40

Perkins, D., Yusuf, S., 1984: Rural Development in China. Baltimore/London

Piazza, A., 1983: Trends in Food and Nutrient Availability in China, 1950–81, World Bank. Washington D. C.

Qian Xinzhong, 1984: Änderung und Entwicklung der chinesischen Bevölkerung, in: BR, 17. 10. 1984

Reisch, E., ed., 1982: Agricultura Sinica, Gieaener Abhandlungen zur Agrar- und Wirtschaftsforschung des europäischen Ostens, Band 114. Berlin

Reisch, E., 1982: Faktoren und Komponenten der Entwicklung der chinesischen Landwirtschaft, in: Reisch, ed., 1982; 151–190

Ren Tao/Yue Bing, 1983: Bevölkerung und Beschäftigung, in: BR, Vol. 20, No. 30 (March 29, 1983); 19–24

Schinke, E., 1985: Der Agrarsektor in der Volksrepublik China: Wandlungen und Möglichkeiten, in: Schüller, A., ed., 1985; 141–157

Schüller, A., ed., 1985: China im Konflikt zwischen verschiedenen Ordnungs- konzeptionen. Berlin

Sheng Li, 1985: New Forms of the Rural Cooperative System—Shareholders Cooperative (chinese), in: Nongcun Gongzuo Tongxun, No. 3 (1985); 21–22

Skinner, G. W., 1985: Rural Marketing in China: Repression and Revival, in: The China Quarterly, September 1985; 393–413

Smil, V., 1986: Chinas Ernährung, in: Spektrum der Wissenschaft, No. 2 (1986); 112–121

Song Linfei, 1984: The Present State and Future Prospects of Specialized Households in Rural China, in: Social Sciences in China, No. 4; 107–130

Wädekin, K. E., 1984a: Agrarian Structures and Policies in the USSR. China and Hungary, A Comparative View, Paper for the Seventh International Conference on Soviet and East European Agriculture. Grignon

———, 1984b: "Verantwortlichkeitssystem" für Chinas Bauern, in: Neue Zürcher Zeitung (Fernausgabe), November 8, 1984

Walker, K. R., 1984: Chinese Agriculture during the Period of the Readjustment, 1978–83, in: The China Quarterly, December 1984, No. 100; 783–812

Watson, A., 1983: Agriculture Looks for "Shoes that Fit." The Production Responsibility System and its Implications, in: World Development, Vol. 11, No. 8; 705–730

Widmer, U., 1986: Neue Strukturen im ländlichen China, in: Geographische Rundschau, No. 3, March 1986; 138–1457

Woodward, D., 1982: A New Direction for China's State Farms, in: Pacific Affairs; 231–251

World Bank, 1983: China's Socialist Economic Development, Vol. II, The Economic Sectors Agriculture, Industry, Energy, Transport, and External Trade and Finance. Washington D. C.

Yuan Chongfa, 1984: Specialized Households are the Representatives of the Most Advanced Productive Forces in the Countryside (chinese), in: Guangming Ribao, July 16, 1984

Yuan Ruizhen, 1984: Three Basic Questions in Restructuring the Commodity Circulation System in Rural Areas (chinese), in: Nongye Jingji Wenti, No. 7 (1984); 23–26

Zhou Qiren/Du Ying, 1984: Specialized Households: A Preliminary Study, in: Social Sciences in China, No. 3 (1984); 50–72

Zhu Weiwen, 1983: Specialized Households in the Province Guangdong (chinese), in: Jingji Ribao, May 5, 1983